# Anthropology and Mental Health

# World Anthropology

*General Editor*

SOL TAX

*Patrons*

CLAUDE LÉVI-STRAUSS
MARGARET MEAD
LAILA SHUKRY EL HAMAMSY
M. N. SRINIVAS

MOUTON PUBLISHERS · THE HAGUE · PARIS
DISTRIBUTED IN THE USA AND CANADA BY ALDINE, CHICAGO

# Anthropology and Mental Health

*Setting a New Course*

*Editor*

JOSEPH WESTERMEYER

MOUTON PUBLISHERS · THE HAGUE · PARIS
DISTRIBUTED IN THE USA AND CANADA BY ALDINE, CHICAGO

# *General Editor's Preface*

In the half-century since Malinowski's Trobriand Islanders provided a dramatic correction to Freudian theory, related information from non-Western cultures has increasingly interested psychiatrists. Development of theory has been pursued by both psychiatrists and anthropologists, and the recently burgeoning interest in therapy has added a very important dimension to this area of study. Generally — inspired by the famous and productive Linton-Kardiner Seminars in the 1930's — the work has been cooperative and interdisciplinary. The present book brings together all of these elements as they have coalesced over the past few years. Its origin in an international Congress which brought together scholars from the whole range of the world's cultures adds vigor to the discussions of some difficult issues.

Like most contemporary sciences, anthropology is a product of the European tradition. Some argue that it is a product of colonialism, with one small and self-interested part of the species dominating the study of the whole. If we are to understand the species, our science needs substantial input from scholars who represent a variety of the world's cultures. It was a deliberate purpose of the IXth International Congress of Anthropological and Ethnological Sciences to provide impetus in this direction. The *World Anthropology* volumes, therefore, offer a first glimpse of a human science in which members from all societies have played an active role. Each of the books is designed to be self-contained; each is an attempt to update its particular sector of scientific knowledge and is written by specialists from all parts of the world. Each volume should be read and reviewed individually as a separate volume on its own given subject. The set as a whole will indicate what changes are in store for anthropology as scholars from the developing countries join in studying the species of which we are all a part.

The IXth Congress was planned from the beginning not only to include as many of the scholars from every part of the world as possible, but also with a view toward the eventual publication of the papers in high-quality volumes. At previous Congresses scholars were invited to bring papers which were then read out loud. They were necessarily limited in length; many were only summarized; there was little time for discussion; and the sparse discussion could only be in one language. The IXth Congress as an experiment aimed at changing this. Papers were written with the intention of exchanging them before the Congress, particularly in extensive pre-Congress sessions; they were not intended to be read aloud at the Congress, that time being devoted to discussions — discussions which were simultaneously and professionally translated into five languages. The method for eliciting the papers was structured to make as representative a sample as was allowable when scholarly creativity — hence self-selection — was critically important. Scholars were asked both to propose papers of their own and to suggest topics for sessions of the Congress which they might edit into volumes. All were then informed of the suggestions and encouraged to re-think their own papers and the topics. The process, therefore, was a continuous one of feedback and exchange and it has continued to be so even after the Congress. The some two thousand papers comprising *World Anthropology* certainly then offer a substantial sample of world anthropology. It has been said that anthropology is at a turning point; if this is so, these volumes will be the historical direction-markers.

As might have been foreseen in the first post-colonial generation, the large majority of the Congress papers (82 percent) are the work of scholars identified with the industrialized world which fathered our traditional discipline and the institution of the Congress itself: Eastern Europe (15 percent); Western Europe (16 percent); North America (47 percent); Japan, South Africa, Austrlia, and New Zealand (4 percent). Only 18 percent of the papers are from developing areas: Africa (4 percent); Asia-Oceania (9 percent); Latin America (5 percent). Aside from the substantial representation from the U.S.S.R. and the nations of Eastern Europe, a significant difference between this corpus of written material and that of other Congresses is the addition of the large proportion of contributions from Africa, Asia, and Latin America. "Only 18 percent" is two to four times as great a proportion as that of other Congresses; moreover, 18 percent of 2,000 papers is 360 papers,

10 times the number of "Third World" papers presented at previous Congresses. In fact, these 360 papers are more than the total of ALL papers published after the last International Congress of Anthropological and Ethnological Sciences which was held in the United States (Philadelphia, 1956).

The significance of the increase is not simply quantitative. The input of scholars from areas which have until recently been no more than subject matter for anthropology represent both feedback and also long-awaited theoretical contributions from the perspectives of very different cultural, social, and historical traditions. Many who attended the IXth Congress were convinced that anthropology would not be the same in the future. The fact that the next Congress (India, 1978) will be our first in the "Third World" may be symbolic of the change. Meanwhile, sober consideration of the present set of books will show how much, and just where and how, our discipline is being revolutionized.

Readers of this book will be especially interested in others in this series which deal with psychological and medical anthropology; health-care delivery; social and mental health problems like alcoholism, drug use, and — on a different scale — ethnicity, competition, agression, and war; religion and shamanism; and the cultures of most parts of the world.

*Chicago, Illinois*                                                                 SOL TAX
*September 1, 1976*

# Foreword

The presently developing close and formal relationship between anthropology and the mental health field has its antecedents in the considerably long history of anthropological interest in psychological concomitants of culture and in the somewhat more recent psychiatric interest in the cultural stimulus events of human behavior. As the mutuality of interests is receiving increased recognition in both fields, areas of overlapping concerns have also expanded widely. In fact, Laura Nader said recently that "Perhaps the major contribution of the social sciences, and particularly we would argue of anthropology, is a broadening of our conception of what the health field comprises."[1] There is much support to this statement in the volume before us.

The history of this book may be considered an illustration of the burgeoning interest in the interface of anthropology and mental health. It was late in the spring of 1973 when Professor Joseph Westermeyer was invited to organize a symposium on anthropology and mental health for the IXth International Congress of Anthropological and Ethnological Sciences. His professional zeal and organizational skills were rewarded by prompt responses from 44 scholars who expressed willingness to prepare contributions on a relatively short notice. This was even more pleasing because no foundation or government support funds were available.

On the day before the opening of the Congress, most of the authors

[1] See Laura Nader and Thomas W. Maretzki 1973 (*Cultural illness and health: essays in human adaptation.* Anthropological Studies 9:1. Washington, D.C.: American Anthropological Association.)

of papers on anthropology and mental health, together with some 30 other interested scholars assembled in Chicago and discussed the topics in an all-day session cochaired by Westermeyer and Maday. Papers were distributed in advance and not read in the session. The substance of the papers and the discussions was then reported to the Congress during a two-hour-long symposium on September 4, 1973.

In addition to Professor Westermeyer, profound thanks are due to the formal discussants of papers, to Professor H. Warren Dunham, Department of Community and Family Medicine, Wayne State University School of Medicine; to Professor Francis L. K. Hsu, Department of Anthropology, Northwestern University; and to Dr. Nancy Rollins, Department of Psychiatry, The Children's Hospital Medical Center, Boston.

Our appreciation for assistance in the preparation of this volume goes to all contributors of papers, discussants, and commentators. Special thanks are extended to Mrs. Rachel Westermeyer for inspiration and logistic support.

BELA C. MADAY

*National Institute of Mental Health and*
*The American University*
*Washington, D. C.*

# *Preface*

This volume is meant to serve as a review of major developments in the field over the last five years. Some of the articles are primarily summaries of an investigator's work, his or her own thoughts on a current issue, or the present state of the art as reflected in the literature. Other papers, more limited in scope, represent activities now at the cutting edge in this field. Some of the papers toward the end of this volume may anticipate new directions for us. They suggest modifications in our theories and methods which — while yet untried in some cases — may move us toward grappling with problems we have so far avoided.

As you read, you will note some authors referring to the comments or papers of other authors. This results from (1) our having read one another's papers, (2) our subsequent meeting for a full day to discuss the papers, and (3) the opportunity to revise our papers after the discussion. As a result, the papers are more than a collection of individual authors' thoughts. In large part, they are an admixture of both our individual efforts and the influence of our colleagues' ideas upon us. Out of this experience grew certain themes which may be evident to you during your reading. In the final summary chapter, Dr. K. J. Pataki-Schweizer attempts to capture what consensus evolved from our discussions in Chicago.

In order to spur discussion at the symposium, three eminent people in the field were asked to read the papers and prepare comments. One of these comments is included as a paper (Hsu, this volume). Comments by Drs. Dunham and Rollins which enhance the critical evaluation of several papers are appended to these papers. An appendix has been added for certain of Dr. Dunham's comments which have particular value, coming from a sociologist-epidemiologist with four decades of active work in this field. You will note that many of their statements included here contain critical remarks of a negative nature. Of course, they also had much positive to say in our discussions as well. However, unless we attend to their remarks and carefully consider them, we run the risk that not only we but also the field may stagnate.

*Acknowledgments*

On remarkably short notice the authors of this volume responded to my call for their best and most recent work. In order to make their work available to you, they were further asked to submit final revisions of their papers within a few weeks following the Congress. Their efforts under this duress of time are greatly appreciated.

Dr. Bela Maday's contribution transcended that of cochairman for the symposium. He also provided logistical support in distributing the papers prior to the symposium and moral leadership in organizing the symposium and subsequent volume. Drs. H. Warren Dunham, Francis L. K. Hsu, and Nancy Rollins also influenced the symposium — and hence this volume — in a major way. Their comments, and the discussion stimulated by their comments, are reflected in my introduction to the volume and in the introductions to the various sections. They are also reflected in many of the revisions made by authors in their papers following the symposium.

Other participants in the symposium also contributed to our efforts by their comments. Among those most active were Drs. Helmut Hoffman, Frank Johnson, Barbara Lex, Masafumi Nakakuki, and Ms. Jeanne Snow. The nature of this format precludes ascribing direct quotations to them, but their impress on the volume can be felt.

In addition, I want to thank Dr. Sol Tax, president of this year's World Congress and the staff of Mouton whose efforts assisted in the evolution of this work. The secretatial efforts of Ms. Gloria Wolf far exceeded the call of duty in this undertaking. Ms. Rachel Westermeyer and Ms. Jean Kelly contributed invaluable editorial assistance.

*University of Minnesota*                              JOSEPH WESTERMEYER
*Minneapolis, Minnesota*
*November, 1973*

# Table of Contents

INTRODUCTION

# Whither the Fresh Course?

JOSEPH WESTERMEYER

The papers in this volume from the IXth ICAES in 1973 indicate certain new directions in the field when compared to similar reviews and edited publications over the past two decade (see Caudill and Lin 1969; De Rueck and Porter 1965; Eaton and Weil 1955; Murphy and Leighton 1965; Opler 1959). Certainly, there are continued emphases that link us to past investigations and provide further development in important areas. However, the new concerns evident over the last few years suggest that, indeed, new frontiers are appearing in a field which has remained fairly stable since its rapid development in the 1930's and 1940's.

In part, this change may be related to new people entering the field. Until recently most workers have been academicians and researchers trained in anthropology, psychoanalysis, social psychology, and sociology. Contributors to this volume come from these traditional fields and, in addition, from clinical and educational and experimental psychology, community and biological and hospital psychiatry, social work, and pharmacology. An indigenous "healer" from the Caribbeans coauthored one paper. The entry of these new professions into the field has brought the kind of diverse perspectives which you will encounter in this volume.

Also, in part, this transition appears due to a change in topical emphasis. Until now most studies have been concerned with problems primarily of interest to the academician: definitions, prevalence of mental disorders, culture-bound syndromes, cross-cultural comparisons, and social change.

A glance at several titles of papers contained herein reveals a pragmatic concern with addressing urgent problems extant in the world today. Many of the authors purposefully seek out hypotheses which might prove useful to mental health workers and health planners as they set about trying to solve the dilemmas which confront them. By seeking such a specific goal (namely, to be useful in some explicit way) in an *a priori* manner, they eclipse many of their predecessors who sought only to be explanatory after the fact. The *a priori* prediction committed to usefulness can at least be shown false when its execution proves to be useless or detrimental; the *ex post facto* explanatory concepts run no such risk.

## MENTAL HEALTH SERVICES ACROSS CULTURAL BOUNDARIES

Mental health care across cultural boundaries no longer occurs as an isolated or unusual event. Several factors account for this. Growing appreciation of mental health care as a human right regardless of social class or ethnic background; increased migration; tourism; greater travel of students abroad; availability of "modern" mental health services in "developing" nations: all these bring patients of different ethnic backgrounds to mental health workers everywhere. Both seasoned professional and trainee now need to learn skills for working effectively in the cross-cultural context.

   Several papers here document the lessons to be learned when traditional healer and mental health clinician collaborate for mutual learning and, especially, for benefit to their patient-in-common. Such learning requires time and commitment, but it can bring professional and personal rewards. Together, traditional healers and middle-class therapists can actually complement each other, providing a diversity of conceptual frameworks within which human behavior can be understood and offering a broader range of resouces to troubled persons than either one could provide alone.

   Techniques elaborated in this volume promise to enable minority communities to regain some control over their own mental health resources. Traditional healers can train professionally educated clinicians in the cosmology and health-and-disease belief systems prevailing within their group. By employing cross-cultural training models, community leaders could assess the competency of the educated professionals — not in professional competency *per se*, but in his or her ability to utilize that competency effectively within the minority community.

   Finally, the numbers of trained mental health professionals are insufficient to meet the need in some places. The discrepancy between need and resources becomes ever more acute under conditions in which cross-cultural provision of mental health services often prevails, as among tribal peoples, disenfranchised minority groups, and "third world" countries with low incomes and limited formal education. Clinicians charged with the responsibility of providing care under these conditions have collaborated with traditional healers and trained indigenous mental health workers. So far this collaboration has depended on the interpersonal relations of healer and mental health worker. Perhaps greater understanding of this relationship might lead to collaboration that does not rest so heavily on the personalities involved.

## SOCIAL SCIENCE IN THE CLINICAL SETTING

The clinical setting has been an anathema to the social scientist interested in mental disorder and, in many respects, with good reason. For example, social dynamics in clinical setting lead to markedly skewed samples, and the clinical setting clearly comprises a subculture with its own initiation rituals and *rites de passage*.

However, some of the clinical studies in this volume do suggest that nuggets can be mined from clinical settings by astute social scientists. For example, such settings provide a site for examining linkage theories between behavioral and psychobiological elements. In addition to studies of patients, there is equal and urgent need to explore those who train in, work in, and direct clinical settings — not merely in the light of an exposé, but in a dynamic fashion, emphasizing characteristics which may be used for social benefit, to produce harm (as perhaps is most often the case) or as a trade-off between harm and benefit.

## ETHICAL ISSUES

It is probably not a coincidence that three American authors NOT of European heritage question the "etic" conceptual framework for mental health disorders now operative in North America. Two Sioux-Americans and one Chinese-American cogently criticize the utility of personality theory, first, in accounting for psychiatric disorder and, second, in using this model as a basis for mental health services which are then made "available to" (or in other terms, "foisted upon") people such as themselves. Their stance argues that it is one thing to search for a constant or "etic" factor in psychiatric disorder; it is another thing to presume its existence and unilaterally apply mental health services to groups who may not share the "emic" belief systems (such as personality theory) of Euroamericans.

Also called into question, by two Canadian investigators, are the "preventive mental health" efforts of many practitioners who seek to instigate social change in child-raising practices, sex taboos, and other altered mores. Might not these instigations accelerate social change, and thereby impair mental health? It is recognized by the authors that practitioners may merely mirror broad-based changes which are afoot in society already, thus only verbalizing or offering rationalizations for changes which are already widely desired. However, the authors nonetheless rhetorically question whether clinicians or social scientists with mental health interests can or ethically should—at this point in our meager understanding—make large-scale recommendations for the primary prevention of mental disorder.

Such questions as these are crucial for societies to understand the roles which mental health services and practitioners play within them. Often the "modern" practitioners discharge social responsibilities previously met by the clergy, the police or other social control forces, healers and medical workers, social change agents, "crisis" helpers, attendants at *rites de passage*, and leaders of face-to-face communities. So, to evaluate the ethical impact of their work, let alone be effective and comfortable in their work, mental health workers need to appreciate these various roles and their accompanying sociodynamics.

## "MENTAL HEALTH" AS A EUPHEMISM; "MENTAL ILLNESS" AS PROFANITY

The title of this volume, *Anthropology and mental health*, itself reflects the influence of social and behavior sciences on the field. Several years ago the title might have been "Anthropology and Mental Illness" (or Mental Disease). Since then, the social morbidity-producing sequelae of treating all psychiatric disorder exclusively as "illness" have become widely appreciated. In our headlong rush to avoid a unitary approach to these problems we have abandoned terms like disease and illness.

Now we have the euphemism "mental health." Perhaps, a continued interest in prevention of psychiatric disorder and in maintenance of mental and emotional well-being may cause this new term to stay with us for a while. At the same time, the work in this field over the past quarter century indicates that incapacitating and disabling mental and emotional problems are not likely to disappear from among men anywhere. As a major cause of human suffering, these problems will in all likelihood continue to occupy our attention.

As social scientists and mental health workers have been trying to remove the "illness" aura from many traditional problems, others have been attempting to label other and new social problems as "illness." Alcoholism, drug addiction, delinquency, criminality, promiscuity, suicide, and violence have been gradually moving from social definitions as moral or legal evils to mental health evils. Hopefully, armed with hard-won wisdom in handling psychiatric disorder within a health care framework, social scientists and clinicians may contribute their considerable expertise in these problem areas without contributing to human misery. A recent volume warns that this latter-day change may not be exclusively beneficial, however (Menninger 1973).

## FIVE YEARS HENCE

Already in this volume one paper offers a systems framework for analyzing drug treatment. We can anticipate in the next volume five years hence that systems analysis will become popular and a variety of problematic behaviors besides addiction will be addressed. Hopefully we will see greater attention to theory, especially theories linking biological, behavioral, and social phenomena. Perhaps a primary preventive emphasis might be reintroduced, this time centered on relatively small social units rather than on the pan-societal mega-units which have been favored by the social philosophers amongst us. The pragmatic emphasis in our work is likely to remain. And the title of the next volume? Again, probably an evanescent euphemism reflecting the movement of the field. We still have too much ground to cover and growth to attain before settling on that sign of maturity (or ossification, if you will), a permanent name.

## REFERENCES

CAUDILL, W., T. Y. LIN, *editors*
  1969  *Mental health research in Asia and the Pacific.* Honolulu: East-West Center Press.
DE RUECK, A. V. S., R. PORTER, *editors*
  1965  *Transcultural psychiatry.* Boston: Little, Brown.
EATON, J. W., R. J. WEIL
  1955  *Culture and mental disorders.* Glencoe, Illinois: Free Press.
MENNINGER, K.
  1973  *Whatever became of sin?* New York: Hawthorn.

MURPHY, J. M., A. H. LEIGHTON, *editors*
  1965    *Approaches to cross-cultural psychiatry.* Ithaca, New York: Cornell
          University Press.
OPLER, M. K., *editor*
  1959    *Culture and mental health.* New York: Macmillan.

SECTION ONE

*Cosmologies and Mental Health*

# Introduction

Peoples' beliefs about the causes of their lifes' problems inevitably affect the symptoms which they manifest as well as the steps which they can take to ameliorate their distress. We tend naturally to view the belief systems of others as conceptual artifacts, esoteric "suspicions" which the enlightened can disregard or view with amused disdain. They have been collected like so many sherds, to be compared with one another, to be assessed at their evolutionary level, and then to be relegated to the back shelves of some library.

De Rios's work postulates a more dynamic, positive perspective. Witchcraft beliefs in Peru can be viewed as licit social theory of causation for psychosomatic disorder. Within such a theoretical framework, the suffering individual can locate the origin of his distress, and his reference group can initiate procedures that bring him relief. In addition, witchcraft beliefs provide a cosmology for understanding the order of things (an "existential" philosophy in contemporary Euroamerican parlance) and a means of governing interpersonal relations, functions that closely interrelate in explaining and curing psychosomatic disorder in any society.

In reading de Rios's paper, think of a "modern" belief system and substitute it for the term "witchcraft beliefs." Choose Pavlovian psychobiology, Roman Catholicism, Freudian psychoanalysis, Frankl's existentialism, or some other. Whichever you choose, you will notice that the explanatory and therapeutic functions of the witchcraft belief system and the belief system of your choice are remarkably similar. Each belief system provides a hypothetical etiology for psychosomatic disorder and treatment regimens logically related to the hypothesized etiology. Examined more closely, your chosen belief system will likely also interdigitate with its own distinctive cosmology and with a theoretical stance for the control of social behavior.

The paper by Teitelbaum also demonstrates the interconnections between social relations, psychosomatic disorder, belief systems, and curing practices. Of particular interest in Tunisia is the apparent lack of congruity between the folk "humoral" theory of psychosomatic and psychoneurotic disorders and the professionally trained clinician's causal theories. Yet, despite this seeming contradiction, the astute clinician, by ackowledging the existence of the "humoral" condition, can sanction the presence of the disorder in order to allow treatment and the reparative social process to ensue. Were he to argue against the patient's cosmology and insist on imposing his own, the clinician would alienate himself as a resource for people in distress. Moreover, the clinician is able to proceed with therapeutic strategies which extricate the patient from his dilemma and reset the social order to functioning again.

In the course of our pre-Congress meeting, Francis Hsu offered an explanation for Teitelbaum's observation regarding the frequent preference of Tunisian patients for foreign physicians and their lesser preference for indigenous Moslem physicians. During Hsu's early work at a teaching hospital in Peking, he found Euroamerican physicians more accepting of Chinese folk theory of disease (and thereby often more therapeutic) than their Chinese colleagues. He posits that isocultural physicians are more apt to be angered at, and embarrassed by, what they take to be the "inferior" (that is, "less scientific") theories of their cultural peers. My own experience with black medical students of middle-class origins in the United States supports this: many of them find considerable difficulty in accepting the idea of "rootwork" theories among rural and ghetto black Americans, while their ghetto black and nonblack fellow students are less apt to have such difficulties. The consistency in these observations suggests that one can expect clinicians to display extreme difficulty in accepting the "nonscientific" or folk theories of disease and suffering among the people with whom they identify.

# The Relationship Between Witchcraft Beliefs and Psychosomatic Illness

MARLENE DOBKIN DE RIOS

The notion of witchcraft, or the ability of individuals to harm or kill others by special medicines or psychic means, has long been of interest to anthropologists, historians, and physicians. The great diffusion of witchcraft beliefs throughout time and space attests to their ubiquitous interest. The function of witchcraft in society — that is, the causality and elaboration of witchcraft beliefs and activities and their interrelations with other parts of culture — has received scientific treatment only during the last fifty years or so (Crawford 1967; Evans-Pritchard 1937; Marwick 1965; Kluckhohn 1944). Durkheim, reacting against prevalent psychological reductionist theories that related all human phenomena to a few specified emotional states, wrote that "when an explanation of social phenomena is undertaken, we must seek separately the efficient cause which produces it and the function it fulfills" (1938:95).

One very neglected aspect of witchcraft research has been the cultural patterning of disease, or simply the physiological disease correlates linked to witchcraft beliefs. When witchcraft exists in a society and especially when witchcraft beliefs reflect individual tensions and anxieties, certain syndromes may be expected to occur frequently with these belief systems.

Psychosomatic infirmities, in general, are emotional or psychological in nature and are believed by Western medical practitioners to be precipitated by stress and conflicts in the interpersonal environment. Folk healing practices throughout the world present the social scientist with an excellent natural laboratory because psychosomatic disease in particular tends to yield successfully to treatment by folk medicine (Kiev 1964). An additional area of interest is how psychosomatic disease can play an adaptive or maladaptive role for man in non-Western society.

As Mayer has pointed out (1970:46), witchcraft beliefs, although by no means universal, are a widespread index of social and psychological strain. Often, witches are believed to cause illness. The indices of ethnopsychiatric studies represent witchcraft as a pathogenic feature of many non-Western cultures. By the same token, psychosomatic illness is seen to be a somatic reaction to socially precipitated stress or conflict. Might there not be some relationship between witchcraft beliefs and psychosomatic disease? Anthropological studies of disease tend to deal with its ecological aspects as revealed in the physical environment, focusing upon biotic components of the environment, nutritional disorders, or maladjustments of growth, function, or control within the human organism (Harrison, et al. 1964: 481). But there is another area of equal concern to the student of human disease — the relationship of man's social relations to his disease pattern.

The well-known psychiatrist Harry Stack Sullivan once called psychiatry the science of interpersonal relationships. Because psychosomatic illnesses are often viewed as infirmities of interpersonal relationships, the correlation between disease patterns and particular types of social stress inherent in witchcraft beliefs should be examined.

## PSYCHOSOMATIC DISEASE

The term "psychosomatic illness" generally refers to psychogenic organic malfunctions, often resulting from emotional and socially precipitated stress or conflict. In many ways, psychosomatic medicine reaffirms the ancient principle that the mind and the body cannot be separated and that they function as interactive, interdependent organs (Alexander 1950:73). Psychosomatic illness usually begins at a time of crisis in a patient's life and correlates strongly with stress-provoking situations. The patient tends to improve when circumstances change for the better or when he learns to adapt to them without undue tensions. As Hambling points out (1965: 37), psychosomatic disorders are essentially diseases of personal relationships. Thus the sick person is not merely a bearer of organs, in Alexander's terms (1950:17), but an indivisible whole.

Simeons (1960:3) has indicated that only recently have psychosomatic interpretations of disease acquired the dignity of a scientific approach. While Simeons focuses upon modern urban man, I shall consider how a belief system per se can be as important a variable as the actual physical stress attendant upon such demographic factors as urban crowding. Thus, we may expect that a set of beliefs could provide a mental environment in which psychosomatic disease flourishes. As Kennedy has stated (1970:6), if an individual lives in a society where witchcraft beliefs exist, thinking that someone has bewitched him when he feels aches and pains does nothing to hasten his cure.

Some Western writers would argue that all disease must be psychosomatic in origin, because disease is due not to tissue pathology alone, but rather to the interaction of psychological and physical factors. In our study of witchcraft beliefs and the patterning of disease, we must be careful not to search for a few simplistic diseases whose covariation with a particular belief system can be clearly delineated. Rather, we should view disease patternings in terms of their interrelationships with beliefs and the conjoint effect on psyche and body.

Weiss and English (1957), Alexander (1950), Simeons (1960), and others would argue that most diseases — including gastrointestinal disorders, infirmities of the endocrine system, chronic fatigue, types of diabetes, various sexual disorders (including frigidity and impotence), menstrual disorders, respiratory disease, asthma, insomnia, skin disorders, and orthopedic problems, to list only a few — fall into the category of psychosomatic illness. In their study of outpatients in an American hospital, Weiss and English estimated that one-third of the patients suffered from clearly chronic illnesses, their symptoms depending in part upon emotional factors; another one-third suffered from clearly psychosomatic infirmities; the last one-third of the sample showed disease patterns in which the interaction of physical and psychological factors was so complex that a clear diagnosis was impossible (1957:5). Certainly, the either/or method of diagnosing functional or organic disorder is passing out of Western medicine as a diagnostic reality. Transcultural psychiatric students, too, are paying more attention to the complex interaction of factors that contribute to disease (Seguin 1970).

Certainly, in non-Western cultures, folk healers are often called upon to treat emotionally precipitated illnesses. These men and women often recognize the important role of emotional factors in disease and give it great prominence in their diagnosis. Western-trained medical personnel, on the other hand, tend to expect physical ailments. Folk healers may indeed be more effective if their training and experience predispose them to look for emotionally and culturally precipitated illnesses.

## ANTHROPOLOGICAL THEORIES CONCERNING THE FUNCTION OF WITCHCRAFT

Early anthropological ideas concerning witchcraft often involved psychological reductionism, wherein certain emotional states, such as anxiety and fear, were seen as the reason that man turned to witchcraft beliefs to explain illness and misfortune. Primitive man was viewed as irrational — in the grip of mysterious, overpowering forces that inspired awe and dread at every turn. Psychological reductionist theories gave way in the late nineteenth century to more sociologically oriented discussions of witchcraft as a reflection of social structural stress. Middleton (1967) has summarized these theories: "Witchcraft activity can be seen as [being] both instrumental and expressive aspects of social behavior. They may achieve particular ends and states and symbolize certain social and cosmological relationships." In recent years, some social psychiatrists have looked at the psychodynamic aspects of witchcraft systems, viewing them as the products of individual psychopathologies that have been accepted, systematized, and institutionalized by members of many groups. These systems are thought to be similar to psychopathological syndromes described in the psychiatric literature today. For example, Kennedy (1970) has examined the similarity between witchcraft systems and paranoid delusions.

## INTERRELATIONSHIP BETWEEN WITCHCRAFT BELIEFS AND ILLNESS

Whatever the function of witchcraft in human society or whatever the complex social and psychological factors contributing to its widespread elaboration, we might agree that everywhere these belief systems occur they reflect certain institutionalized patterns of tension and anxiety. My own work in the Peruvian Amazon has shown an association between witchcraft beliefs and psychosomatic infirmities (Dobkin de Rios 1969, 1970, 1972). We should expect that when anxieties and tensions are reflected in institutionalized witchcraft beliefs, the human organism will respond in predictable ways, through the development of psychosomatic disorder.

Of course, other disease patterns should also be expected to occur. Rather than seeking reliable statistics of incidence and prevalence of psychoneurotic disorders in Western societies, I shall tentatively and at a theoretical level point to covariation between one type of belief system and physiological disorder. I hope that this link between disease and witchcraft will lead to wider examination of these variables in the future.

## WITCHCRAFT DYNAMICS AND FOLK HEALING

In general, folk healers are most successful in treating illnesses that are not indications of psychoses but rather are psychosomatic or emotional in nature. As the social psychiatrist Seguin has noted (1970), it is useless to attempt to transfer diagnostic categories from Western medicine to folk disease. Such illness can only be understood within the context of the social system that harbors it. Kiev (1964), in a study of Mexican-American folk healing, pointed out quite clearly that throughout the world folk healers tend to be most successful in the area of psychosomatic infirmity.

In the Peruvian Amazon, in questions of witchcraft, healers draw upon the visual content of hallucinations produced by the *ayahuasca* vine in order to enable them or their patients to identify the source of evildoing. Only then does the healer use countermagic to neutralize his client's disease and return the evil to its perpetrator (Dobkin de Rios 1970). Elsewhere, I have stressed the patterns of omnipotence that most healers establish *vis-à-vis* their clients and the use of subtle and not-so-subtle boasting. Reassurance, counseling, and using patients' suggestibility during drug sessions also contribute to their healing success. Most folk healers are careful to select their patients in order to avoid taking on cases that would fall into Western diagnostic categories of psychoses, because their chances of cure there are indeed quite slim.

If we try to examine witchcraft beliefs from an adaptive or maladaptive standpoint, the model shown in Figure 1 is helpful. We can see that the very beliefs in the ubiquitousness of witchcraft can contribute to disease patterning and treatment. The healer's counseling, advising, and use of

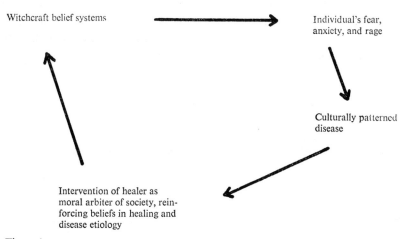

Figure 1.

the plant hallucinogen *ayahuasca* reaffirm beliefs concerning disease etiology as well as marshal all of his own "force and power" to overcome the evil that has made his client ill. Most folk healers are pragmatically quite wise in the preparation and dispensing of medicines, both natural and pharmaceutical, which they administer to their patients in addition to psychological counseling.

From the point of view of population dynamics, one of the interesting aspects of adaptive versus maladaptive functioning of witchcraft in society can be related to disease patterning and treatment. A general notion exists among anthropologists (discussed at length by British social anthropologists who study African societies) that witchcraft can contribute to the dispersal of populations who fear that they are endangered by evil willing from witches in their community. Witchcraft is often believed to work only over short distances. Thus, a population that has grown beyond the resources of its environment may fission and set up a new village because of witchcraft fear. As Kennedy (1970) has noted, these witchcraft systems can then be viewed as highly adaptive in ecological terms.

I would like to argue the point even further. Folk healers throughout the world tend to utilize techniques and plants that enable them to induce emotional abreaction or catharsis in their patients. By means of his ritual paraphernalia, techniques, or symbols, a healer is assured of relative success in those cases where psychoses are absent or where disease syndromes with organic damage are not too well developed. Despite the heavy toll that witchcraft beliefs can take upon those who internalize mystical theories of disease etiology, including the "voodoo death" that Cannon (1942) described, one could argue that ecological benefits are derived by populations sharing these beliefs. This is especially the case when disease patterns that arise from the belief systems are amenable to healing resources, either psychological or botanical, that folk practitioners can draw upon in their treatment of disease.

## REFERENCES

ALEXANDER, FRANZ
   1950   *Psychosomatic medicine: its principles and applications.* New York: Norton.
CANNON, WALTER
   1942   Voodoo death. *American Anthropologist* 44:169–181.
CRAWFORD, J. R.
   1967   *Witchcraft and sorcery in Rhodesia.* International African Institute. London: Oxford University Press.

DOBKIN DE RIOS, MARLENE

1969   La cultura de la probreza y la mágia de amor: un síndrome urbano en la selva Perúana. *América Indígena* 29:1.

1970   *Banisteriopsis* used in witchcraft and healing activities in Iquitos, Peru. *Economic Botany* 24:296–300.

1972   *Visionary vine: psychedelic healing in the Peruvian Amazon.* San Francisco: Chandler.

DURKHEIM, EMILE

1938   *The rules of sociological method.* Translated by S. A. Solovay and J. H. Mueller and edited by E. G. Catlin. Chicago: University of Chicago Press.

EVANS-PRITCHARD, E. E.

1937   *Witchcraft among the Azande.* Oxford: Clarendon.

HAMBLING, J.

1965   "Are guilt and anxiety experienced differently in patients suffering from psychoneurotic and psychosomatic illness?" in *The role of psychosomatic disorder in adult life.* Edited by J. Wisdom and H. H. Wolff. New York: Pergamon.

HARRISON, G. A., J. S. WEINER, J. M. TANNER, N. A. BARNICOT

1964   *Human biology: an introduction to human evolution, variation and growth.* New York: Oxford University Press.

KENNEDY, J. G.

1970   Psychosocial dynamics of witchcraft systems. *International Journal of Social Psychiatry* 15(3):165–178.

KIEV, ARI

1964   *Magic, faith and healing.* New York: Free Press.

KLUCKHOHN, CLYDE

1944   *Navaho witchcraft.* Boston: Beacon.

MARWICK, M. G.

1965   *Sorcery in its social setting: a study of the Northern Rhodesian Cewa.* Manchester: Manchester University Press.

MAYER, PHILIP

1970   "Witches," in *Witchcraft and sorcery.* Edited by M. Marwick. Baltimore: Penguin.

MIDDLETON, J., *compiler*

1967   *Magic, witchcraft, and curing.* Garden City, New York: Natural History Press.

MIDDLETON, J., E. WINTER, *editors*

1964   *Witchcraft in East Africa.* New York: Praeger.

1967   *Gods and rituals.* American Museum of Natural History Sourcebooks in Anthropology. New York: Natural History Press.

SEGUIN, CARLOS A.

1970   "Folk psychiatry," in *World biennial of psychiatry and psychotherapy,* volume one. Edited by S. Arieti. New York: Basic Books.

SIMEONS, A. T.

1960   *Man's presumptuous brain.* New York: Dutton.

WEISS, E., O. ENGLISH

1957   *Psychosomatic medicine.* Philadelphia: Saunders.

# Humoral Theory and Therapy in Tunisia

JOEL M. TEITELBAUM

A people's basic health concepts are essential to understanding and treating their health problems, be they organic and/or psychic conditions. For example, persistent headache means various things to and in different cultures. In France it raises fears of brain tumor; in Tunisia it is thought to result from "blood" problems; Americans often ascribe it to the tensions of modern living. Anthropology can contribute to medical science a set of insights into the relationship between the beliefs and the "interpersonal nexus" (in Hsu's terms) of the patient. If anthropological concepts of illness are applied, the physician's capacity to diagnose, treat, and comfort persons, especially those who have non-Western or traditional views, is increased.

In Tunisia, a small Arabic-speaking Muslim country of North Africa, the inhabitants maintain a lively attachment to their Mediterranean culture. Originally a Berber population, they have, over the centuries since 900 B.C., accommodated repeated invasions and colonizations by Carthaginians (Phoenecians), Romans, Vandals, Arabs, and Turks. Most recently during the French colonial protectorate (1882–1956), European technology and science were introduced and a variety of southern Europeans from Spain, France, Italy, and Greece emigrated to Tunisia. A Western system of higher education and medicine was established and sanitary measures were introduced to combat infectious disease through prevention and innoculation. However, many traditional remedies continued to be used by the indigenous Muslim population. Since the achievement of independence, Tunisia has evolved as a dual society — one sector modern, pragmatic and urban, economically geared to the West and the other part rural and technologically backward, looking inward toward the family group and small-scale village community, which includes the majority of the population.

Many individuals respond ambivalently to these two worlds. Their social perception of illness is linked mystically to the interpersonal nexus of the primary group, but they are consulting the Western-educated health professionals more and more for medical care. Although the traditional use of the leech (extraction of "rotten" blood from the head and neck as practiced by barbers and midwives) has been declared illegal, the practice continues in secret in accordance with the people's belief in the humoral theory of "blood" as the medium of bodily and spiritual disease. On the other hand, the physician's drugs and diagnostic tools, especially the injections and innoculations which penetrate the skin and enter the blood stream, are recognized as efficacious in treating disease. It has been suggested by Huessy (this volume) that bleeding a patient, although culturally different, might be a functional equivalent of American psychotherapy because it allows for the "expression" of inner problems and provides a context for the confidential talking-out of conflicts with a customary practitioner, thereby stimulating catharsis and alleviating symptoms.

## HUMORAL THEORY AND TREATMENT

Analgesic use of the humoral theory links the body and the emotions in Tunisian belief. It is a crude folk model of ancient Mediterranean philosophy and medicine espoused by Egyptian, Greek, and Roman thinkers and developed by Arab physicians during the Middle Ages as a therapeutic tool. This cosmology gives an alchemical explanation that matter and the world are composed of mixtures of basic substances — earth, air, fire, and water — having certain properties. All things, including foods and medicines which enter or touch the body, are thought to be composed of these opposing principles. Thus the blood can be "heated" by certain foods and "cooled" by others to counteract chills or fever. Human temperament is also thought to be affected by these humoral properties, hence the "cold-blooded" (calm) person, the "hot-blood" (irritable) person, the weak-blooded and the strong-blooded, etc.

In treating illness certain foods must be avoided if they conflict with health beliefs about blood. Sudden shifts such as going from warm, dry places into the cold, humid outdoors must be accompanied by slow acclimatization in order to prevent illness caused by the "airs." Once provoked, chills and fevers are treated by bloodletting and humoral antidotes. Compared to the Daltonian concept of atomic composition of matter and the experimental method of the sciences of physiology and bio-chemistry, these humoral beliefs are outmoded. They are often ridiculed by the Western-educated Tunisian physician. However, because most of his patients interpret their symptoms in this manner, insight into their mode of thought is necessary for him in order to treat conditions attributed to "bad blood." The following summarizes the relationship between "blood" beliefs and social relations in Tunisian perceptions of illness.

"Anger" is considered the major cause of rotten blood. Outbursts of anger fatigue the individual in the same way as do shock and over-exertion. In cases of acute weakness after a display of anger, a person is rushed to the hospital complaining of a "broken heart," due to the rapid pounding of his blood. The psychosocial element in this set of "causal" beliefs is that "anger in the blood" is preceded by worry; thus a man who constantly worries is considered a prime target for blood affliction.

## ILLNESS AND THE INTERPERSONAL NEXUS

The blood-affliction beliefs are linked with the field of small-scale social relations within the community. Close kin or associates who have broken customary obligations are thought to bring on worry and anger in the affected person. To have someone close to you harboring these ill feelings is immoral and a source of active concern because it can disrupt daily life. Expected norms of behavior are interpreted in terms of sentiments of love, hate, and jealousy and, if someone acts disrespectfully or shamefully and hurts the feelings of a companion, the latter may sicken with the blood affliction from worry and anger. Treatment by a physician is a means of obtaining partial relief from the symptoms of the illness as well as a way of demonstrating the gravity of the affliction to others. Visits to religious shrines such as *marabouts* [saints' tombs] and watering places widely known for their curative properties afford physical and emotional relief and also serve to communicate the immediacy of the problem to kin and friends in the community. These visits are social acts which correspond to the value system of the community. Thus the tendency to expend time and money by leaving the village for treatment reflects the seriousness of the social breach which is thought to have caused the affliction and weighs the status of the invalid and the person(s) who has wronged him on the scale of communal values.

Real recovery can come only when the person who is responsible for the anger or excessive worry comes to beg forgiveness, make amends and acknowledge customary duties to the invalid. If these acts are refused, the illness may persist and visitors to the sickbed, who according to custom must come to wish the invalid well and demonstrate their goodwill toward him, are told the story of how he has been wronged and who has "sickened" him. Thus, behavior during illness is associated with social disruption and in order to be complete, therefore, the cure must include a reordering of human relationships and a redress of the injured feelings.

## DISCUSSION

In sum, beliefs about illness and improper human conduct form a cyclical system of perceptions which fits neatly into the framework of modern medical practice and the tendency to employ doctors for social ends. The humoral theory of disease through blood affliction gives a personalized causation theory which complements the scientific explanation with accounts of the why and the particularly of an illness. This *post hoc* system of belief incorporates disease into the small-scale social contest of kin groups and communities and tends to reinforce the constraints surrounding the application of customary norms of behavior.

That illness produces feedback effects on the interpersonal nexus of the patient is a concept not far removed from modern psychiatric analysis of the interpersonal context for mental illness. Hence, placebo injections can elicit a positive response to a variety of symptoms of illness; mere use of elaborate diagnostic instruments by a physician allows the patient to bring pressure to bear on his primary kin group in order to redress his grievances. In addition, fears about the blood can be involved. For example in certain types of female hysteria, such as that exhibited by girls at the onset of menstruation and by women reaching menopause, the flow of blood becomes an important "cause" of their abnormal behavior during which mystical powers are invoked and interpersonal conflicts are expressed. Such responses may have to do with disturbance of the patient's network of close ties to family and peers.[1]

As modern Tunisians become increasingly mobile, individuals grow more isolated from their kin. They are shifting from the traditional toward the modern sector of this developing society while retaining many of their humoral beliefs and psychosomatic responses toward health and illness.

[1]  Pedro Ruiz this volume has supplied valuable information on this point.

# REFERENCES

DESPOIS, J.
1955    *La Tunisie orientale, Sahel et Basse Steppe.* Paris: PUF.
DE MONTETY, H.
1958    *Femmes de Tunisie.* Paris: Mouton.
FERCHIOU, S.
1969    "Differenciation sexuelle d'alimentation au Djerid (Sud Tunisien)."
        *l'Homme* 1969:64–85.
GALLAGHER, CHARLES F.
1957    *Modern medicine in North Africa.* American Universities Field
        Staff Reports, North Africa CFG–2.
MALINOWSKI, B.
1948    *Magic, science and religion and other essays.* Glencoe: The Free Press.
MONTAGUE, J.
1970    "Disease and public health in Tunisia: 1882–1970; an overview of the
        literature and its sources," in *A current bibliography on African
        affairs*, series II (4):250–260.
SHIVOH, AILON
1968    "The interaction of Middle Eastern and Western systems of medi-
        cine," in *Social science and medicine*, 235–248. London: Pergamon.
TEITELBAUM, J. M.
1969    "Lamta: leadership and social organization of a Tunisian commun-
        ity." Unpublished doctoral dissertation, University of Manchester.
TOMICHE, F. J.
1971    Tunisia: how to make the most of health services. *World Health*
        (December):16–21.

# SECTION TWO

*Culture and Psychopathology*

# Introduction

The decussation between culture and psychopathology continues to hold considerable interest for those working in this field. Unfortunately, many of these studies have continued to draw correlations in a crude manner which have shown more evidence of the investigator's ability to free associate than of his ability to employ rigorous scientific methods. Happily, the authors in this section have begun to reverse this trend.

Clearly stating his hypothesis at the outset, Yamamoto sets out to show ways in which suicide among Japanese-Americans resembles this same phenomenon in Japan. In part, the suicide patterns among Japanese people in both places resemble each other and in part they do not. Operationalizing his ideas in a most innovative way (using Japanese and Euroamerican first names), he suggests that the Japanese style of suicide persists among those still highly enculturated to their country of origin (or lowly acculturated to the new country of migration).

In another study focused on Japanese suicide, Iga uses the intensive care study method to dissect out the factors perhaps operant in the deaths of two prominent authors. The paper is unusual for a case study approach in that the author is a sociologist rather than a clinician. Thus he stresses the sociodynamics which are so often ignored or glossed over in case studies. In addition to elaborating certain psychological characteristics which might have made these two men prone to suicide, Iga also posits several social variables: problems in interpersonal relationships, with manifest loneliness; difficulties with social identity; a confluence of sociocultural events which were odious to each individual. It is refreshing that Iga accomplishes his task without employing clinical terms which, while appearing to explain poorly understood phenomena, more often serve to confuse.

Unlike the former two studies, that by Katz and Sanborn occurs in a clinical setting. As such, it is subject to all the sampling bias which confronts such studies, especially when they are done in a cross-cultural context. Regrettably, the raters and the rating instruments were mostly Euroamerican despite the fact that Japanese-Americans and Malay-Americans were studied in addition to Euroamericans. However, the authors have added a most desirable component: the patient's cultural peers (family members and neighbors) were utilized for ratings, in addition to clinicians. Despite its methodological problems, the study still is an advance over its predecessors which have often simply ignored the intracultural or "emic" aspects of psychopathology in a gross ethnocentric manner.

Jilek-Aall's paper is "action research" at its best — and done in an "emic" manner utilizing the tribal name for the condition being studied (*kifafa*) Many *kifafa* cases strongly resemble untreated epilepsy, with its incapacitating and malignant course. Local folk theories regarding its causes and its contagious nature had made the disorder most difficult to study. By undertaking its treatment (using primarily antiseizure and sedative medication), Jilek-Aall was able to learn the folk theories about the disorder and examine several score people with *kifafa*. Both she and clinician-discussant, Dr. Nancy Rollins, raise the issue of "etic" comparability with data from other ethnic groups: specifically, is *kifafa* primarily a seizure disorder (using the term seizure in its "Western" medical context)? Or, as a folk disorder with well-known social concomitants, does *kifafa* also include other disorders within the "Western" diagnostic categories, such as conversion reaction or hysterical psychosis? While this question could be answered only with an extensive interdisciplinary project, it nonetheless addresses important issues. If *kifafa* does indeed comprise a variety of organically induced and psychosocially induced problems, then it would appear that the social "labelling" process can occur without designated societal experts to do the labelling and "institutionalization" can occur without a building and without a corps of staff to teach institutionalization behavior. That is, psychosocially disordered people might also be "labelled" and "institutionalized" as a function of their own behavior and the behavior of those about them, rather than only by professionals outside of the patient's reference group. Hopefully, Jilek-Aall's work in this vital area will continue.

# Japanese-American Suicides in Los Angeles

JOE YAMAMOTO

I grew up as a Japanese-American, born in Los Angeles. The first language I learned was Japanese. During my early years I was told the usual folklore about suicide by my parents, and this led to my belief that the general attitude of the Japanese toward suicide is unique. In the following pages I will examine this early belief in a comparison of suicides among the Japanese and other Orientals in Los Angeles.

Because many Japanese planned to return to ancestral lands after having made their fortunes, they felt it was unnecessary to learn English or to adopt American ways. This motivated the Japanese to stay together and form little communities, where the old ways, customs, language, and values were maintained.

These attitudes continued until World War II, when the Japanese were forced to move from the Pacific Coast. A total of 117,000 were detained in the relocation centers (Thomas 1952). The parental authority was diluted for many reasons, and there was a general breakdown of the rigid family hierarchy.

## THE SAMURAI: SUICIDE WITH HONOR

While growing up in a Japanese-American community in Los Angeles, I learned about the samurai and their concept of suicide with honor. Three examples are particularly significant in the Japanese experience.

The author extends sincerest thanks to Dr. Thomas Noguchi, coroner and chief medical examiner of Los Angeles County. Without the help of the coroner and his staff, this study could not have been carried out.

The first is the eighteenth century tale of the forty-seven *ronin*. This is a story, oft-repeated, about forty-seven masterless samurai (*ronin*) who suffered from what they considered the unjust fate of their leader. After suffering from the disadvantage of being masterless samurai, they became honored in the history of Japan. The manner in which they became famous is remarkable in that it contributes valuable understanding of the Japanese. The forty-seven *ronin* avenged the death of their leader by killing the responsible samurai. Having thus achieved their mission, they were free to commit *seppuku*, commonly called harakiri (Iga and Yamamoto 1973). The point of the story was that they had carried out their obligation to their leader, avenged his wrongful death, and atoned for their acts with honor.

The second example is of Nogi Taisho (General Maresuke Nogi) who had led the Japanese forces to victory in the Russo-Japanese War of 1904–1905. He was honored and became famous for his feats as a military conqueror. However, guilt feelings about the massive mortality among his troops led him to wish that he could commit *seppuku*. But his emperor commanded him to continue his work. Therefore, he did not feel free to commit ritual suicide until after his emperor had died of natural causes in 1912. Only then could he commit *seppuku* and be followed by his wife. General Nogi is revered and honored by the Japanese not only for his victory over the Russians, but because he had cared enough to atone for the death of his troops by his heroic act of suicide.

During the Manchurian war, prior to World War II, there was a group of three infantrymen who sacrificed their lives. They were members of an infantry troop attacking an entrenched Chinese position. Wave after wave of Japanese attacked the position, only to be thrown back, for the Chinese troops had skillfully laid barbed wire and established a deadly machine gun cross fire. Seeing so many of their fellow infantrymen thrown back, they could only pray for them. Finally, in desperation, the three soldiers tied explosives to their waists; flinging themselves along the barbed-wire perimeter, the three human bombs opened the way for the assault wave to overrun the enemy position. Again in their final courageous suicidal act, the *niku dan san yu shi* will be honored and remembered for their heroism and adherence to the Japanese warrior code.

These examples of heroism and suicidal behavior which I had learned in the Japanese community in Los Angeles led me to hypothesize that we Japanese would commit suicide more frequently than other Asians or Caucasians. This, then, was the initial basis for this cross-cultural study of suicides.

## JAPANESE-AMERICAN VALUES

Japanese-Americans who grew up in the Little Tokyo section of Los Angeles were not of the samurai class. But they could develop a samurai identity through a code of conduct which greatly emphasized patience, perseverance, consideration for one's family, clan, and nation, courage and devotion to duty (Suzuki, et al. 1972). Hence, the emperor was the god.

This fierce pride in the Japanese identity and heritage was a most useful defense against the feelings of prejudice in the larger American community. Acts of discrimination could be neutralized by countervailing beliefs in the superiority of the Japanese: one expects more from a Japanese because he is more honest, reliable, conscientious, ambitious, thorough, hardworking, considerate, and clean (Caudill 1952; Light 1972; Yamamoto and Iga 1973; Breslow and Klein 1971; Dator 1966).

## HYPOTHESES

Have these Japanese ideals persisted in reference to suicide? In order to study this question, the incidence of suicide in Los Angeles among Japanese was compared with that of other Orientals and Caucasians who do not have the same tradition of suicidal behavior.

My first hypothesis was that the rate of suicide would be higher among Japanese. My second hypothesis was that the Japanese would more often cut themselves, like the samurai of the old tradition.

## DATA IN LOS ANGELES

The 1960 census showed that out of a total population of 6,038,771 in Los Angeles County, Japanese comprised 77,314 and other Orientals 31,408. It was hypothesized that the percentage of suicides would be higher among the Japanese.

Table 1 shows that there were, from 1959 to 1969, almost as many other

Table 1. Suicides of Japanese and other Orientals*

|  | Population in Los Angeles (1960) (U.S. Census data) | Suicides (1959–1969 (Coroner's data) |
|---|---|---|
| Japanese | 77,314 | 83 |
| All other Orientals | 31,408 | 66 |

* With a test of proportions, the above differences are significant with a probability of less than .01.

Orientals committing suicide as there were Japanese despite a smaller population in the area. Thus, this hypothesis was not confirmed. I will discuss this and other findings later on.

In evaluating the age distribution and modes of suicide, there were notable differences. The age distribution of Japanese is compared with the Caucasian population in Table 2.[1]

Table 2.   Age distribution of suicides — Caucasians and Japanese*

| Age | Caucasians (1969 only) | | Japanese (1959–1969) | |
|---|---|---|---|---|
| | Percent | Number | Percent | Number |
| 10–19 | 6.3 | 75 | 4.8 | 4 |
| 20–29 | 18.9 | 224 | 16.9 | 14 |
| 30–39 | 14.2 | 169 | 24.1 | 20 |
| 40–49 | 19.0 | 226 | 21.7 | 18 |
| 50–59 | 17.9 | 212 | 4.8 | 4 |
| 60–69 | 12.0 | 142 | 12.0 | 10 |
| 70–79 | 11.5 | 137 | 9.6 | 8 |
| 80–89   unknown | 0.2 | 2 | 3.6 | 3 |
| Totals | 100.0 | 1,187 | 97.5 | 83 |

\*   The above differences are not significant with the *chi* square test. The lowest probability is at the level of 0.10.

The mean age for Japanese suicides was 44.5, with a range from 17 to 91. The median age was 40. Surprisingly, the mode was 35 with some 24 percent (20/83) of the suicides being in the age range of 30 to 39. Thus, the Japanese seem to be greater risks for suicide at a slightly younger age than Caucasians.

When the method of suicide is analyzed, there are clearly Japanese methods of suicide. Table 3 shows that the frequency of suicide by hanging is much greater among the Japanese. Suicide by cutting, jumping, suffocation, and burns, is also relatively more frequent. In contrast, the most popular method used by Caucasians is taking overdoses of barbiturates, namely, 38.8 percent; among the Japanese it is only 19.3 percent. Gunshot wounds are similarly less frequent, with 28.6 percent of Caucasians and only 13.3 percent of Japanese. The less frequently used means of suicide, such as poisons, carbon monoxide inhalation, vehicles, narcotics, etc., are used even less often by the Japanese.

The incidence of cutting is higher among Japanese — 10.8 percent as compared to 2 percent among Caucasians. This tended to confirm the second hypothesis that the Japanese more often commit suicide by cutting.

---

[1]   The data on Caucasians were for the year 1969 only.

Table 3. Methods of suicide — Caucasians and Japanese*

| | Caucasians (1969 only) | | Japanese (1959–1969) | |
| | Percent | Number | Percent | Number |
|---|---|---|---|---|
| Barbiturates | 38.8 | 460 | 19.3 | 16 |
| Gunshot wounds | 28.6 | 339 | 13.3 | 11 |
| Other poisons | 9.9 | 117 | 2.4 | 2 |
| Hanging | 7.3 | 87 | 36.0 | 30 |
| Carbon monoxide exhaust | 5.3 | 63 | 3.6 | 3 |
| Jumping | 3.0 | 36 | 4.8 | 4 |
| Cutting | 2.2 | 26 | 10.8 | 9 |
| Suffocation | 1.4 | 17 | 4.8 | 4 |
| Drowning | 1.0 | 12 | 2.4 | 2 |
| Miscellaneous | 0.8 | 10 | — | — |
| Burns | 0.8 | 9 | 2.4 | 2 |
| Vehicles | 0.6 | 7 | — | — |
| Narcotics | 0.3 | 4 | — | — |
| Totals | 100.0 | 1,187 | 99.8 | 83 |

* Combining in the Caucasian group burns, vehicles, and narcotics, the above differences are significant with the *chi* square test with a probability of less than 0.01.

Table 4. Methods of suicide among Japanese with Japanese and American given names

| | Given names | | |
| | Japanese | American | Total |
|---|---|---|---|
| Overdose | 6 | 10 | 16 |
| Gunshot wounds | 6 | 5 | 11 |
| Hanging | 23 | 7 | 30 |
| Cutting | 7 | 2 | 9 |
| Jumping | 4 | 0 | 4 |
| Suffocation | 3 | 1 | 4 |
| Carbon monoxide exhaust | 0 | 3 | 3 |
| Drowning | 1 | 1 | 2 |
| Burns | 1 | 1 | 2 |
| Poison | 1 | 1 | 2 |

* With the *chi* square test, there are no significant differences due to the small numbers.

Because one index of acculturation is having an American first name, the data were analyzed to compare persons having Japanese given names with those having American first names. Table 4 gives the results. As is apparent, when the method of committing suicide is more frequent among the Japanese, for example, hanging, cutting, suffocation, jumping, drowning, and burns, there is a distinct tendency toward Japanese given names. This suggests that those Japanese who are less Americanized use suicide methods common to the Japanese.

Table 5 shows that when comparing Japanese ways of suicide (hanging, cutting, suffocation, jumping, drowning, burns) and American ways (overdose of barbiturates, gunshot wounds, other poisons, etc.) there is a remarkably direct relationship. Most of those using Japanese methods have Japanese first names. On the other hand, the majority of those using American methods had American first names. Thus, it appears that acculturation influences the mode of suicide.

Table 5.   Relation of method of suicide to given names*

| Method of suicide | Given names | | |
| --- | --- | --- | --- |
| | Japanese | American | Total |
| "Japanese" (e.g. hanging, cutting, jumping, suffocation, drowning, burns) | 39 | 12 | 51 |
| "American" (e.g. barbiturate overdose, gunshot wounds, carbon monoxide exhaust, poison) | 13 | 19 | 32 |

*   With the *chi* square test, the above differences are significant with a probability of less than .01.

## SUMMARY

Being an American born of Japanese parents, I recalled the cultural attitudes toward suicide as taught by my parents and the media. Having also been influenced by extensive exposure to American ways, I have a combination of values as do other Japanese in Los Angeles. The proportion may vary, but the ingredients are the same.

I hypothesized that because suicide in Japan is accepted as an honorable solution to life's vicissitudes, the Japanese even in Los Angeles are more likely to commit suicide. However, a comparison study of suicides among Orientals showed that the Japanese do not commit suicide more frequently. The data substantiated my second hypothesis that the Japanese more often cut themselves.

Analysis of eighty-three Japanese suicides showed that in this group, the age of suicide in a substantial group may be younger because the most frequent age group was 30 to 39. Suicide occurred only one-third as often among those 50 to 59 (4.8 percent compared to 17.9 percent of Caucasians in the same age group).

There are typical ways to commit suicide among the Japanese: hanging cutting, jumping, suffocation, drowning, and burns. In contrast, Caucasians more frequently die of barbiturate overdose and gunshot wounds. Comparison of the given names of those Japanese who used hanging, cutting, and other Japanese methods showed they had Japanese first names. As might then be expected, those who used Caucasian methods such as barbiturate overdose and gunshot wounds had American first names. This shows the importance of culture in determining the method of suicide. In Japan, *seppuku* was the religious ceremonial ritual used by samurais in suicide. The masses either hanged themselves or drowned in suicide attempts, according to Dr. Thomas Noguchi. Thus, many more used hanging, but a substantial number committed suicide by cutting. Perhaps these latter were influenced by the samurais of old Japan.

## REFERENCES

BRESLOW, L., B. KLEIN
1971   Health and race in California. *American Journal of Public Health* 61: 763–775.
CAUDILL, W.
1952   *Japanese-American personality and acculturation.* Genetic Psychology Monographs 45.
DATOR, J. A.
1966   The "Protestant ethic" in Japan. *Journal of Developing Areas* 1:23–40.
IGA, M., J. YAMAMOTO
1973   "The chrysanthemum and the sword in suicide: Yasunari Kawabata and Yukio Mishima," in *Life-threatening behavior*, volume three.
LIGHT, I. H.
1972   *Ethnic enterprise in America.* Berkeley: University of California Press.
SUZUKI, T., *et al.*
1972   A study of Japanese-Americans in Honolulu, Hawaii. *Annals of the Institute of Statistical Mathematics (supplement).*
THOMAS, DOROTHY S.
1952   *The salvage.* Los Angeles: University of California Press.
YAMAMOTO, J., M. IGA
1973   Japanese enterprise and American middle-class values. American Journal of Psychiatry 131:577–579.

## COMMENT by H. Warren Dunham

I found Dr. Yamamoto's paper on suicide most interesting, particularly because of his own personal account of the formation of the problem. Dr. Yamamoto, of course, was concerned as to whether he could establish a higher rate of suicide among the Japanese in Los Angeles as compared to other Orientals. He fully expected the Japanese to have a higher rate because of the high rate of suicide in Japan. However, he found just the reverse, namely, that the other ethnic groups had a rate twice as high as the Japanese. I cannot help but note, however, that he misses the point that his data help to establish, namely, that the acculturation and assimilation of the Japanese in America have been most successful and that they are likely to exhibit traits and adjustment patterns much closer to the Americans than to the Japanese living in Japan.

## REPLY by Joe Yamamoto

Dr. Dunham's comments are well taken. The progress in education and enterprise of the Japanese in America are well known to all of us. My point was related to those who may not have succeeded in adapting and who may then have resorted to suicide because of the cultural approval of suicidal behavior.

Not all the acculturation has been due to assimilation, it has been influenced also by congruence of values. Suzuki's survey of national character and comparison in Honolulu illustrates this point.

# Personal Situation as a Determinant of Suicide and Its Implications for Cross-Cultural Studies

MAMORU IGA

## SOCIOLOGICAL STUDIES OF SUICIDE

Sociological studies of suicide are not generally applicable to a cross-cultural study, largely for two reasons. First, sociologists explain suicide primarily in terms of social condition, such as cohesiveness (Durkheim 1951), status integration (Gibbs and Martin 1964), and external restraint (Henry and Short 1954; Maris 1969). Because these factors may be both directly and inversely related to suicide rate, it is necessary to find intervening factors, which distinguish a high-suicide-rate society from a low-suicide-rate one, with the above factors controlled. Second, in cross-cultural studies, statistics are not generally comparable, and case analyses therefore are necessary. However, the tendency among sociologists to emphazise the environmental situation at the expense of a personal one — a series of fields in which the self and physico-sociocultural environments interact — makes for difficulty in applying sociological theories to individual cases.

The most notable example is Durkheim's typology of suicide, which has been the fountainhead of numerous sociological studies. Because of its inapplicability, Douglass (1967) attempted to relate it to the individual by interpreting Durkheim's types as social forces, which exist in all individuals. The loss of the equilibrium among them makes for a suicidal motivation, which is characterized by the most dominant force, whether it be egoistic, altruistic, anomic, or fatalistic. However, the interpretation has not been converted into behavioral indicators, which are necessary for relating to cases.

The Durkheimian types of suicide seem to be represented by behavioral traits on four levels: personality, social relations, crisis situation, and psychological condition. The personality system is represented by self- or collectivity-oriented values and by individually characteristic means for goal attainment. The social-relational system is divided into relational (as indicated by the degree of social restraint), attitudinal (as shown by the degree of self-assertiveness), communicational (degree of communication with social objects), and evaluational (criteria for evaluation of received communication).

A suicide type is interpreted as a pattern produced by the combination of these traits. For example, the egoistic suicide is indicated by (1) self-oriented goals and nonconforming means for goal attainment (personality), and (2) weak (or weakly felt) social restraint, a high degree of demands and self-expression, a low degree of received communication, and highly individualistic criteria for evaluating received communication (social relation). This type of person may crave for the meaning of life, which is obtainable only by social attachment (Durkheim 1951:212). He may suffer from the conflict between selfish goals and unconscious wishes for response and recognition (crisis). In a frustrating situation, he may have a difficulty in finding a meaningful communication, and may lose the courage to live (psychological condition).

In a previous work, these indicators were applied to sixty-eight completed suicides by Kyoto University students, which had occurred during the period from 1953 through March 1968. There was no egoistic suicide, in comparison with three altruistic, thirteen fatalistic, and fifty-two anomic suicides (Iga 1971). The same indices were applied to the suicides of two prominent Japanese writers: Yasunari Kawabata, the Nobel Prize winner for literature in 1968, and Yukio Mishima, a Nobel Prize candidate in the same year. Kawabata left his home in Kamakura in the afternoon of April 16, 1972, for his workroom in nearby Zushi. There was no sign of suicidal intention. That evening he was found dead with a gas conduit in his mouth in the room, which commanded magnificent views of an ocean and mountains. He was seventy-two years old.

Mishima committed *harakiri* [self-disembowelment] on November 25, 1970, with one of his male admirers, following the traditional samurai ritual. He did so after delivering an impassioned plea to 1,200 members of the Self-Defense Forces from the balcony of its Tokyo headquarters, for an uprising to produce a constitutional change, which would revive the Imperial Army. He was 45 years old. The application found that both suicides were "egoistic," although the writers were diametrically opposite in personality, philosophy of life, and experiences. Apparently, the Durkheimian typology, like most other sociological theories, lacks the power to discriminate individual cases.

## PSYCHOLOGICAL STUDIES OF SUICIDE

Psychological studies of suicide seem to be classified into five categories:
1. Personality traits, e.g. impulsiveness, narcissism, dependence.
2. Psychological condition, e.g. loss of self-esteem; perturbation, anguish, rage; and feelings of powerlessness, worthlessness, loneliness, and hopelessness.
3. Inferred motive, e.g. wishes to kill, to be killed, and to die; and wishes for ego maintenance, rebirth and reunion, communication, revenge, escape from fear and doubt, and for control of "significant others."
4. Learning of inadequate social techniques (for handling others) and adjustment mechanisms (for tension reduction), together with rigidity.
5. Thinking pattern, e.g. narrowing perception; semantic confusion, e.g. "If anyone kills himself, he will get attention. If I kill myself, I will get attention."

These concepts are applicable to suicidal individuals. However, they are mostly symptoms rather than causes. Nor do they really distinguish suicidal individuals from each other, because suicidal persons show a combination of the same traits. The major difficulty here seems to be that the psychological explanations are generally segmentalistic and neglect the total situation in which the victim is enveloped. Especially the tendency among psychologists to disregard values produces a difficulty in cross-cultural studies, because values largely determine any behavior, including suicide.

## PERSONAL SITUATION AS A PROCESS

The personal situation is considered to consist of two phases: definition of the situation and adjustive effort. The suicidogenic definition of the situation is produced by the interaction between three factors: (1) wide goal-means discrepancy, (2) the lonely self, and (3) perception of the immediate condition as overwhelming and inescapable. The self-destructive adjustment is composed of (1) inadequate coping mechanism, (2) the inaccessibility to effective alternative outlets for aggression, (3) a negative view of life and accepting views of death and suicide, and (4) perception of others as unreliable for problem solving. Each of these components is not determined solely by psychology or by society but by their interaction in a particular situation. Individual uniqueness among suicidal victims comes from a unique combination of the components.

The objective of this study is to apply these components to the suicides of Kawabata and Mishima. If they are applicable to the suicides and if they show the difference between them, the components may suggest a model for comparative study of not only suicide but also mental health in general.

## DEFINITION OF THE SITUATION

### Goal-Means Discrepancy

When writers finally attain the gratifications of a high level of self-esteem, public success, and power which accompany their success, they will establish a new standard to repeat the past achievement (Weissman n.d.). This applied to both Kawabata and Mishima. The difference between them was in the means available for their goal attainment.

Kawabata's difficulty was partly due to his declining physical strength and partly, however ironic it may sound, to his great popularity among the public as a result of the Nobel Prize. The popularity was utilized by politicians, and Kawabata, whose whole life had been devoted to aestheticism, was suddenly thrown into "dirty" politics. He campaigned vigorously and conscientiously, but in vain, for Hatano, a conservative mayoral candidate for Tokyo. The involvement was very emotional because of his hostility toward progressivism, and it produced a psychological disequilibrium (Hirano 1972).

The deflated self-conception of Mishima came basically from his highly narcissistic temperament. He was reared by his sickly grandmother, who loved him so much that she took him away from his parents when he was forty-nine days old. Because of his poor health she was extremely indulgent, producing the infantile sense of omnipotence. She reared him as if he were a girl until he was fourteen years old, when she died. Until his senior high school age he spoke girls' language. The Peers School, which he attended from elementary through high school, placed a particular emphasis on masculinity, primarily because of the tendency among upper-class Japanese families to produce effeminate boys. This emphasis made him feel particularly ashamed of his own girlish language and behavior.

To his frail physique and feminine identification he reacted with compulsive masculinity and narcissism. The narcissism was furthered by a series of easy successes during his adolescence and young adulthood. The masculine physique which he developed by body building reinforced this narcissism. Highly characteristic was a boastful declaration in August, 1970: "I cannot see any cultural development in postwar Japan of any significance. Poetry? No... In literature, there is only myself" (Shabikoff 1970). With this attitude, the failure to receive the Nobel Prize must have been a severe blow. In addition, even during his last several years, when many critics believed that Mishima's creativity was already exhausted, he continued to be a superb critic *(Shūkan Gendai* 1970). His critical competence must have produced diffuse but keen dissatisfaction with himself, which his narcissism did not admit.

The dissatisfaction was probably due basically to his limited life experience. The grandmother reared him in almost complete isolation from his peers, particularly from boys, lest he should learn "bad things" from them. His whole world consisted of picture books and children's stories, and his upbringing was confined to an atmosphere of rigidity, fanaticism, indulgence, and detachment from reality. His limited life experiences are reflected by his knowledge of Japanese society which was limited to his narrow circle of life in upper- or upper-middle-class Tokyo. Even his knowledge of samurai culture, which he romanticized, was limited to an abstract conception of their culture in the latter part of the Tokugawa period in the eighteenth century. His samurai identification and detachment from reality were probably handicaps as a writer. His hostility toward realistic description, relying almost entirely on his own imagination for his work, must have been a constant source of strains and anxiety.

## The Lonely Self

Both Kawabata and Mishima felt alienated from the social reality surrounding them. The individualistic, materialistic, and rationalistic "democracy" of postwar Japan produced an overwhelming frustration and intense hostility in both, and advocacy of particularism, familism, traditionalism, intuitionism, and mysticism. Kawabata's inability to form intimate relationships is reflected in his character Komako in *Snow country*, who "seemed to live alone reading books, without much friendship with fellow villagers" (Kawabata 1970). His loneliness was rooted in his childhood experiences. During his first year of life, both his parents died, and he was separated from his only sister, with whom he had no subsequent contact. The sister died when he was ten years old. His grand-mother died when he was seven and his grandfather when he was sixteen years old. He had little contact with other relatives. One of his novels, *Nemureru Bijo* [*House of the sleeping beauties*], symbolizes a wish to be warmed by a maternal figure. Mishima had no really intimate friend. He felt that "he had been betrayed by his seniors and friends repeatedly" (Muramatsu 1970:53) (Ōka 1971:110). His perception of the happy family as an "enemy" (Muramatsu 1970:53), was probably a projection of his own alienation.

*Perception of Immediate Condition as Overwhelming and Inescapable*

Kawabata's despair is expressed in his statement: "Since the defeat in the last war, I have nothing but to return to *Nihon korai no kanashimi* [traditional pathos of Japan]. I do not believe in postwar conditions, not do I believe in reality" (Kawabata 1970:702). Shortly before the reception of the Nobel Prize, he felt that his body was "crumbling down all over" and he was "almost giving up" (Nakamura 1972:23).

In 1965, five years before his death, Mishima was "disgusted with literature," and suffered from a feeling of helplessness. He thought that nothing he attempted was useful (Fukushima 1971:258). In March 1970 Mishima thought, "Life is a nosedive to decay without any alternative potential left" and he wanted to die quickly (*Bungei Shunju* 1971:238). Just about a week before his death, he said, "I am exhausted... I am disgusted.... There is no way out" (Mizutsu 1971:125).

Thus far, three elements of the suicidogenic definition of the situation have been discussed. Once a person has defined the situation, his response to the definition marks the difference between suicide and survival. The response is determined by the interaction between the elements below.

## ADJUSTIVE EFFORT

*Inadequate Coping Mechanism*

The mechanisms which Kawabata and Mishima used can be inferred only through their behavior. Mishima's heightened narcissism toward the end of his life apparently was related to a weak ego control, i.e. an ineffective coping mechanism in a frustrating situation. Narcissistic dependence upon others for constant admiration, without a capacity to love them, interacts with the wish for self-inflation, forming a vicious cycle. The cycle impairs social relations, and ultimately makes for increasingly less effective coping mechanisms.

The growing ineffectiveness of Kawabata's coping mechanism was indicated by his unusually emotional expression of hostility toward "progressive" Mayor Minobe, (Mizutsu 1971:57; Seidenstecker1972:344). who was generally favored by Japanese intellectuals. The decline of his self-control possibly came from two sources. One was his habit of taking sleeping pills, in combination with his physical weakness. Kawabata often suffered from insomnia and needed sleeping pills to ease his tension. He frequently was found in a daze (Nakamura 1972:23). It is probable that when he had to operate in reality without the influence of pills, he became more easily irritated. The other is the impetuosity which often accompanies a great success. A success, such as the Nobel Prize, tends to produce and promote narcissism and the sense of omnipotence. Kawabata might have unconsciously placed himself in the position of a demigod in his evaluation of others. The more narcissistic the less effective is the coping mechanism in frustration.

### Inaccessibility of Effective Alternative Outlets for Aggression

Japanese people generally show three patterns of behavior for ego defense: *gurūpu maibotsu shugi* [identification with the group], *dentō maibotsu shugi* [merging oneself in tradition], and *kōdō maibotsu shugi* [forgetting frustration by becoming absorbed in compulsive action] (Ishikawa 1965:39). Mishima's behavior may be explained in terms of *dentō* and *kōdō maibotsu shugi*, as indicated by his glorification of samurai tradition and his belief in *chiko gōitsu* [identity of knowledge and action]. However, ultimately all activities short of suicide proved ineffective in satisfying his narcissistic ego.

Kawabata was an individualist, as he called himself *burai no to* [villain or nonconformer]. He was a nihilist (Nakamura 1972:23). Therefore, group identification was not functional for his tension reduction. Neither was traditionalism. Despite his traditionalistic appearance, tradition was not to supply materials for his self-expression. Probably, such activities as writing and making a trip could have alleviated his tension. However, his old age and declining physical strength deprived him of these pleasures.

*Negative View of Life, Negative Views of Death and Suicide*

The basic philosophy of life of both Kawabata and Mishima was traditionally Japanese: life and death are determined by *tenri* [natural law]. Because life came from eternal Nature, one should be ready to return there. To live according to Nature is to die according to it (Ben Dasan 1971:134). Beyond this basic orientation, Kawabata was strongly influenced by Heian literature, which was characterized by the almost exclusive concern with sensual pleasure and the beauty of Nature (Yamada 1972:18), by the pessimistic view that life was suffering and death was sweet, and by an animistic belief in the existence and influence of spirits — all contributed to his suicide.

Mishima was attracted by Wang-Yangmin's philosophy with its spiritualism and activism. According to the philosophy, the ultimate significance of life is in attaining the "great nothingness," which can be attained only be rejecting one's self for a great cause. The great cause, in Mishima's eyes, was an action characterized by "solitude, tension, and tragic resolution" (Mishima 1970:56), as exemplified by his suicide.

*Perception of Others as Unreliable for Problem Solving*

As long as a person feels that other people are helpful, the feeling is a deterrent to suicide. However, Japanese people generally avoid being involved in other persons' troubles (Trumbull 1958:74), thus breeding mistrust against one another. Mishima's mistrust was shown by the aforementioned belief that he had been betrayed repeatedly by his seniors and friends. The protagonists in Kawabata's novels and stories are lonely figures, probably suggesting his attitude toward people in general. He was a fatalist and believed that human endeavor could not change fate.

## SUMMARY AND IMPLICATION OF CROSS-CULTURAL STUDIES

It was indicated here that the personal situation — the series of fields of constant interaction between the self and the physico-sociocultural environments — is a determinant of suicide. The personal situation, it was stated, consists of a definition of the situation and adjustive effort. The former is determined by wide goal-means discrepancy, the lonely self, and the perception of the immediate condition as overwhelming and inescapable. The self-destructive adjustment is due to an inadequate coping mechanism; inaccessibility of effective outlets for aggression; a negative view of life and accepting views of death and suicide; and the perception of others as unreliable for problem solving. According to this analytical scheme, the similarities and differences between the suicides of Kawabata and Mishima were explained.

In conclusion, the concept of personal situation seems to be useful in explaining suicide as a process and a situation. The difference between the suicides of the two writers was found to be largely due to differences in basic value orientation. The analysis of goal-means discrepancy; alternative outlets for aggression; views of life, death, and suicide; and the availability of social resources revealed directly the societal values. The other element of personal situation — the self-conception, perception of conditions, and coping mechanism — reflected societal values indirectly through the childhood experiences of the writers.

## REFERENCES

BEN DASAN, ISAIAH
1971 *Nihon-jin to Yudaya-jin* [The Japanese and the Jew]. Tokyo: Kadokawa Shoten.
*Bungei Shunjū*
1971 Article appearing in *Bungei Shunjū* 49(2):238 (February 1971).
DOUGLASS, JACK D.
1967 *The social meanings of suicide*. Princeton: Princeton University Press.
DURKHEIM, EMILE
1951 *Suicide*. Translated by J. A. Spaulding and G. Simpson. Glencoe, Illinois: Free Press.
FUKUSHIMA, AKIRA
1971 Mishima Yukio no naiteki sekai [Inner world of Yukio Mishima]. *Gendai no esupuri; L'Esprit d'aujourd hui* 9 (51):258 (July).
GIBBS, JACK R., W. T. MARTIN
1964 *Status integration and suicide*. Eugene: University of Oregon Press.
HENRY, A. F., J. F. SHORT
1954 *Suicide and homicide*. Glencoe, Illinois: Free Press.
HIRANO, KEN
1972 Bungei Jihyōka: Kawabata Yasunari [Yasunari Kawabata: commentator on current literature]. *Sekai* (319) 261–265.
IGA, M.
1971 A concept of anomie and suicide of Japanese college students. *Life-Threatening Behavior* 1:4.
ISHIKAWA, HIROYOSHI
1965 *Nihonjin no shakai shinri* [Social psychology of the Japanese people]. Tokyo: Sanichi Shobo.

KAWABATA, YASUNARI
   1970   *Kawabata Yasunari zenshu* [Works of Yasunari Kawabata], Tokyo: Shinchosha.
MARIS, R. W.
   1969   *Social forces in urban suicide.* Homewood, Illinois: Dorsey Press.
MISHIMA, YUKIO
   1970   *Kōdō-gaku Nyūmon* [Introduction to the study of action], Tokyo: Bungei Shunjū-sha.
MIZUTSU, KENJI
   1971   *Mishima Yukio no higeki* [Tragedy of Yukio Mishima]. Tokyo: Toshi Shuppan-sha.
MURAMATSU, TSUYOSHI
   1970   Watashi wa sore o yochi shite ita [I foresaw it].   *Shūkan Gendai,* December 12.
NAKAMURA, SHINICHIRO
   1972   Kyomu o mitsumeru bigaku [Aesthetics gazing at vacuum]. *Asahi Jānaru* [Journal] 14(17):23 (April 28, 1972).
ŌKA, SHŌHEI
   1971   Ikinokotta mono e no shogen [Testimony to those who remain alive]. *Bungei Shunjū* 94(2):110.
SEIDENSTECKER, E. G.
   1972   Kawabata Yasunari to tomo ni hitotsu no jidai wa satta [With Yasunari Kawabata an era is gone]. *Chūo Kōron* 87(6):344 (June).
SHABIKOFF, P.
   1970   "Yukio Mishima." *New York Times Magazine,* August 2.
*Shūkan Gendai*
   1970   Article appearing in *Shūkan Gendai.* December 12.
TRUMBULL, ROBERT
   1958   "Japan turns against the 'Gyangu'." *New York Times Magazine,* November 30.
WEISSMAN, PHILLIP
   n.d.   "The suicide of Hemingway and Mishima: a study of the narcissistic ego ideal." Unpublished, undated manuscript.
YAMADA, MUNEMUTSU
   1972   "Yuki-tsuki-hana no shisō" [Ideology of the snow-moon-flower]. *Asahi Jānaru* (Journal) 14(17):18 (April 28, 1972).

## ADDITIONAL REFERENCES

BOHANNAN, PAUL, *editor*
   1960   *African homicide and suicide.* Princeton: Princeton University Press.
DUBLIN, LOUIS I.
   1963   *Suicide: a sociological and statistical study.* New York: Ronald Press.
FARBEROW, N. L., E. S. SHNEIDMAN
   1961   *The cry for help.* New York: McGraw-Hill.
GIDEON, ANTHONY
   1971   *The sociology of suicide.* London: Frank Cass.

HENDIN, H.

1964 *Suicide and Scandinavia: a psychoanalytic study of culture and character.* New York: Grune and Stratton.

1969 *Black suicide.* New York: Basic Books.

JACOBS, JERRY

1971 *Adolescent suicide.* New York: Wiley-Interscience.

KOHLER, A. L., E. STOTLAND

1964 *The end of hope.* Glencoe, Illinois: Free Press.

MEERLOO, J. A. M.

1962 *Suicide and mass suicide.* New York: Grune and Stratton.

RESNIK, H. L. P., *editor*

1968 *Suicidal behaviors.* Boston: Little, Brown.

SEIDEN, RICHARD H.

1969 *Suicide among youth. A review of literature, 1900–1967.* Washington: U.S. Government Printing Office.

SHNEIDMAN, E. S.

1967 *Essays in self-destruction.* New York: Science House.

1969 *On the nature of suicide.* San Francisco: Jossey-Bass.

SHNEIDMAN, E. S., N. L. FARBEROW

1957 *Clues to suicide.* New York: McGraw-Hill.

# Multiethnic Studies of Psychopathology and Normality in Hawaii

MARTIN M. KATZ and KENNETH O. SANBORN

Psychosis, the most extreme form of mental disorder, is expressed through social behavior, through the expression of emotions, through the manner in which human beings perceive the outer world, and how they think about it. When someone is judged to be "psychotic," we identify or diagnose it not through any tests of biological functioning, but by the outer behavioral manifestations of this inner disturbance; certain emotions like anxiety and depression are exaggerated beyond normal limits, or the capacity to distinguish fantasy from reality appears to be weakening, or there may be highly defined disturbances in thought, false ideas we identify as delusions. There are obviously many ways to express severe inner psychological disturbance – we know that how it gets expressed in any one person is the result of many varied psychological, biological, and cultural forces.

Since it is not likely that psychosis is "caused" by any one of these major influences, most clinical research on the mental disorder proceeds as if it is the outgrowth of many forces; culture, specific environmental stress, the personality of the individual, his constitution, his biology, his capacity to endure stress, and his psychological history and development. Of all these factors, it would be fair to say that we know least about the contribution of culture to the development and expression of psychosis. There are a number of practical reasons why this is so. To study such factors, we have, for example, to be in a position to compare the mentally ill in widely separated geographic settings. We also require methods for studying behavior that are both relevant to and can be translated within these cultures. Such methods have only recently been developed and most are relatively untried in cross-cultural research situations.

In the past, most such research has been carried out by anthropologists or culturally oriented psychiatrists and psychologists who relied very heavily on observation and on interview techniques. Most of the data we have are therefore impressionistic in quality. More recently, some of the newer devices for the systematic recording of symptoms and social behavior and for the quantification of observational data of this type have become available for application to the problem. These techniques were not designed for studies of "cultural influence" but lend themselves to systematic study of abnormal behavior across cultures.

With these developments, that is, both the increase in interest in the past few years in appraising the role of culture, and the availability of certain methods, it becomes possible to reapproach some of the critical questions in this area and to expect to obtain more definitive answers. It was in this spirit and in relation to some new findings on the variations of schizophrenia (Katz 1968; Katz, Cole, and Lowery 1964) that we began some years back to study the ways in which people from very different cultural backgrounds express psychopathology.

The findings related, for example, in some unusual ways to earlier differences that had been uncovered in an intensive investigation of the behavior and symptoms of Hawaii-Japanese and Hawaii-Filipino paranoid schizophrenics (Enright and Jaeckel 1963). The Japanese presented a more contained, restrained psychosis marked by suspiciousness and seclusion; the Filipino, a more manic, aggressive form of what appeared to be the same underlying condition. In a large group of mainland schizophrenics studied in the National Institute of Mental Health Collaborative Studies of drugs and schizophrenia (National Institute 1964), we had uncovered a similar variety of forms within the category of paranoid schizophrenia, and the fact that certain of these types were predominant in certain ethnic groups we found intriguing.

It was intended, therefore, in what later became a very extensive study of psychopathology and normality in Hawaii, to compare Japanese, Caucasians, Hawaiians, Filipinos, and Portuguese, to examine the influence of ethnicity on the causation and on the shaping of symptoms and behavior, and to see whether certain improved methods which had been developed in the field of psychopharmacology could be applied to achieving more definitive answers on these cross-cultural questions.

If one is interested in the ways in which psychopathology is manifested in different cultural groups, then it is easy to see why Hawaii provides a very convenient laboratory. For one thing, the islands have representatives of such disparate cultural groups as the Western, the Oriental, the Malay, and the Polynesian. Further, in this particular setting, they all speak a common language. Finally, where severe functional mental disorders are the focus of interest, we note that there is only one state hospital in the islands and only one general hospital to which most of the severely disturbed are referred. Although we identify these aspects of the situation in Hawaii as advantages for cross-cultural research, we are also aware that the relatively uniform environmental conditions also contribute to a somewhat rapid assimilation of these groups and thus contribute to the blurring of lines among them.

The primary aim in this research, as a comparative study in culture and psychopathology, is the development of VALID OBJECTIVE PICTURES of the psychopathology of particular ethnic groups. There was interest in (1) whether various ethnic groups (in this case, Hawaii-Japanese, Hawaii-Filipinos, Hawaii-Caucasians, and part-Hawaiians) express psychosis differently; (2) whether these differences are consistent with those found in previous studies or consistent with what might be expected from an understanding of normal personality in these ethnic groups; and (3) for important theoretical reasons, whether there are ways in which all these groups of functional psychotics are the same (Katz, Sanborn, and Gudeman 1969a, 1969b).

To determine whether ethnic background influences psychopathology, it was clear that we first had to describe and to measure in reliable fashion the nature of each group's behavior and symptoms, and to work towards the development of valid "objective" pictures of the nature of their psychoses. This aim turned out to require a much more complicated approach than we initially had any reason to expect. In our studies we were going to rely almost exclusively on observational procedures, but we were going to extend this approach so that we could obtain several perspectives on the nature of the patient's behavior, e.g. using both professionals and lay people and studying the patient in more than one setting, in the hospital and in the community. We introduced a number of relatively new methods into this investigational approach.

If one wishes to develop "valid, quantitative pictures" of the behavior of patients through the observational method one has to cut through a number of natural perceptual biases to arrive at an "objective picture" of psychopathology. The overall assessment of a patient that one gets at any point in time is influenced by such factors as the following:
1. The nature and background of the interviewer or diagnostician himself: In clinical studies, it is always difficult to estimate the influence of the observer himself on his observations and judgments of patients, e.g. his experience, age, national background, etc. The complications these factors introduce are even more exaggerated in cross-ethnic and in

cross-cultural studies (Katz, Cole, and Lowery 1969).

2. The nature of the method for obtaining information, i.e. whether it be a "structured research" or the more conventional "unstructured clinical interview": The difference in what actually gets expressed by the patient, as a function of the type of interview, was clearly demonstrated in a study we carried out a couple of years ago using large groups of experienced clinical psychologists. Although only single case studies were involved, it was clear that the clinically oriented unstructured interviews were capable of bringing out more emotionality and more psychopathology than the standard or structured research interview.

3. The setting in which the research is carried out, i.e. where the patient is studied: Our early comparison in the Hawaii study of Japanese versus mainland schizophrenics exemplified that problem. For example, the Japanese looked more obstreporous and excited than the Caucasians in the community. The pictures these two groups presented were almost reversed following their entrance into the hospital (Katz, Sanborn, and Gudeman 1969a).

These methodological influences have to be controlled or their extent estimated in order to assess directly the actual nature of the differences between ethnic groups. We tried to overcome some of the obstacles by:

a. using a clinical interview with a standard set of questions across all ethnic groups, e.g. Mental Status Schedule (Spitzer, et al. 1967);

b. using a standard set of scales for rating psychiatric symptoms, e.g. IMPS (Lorr, et al. 1962);

c. investigating psychopathology in more than one setting, i.e. measuring social behavior and symptoms in the hospital and in the community through the use of a standard method, e.g. KAS (Katz and Lyerly 1963).

Further controls relevant to cross-cultural studies were also instituted, e.g. controls for social class, generation, etc. Finally, after becoming convinced that "normal" baselines were essential to answer the critical questions about the influence of culture, we introduced a second major study. This investigation was aimed at deriving baselines of social behavior and symptoms for each of the ethnic groups, and required the administration of one of the descriptive methods, the adjustment scales, to representative "normal" samples of each of the ethnic groups in the community. With this unique facet for a cross-cultural study, we would be able to consider the problem of how the community itself defines mental disorder.

Our sample of 300 consisted of all patients from selected ethnic groups between the ages of 20 to 50 who were admitted for severe functional psychotic disorders to Hawaii State Hospital over a period of two years. Our "normal" sample was drawn from a representative sample of 1300 households in Hawaii and provided subsamples for all of the ethnic groups included in the patient group.

## MAJOR FINDINGS

The results that have emerged from this series of studies are the following:
1.  Patients from different ethnic groups do manifest psychosis differently when judged by a varied group of experienced clinicians in the hospital setting. The contrast was most marked between the Hawaii-Japanese and the Hawaii-Caucasian patients, but there were variations in emotional and behavioral patterns between all groups.
2.  The differences are most pronounced in the expression of emotional states, i.e. hostility, anxiety, depression, and apathy.
3.  The Hawaii-Caucasian psychotic is viewed as significantly more "emotional" in quality — the Hawaii-Japanese, more schizoid, more withdrawn and retarded.
4.  The Japanese and the Filipinos do differ primarily on a factor called "disorganized hyperactivity" — one that indicated the Filipino psychotic to project a significantly more excited, hyperactive, manic quality. The findings tend to confirm previous findings concerning these two groups.
5.  There is less contrast between the ethnic groups in the cognitive and perceptual aspects of the psychosis — all have similar levels of disturbance in these spheres.

*On the Analysis of "Normal" and "Socially Deviant" Behavior in the Community*

The subsequent study of "normal behavior" in the community provided a baseline for each of the ethnic groups. These baselines could be used as a control and thus markedly increase the sensitivity of the relatives' ratings in the description of the patient sample. It was then possible to return to the community data on the patients and to reanalyze it.

Techniques which involve analysis of the patient's behavior in the community by controlling for specific ethnic norms (a) reveal the ethnic community's own definition of mental disorder, i.e. how they view the nature of the hospitalized patients' behavioral and emotional conditions, and (b) provide a profile for each patient which describes his specific "deviance" pattern.

This measure, which we call "social deviance," when compared across ethnic groups indicates wide differences in the way the various communities view and judge emotionally disturbed behavior.

The Hawaii-Japanese psychotic, for example, is viewed as highly suspicious and anxious — the emotional side of this picture contrasting markedly with the clinician's appraisals. The Caucasian and the Portuguese community portraits specifically are seen, however, more in accord with the anxious, depressed quality identified by the clinicians.

Finally, using this approach to retest the specific hypothesis concerning the nature of the Japanese and Filipino psychoses, the Japanese and Filipino are viewed by their own communities as highly paranoid — more so than the other groups — but the distinction is clearer that the Japanese paranoia is of a more fearful, agitated type, and the Filipino is a more belligerent, "helpless" type. These characteristics fill out somewhat the picture provided by the clinical ratings. They also are in accord with earlier findings and provide a more complete picture of the contrasting features.

What are the theoretical and clinical implications of these findings?

## On Culture and Psychopathology

If we were to review the way clinicians observe and judge psychopathology, we would say that the main impact of culture is on the manner in which EMOTIONS AND BEHAVIOR are expressed. The impact is less on the "core" psychosis, e.g. on the perception and assessment of reality — the nature of the thought disorder.

In isolating the factor of ethnicity, the findings clearly indicate that the ways in which psychopathology is expressed vary as a function of cultural background. Further, there is support for a theory that psychosis as expressed through behavior is an exaggeration of the normal pattern; that observation would hold particularly for two of the groups, the Hawaii-Portuguese and Hawaii-Filipino samples.

Because of discrepancies in the way the Japanese are perceived by professionals and by their own ethnic community, a similar conclusion that the normal emotional and social behavior pattern is exaggerated in psychosis cannot be drawn about that group. We make note of the fact, however, that Caucasian clinicians may have difficulty in reading, interpreting the emotions of the Japanese, so we are less comfortable about their description of the psychotic pattern.

We confront again a critical problem inherent in this investigational approach. The ways in which our observers perceive behavior are also influenced by their own ethnic background. The influence of culture is, therefore, felt in two ways in such research: its impact on the behavior of the various groups, and on the way our observers perceive behavior.

We are currently attempting through experiment to analyze further the extent of the influence of culture on perception — to study how the various ethnic groups perceive the behavior of others in that community; to investigate the more general problem of how behavior and perception interrelate in multiethnic communities.

It is clear that while multiethnic situations are useful models for cross-cultural research, they are also unique in their own right. As part of one community, each ethnic group's history and patterns of behavior begin to blend with those of the other groups and the difficulties of character-izing its uniqueness increases with time.

Even without complete understanding of how these groups relate and perceive each other, we can already see the clinical implications of a situation in which there is a discrepancy between the views of psychosis held by the professionals and those by particular ethnic groups.

Since both the community and the professionals contribute to identi-fying mental disorder, this discrepancy influences in unknown ways how we diagnose mental disorder and subsequently treat it in a given ethnic group. There are different qualities to the psychosis when one looks at it in the community — and then in the hospital. The problems inherent in cross-perception between ethnic groups are magnified in multiethnic communities like Hawaii and in other major urban centers, where the professionals are likely to be very different in background from the pa-tients they treat. We see the results of this work as contributing to clari-fying these issues by describing the "norms of social behavior and symptomatology" for each of the various groups, as seen through the eyes of the ethnic community and by the professionals, and by providing data on the kinds of patterns of mental disorder typical of these groups.

Cross-cultural and multiethnic studies have in common, then, the capacity to extend our understanding of the role of culture in the devel-opment of psychopathology. They also provide us with more refined information for diagnosing and, consequently, for treating mental dis-orders – thus contributing to the important task of sensitizing those who work in the mental health field to the complexities of conducting clinical work in the multiethnic community.

# REFERENCES

ENRIGHT, J., W. JAECKEL,
1963 Psychiatric symptoms and diagnoses in two sub-cultures. *International Journal of Social Psychiatry* 9:12–17.
KATZ, M. M.
1968 "A phenomenological typology of schizophrenia," in *The role and methodology of classification in psychiatry and psychopathology.* Edited by M. M. Katz, J. O. Cole, and W. E. Barton. Washington, D. C.: U. S. Government Printing office.
KATZ, M. M., J. O. COLE, H. A. LOWERY
1964 The nonspecificity of the diagnosis of paranoid schizophrenia. *Archives of General Psychiatry* 11: 197–202.
1969 Studies of the diagnostic process: the influence of symptom perception, past experience and ethnic background on diagnostic decisions. *American Journal of Psychiatry* (125):109.
KATZ, M. M., S. B. LYERLY
1963 Methods of measuring adjustment and social behavior in the community, I: rationale, description, discriminative validity and scale development. *Psychological Reports* 13:503.
KATZ, M. M., K. O. SANBORN, H. GUDEMAN
1969a "Characterizing differences in psychopathology among ethnic groups. A preliminary report on Hawaii-Japanese and Mainland-American schizophrenics," in *Mental health research in Asia and the Pacific.* Edited by W. Caudill and Tsung-yi Lin. Honolulu: Center Press.
1969b Characterizing differences in psychopathology among ethnic groups in Hawaii. *Social Psychiatry* 47:139.
LORR, M., D. M. MC NAIR, C. J. KLETT, J. J. LASKY
1962 Evidence of ten psychotic syndromes. *Journal of Consulting Psychology* 26:185–189.
NATIONAL INSTITUTE OF MENTAL HEALTH — PSYCHOPHARMACOLOGY SERVICE CENTER COLLABORATIVE STUDY GROUP
1964 Phenothiazine treatment in acute schizophrenia. *Archives of General Psychiatry* 10:246–261.
SANBORN, K. O., M. M. KATZ
1971 "Multiethnic norms of adjustment in Hawaii." Unpublished manuscript.
SPITZER, R. L., J. L. FLEISS, J. ENDICOTT, J. COHEN
1967 The mental status schedule: properties of factor analytically devised scale. *Archives of General Psychiatry* 16:489.

# Kifafa: A Tribal Disease in an East African Bantu Population

LOUISE JILEK-AALL

When working as a physician among the Wapogoro in the hinterland of Tanzania[1] in the 1960's, I noticed that an astonishing number of tribesmen came for the treatment of severe burns. Each time such a patient appeared at the dispensary, I noticed a certain excitement among the other people. They would shy away from the afflicted person, who was feared and treated with contempt. The burns would often cover large areas of the body, and many of these patients had scars from previous accidents. Treatment was difficult, as the patients invariably also were suffering from malnutrition and parasitic infestation to an even greater extent than the average Wapogoro.

Neither the patients nor their families or other tribesmen were willing to give an explanation regarding the origin of these burns; everybody would react with anxiety and try to avoid answering my questions. Because the Wapogoro use open domestic fires, I suspected that the patients had sustained their burns there. As most burns were located on face, hands, arms, chest, and abdomen, I concluded that these patients must have a tendency to fall head-on into the fire.

I soon learned that the affliction which causes these falls, was called *kifafa*. This term may be translated as "being half-dead," or "being rigid," like an insect which has the ability to freeze motionless when in danger. Once I knew this term, I was able to make informal inquiries about the illness.

I found that very few people outside the Wapogoro tribe had heard

[1] Wapogoro, a Bantu tribe populating the Mahenge mountain area of the southeastern interior of Tanzania (see Lussy 1951; Engelberger and Lussy 1954; Murdock 1959; Schoenaker 1965).

about *kifafa*, but every Wapogoro, even when living away from his tribe, seemed to know and fear it. I learned of numerous causes of this illness; such as poisoning, witchcraft, evil spirits, head injuries. I was told of many prophylactic rules, e.g. children should avoid spinning around so they would not get dizzy, as this is a symptom of *kifafa;* the fish-eagle should not be hunted because its diving for prey resembles the falling in an attack of *kifafa;* for the same reason one should not watch the convulsions of dying fowl. I also heard of a foreboding dream in which the dreamer washes himself and pours water over his shoulders with a feeling of great pleasure until the water suddenly turns red like blood. This is so frightening that the dreamer wakes up in a panic, expecting to fall ill with *kifafa*. People call this "the dream of the Wapogoro," and witch doctors prepare a special medicine against it (Jilek-Aall 1964; Jilek and Jilek-Aall 1967). There was such a preoccupation with *kifafa* among the Wapogoro, whose medicine men specialize in the treatment of this affliction, that it may well be called their tribal illness.

## METHOD

Becoming increasingly fascinated with the phenomenon of this tribal disease, I decided to stay among the Wapogoro in order to study *kifafa*, hoping to initiate an effective therapy. I suspected that *kifafa* might be a form of epilepsy and started some of the patients with burns on pheno-barbital medication. No sooner had the word spread that treatment for *kifafa* was available at the dispensary, than patients arrived in ever-increasing numbers. Every morning the most incredible looking wretches lay around the dispensary, dragged there and often abandoned by relatives. They were half-starved, covered with filth and sores, and, over-whelmed by fear and timidity, hardly uttered a word. Before long, crowds of *kifafa* patients threatened to inundate the dispensary. Thanks to the assistance rendered by the local Catholic mission, it was possible to organize a treatment program which developed into the Mahenge Clinic. About 200 patients were examined in the years 1961 to 1963 by myself and my husband, and 175 received anticonvulsive medication, many of them for up to fifteen years now. A Swiss nurse has kept the bush clinic functioning; she has trained African nursing aides to dispense medication and has continued to supervise treatment after we left Africa, informing us regularly on each patient's progress. Approximately 150 patients are still attending the clinic regularly, the majority have benefited from anti-convulsive medication, and many of them have been free of seizures for years.

## DATA

The approximately 200 patients suffering from *kifafa* who have been examined at our clinic in Mahenge belong to a tribal population estimated at 20,000 members, of which about 10,000 are served by the dispensary. We have been told that many more *kifafa* cases exist, tucked away in far-off places. This would mean that at least 2 percent of the Wapogoro population suffer from *kifafa*. By comparison, around 0.4 percent is the prevalence figure usually given for epilepsy in other investigated populations.

Although we assume *kifafa* to belong to the epileptic syndromes, it has sufficient peculiarities to warrant rating as a separate disease entity. After having gathered some experience among the Wapogoro, we found that it was frequently possible to recognize persons suffering from *kifafa* at first glance. Not only did their extremely poor physical condition set them apart from others; they would also display Parkinsonian features, such as a rigid, mask-like facial expression, drooling from the mouth, eyes without luster, grating monotonous voice, stooped posture, stiff shuffling gait, and clumsy movements. Some were limping, had asymetric features or deformed limbs; many showed psychomotor retardation and quite a few impressed one as oligophrenic.

On neurological examination, we often found asymetric, absent, or pathological tendon reflexes; several patients showed monoparesis. The most conspicuous manifestations of *kifafa* were generalized paroxysmal convulsions and acute psychotic episodes. Convulsive seizures were often extremely violent, the patient was thrown around and often remained unconscious for hours after an attack. Prodromal signs were described by nearly half of our patients and were not different from the typical aura experience of epileptics. Seizure frequency varied between once a year and several times daily.[2] Those patients who suffered frequent attacks, deteriorated quickly, both mentally and physically; some of them went into a cataleptic rigidity which lasted for days, terminating in a lethal *status epilepticus*. Age of onset was usually dated around puberty, but we saw many younger children already afflicted.

Wapogoro parents distinguish between common febrile convulsions in children and incipient *kifafa*. Besides *grand mal*-type and psychomotor-

---

[2]   The Wapogoro connect *kifafa* attacks with the lunar phases, claiming that seizures and other manifestations of the illness occur most frequently during the time of the new moon. This is an interesting contrast to Hippocratic and medieval European beliefs that the full moon aggravates epileptic seizure activity and the psychotic manifestations of "lunatics."

type seizures, 27 out of 175 patients presented with what may best be described as myoclonic attacks. This type of ictal manifestation occurred only in children and was called "nodding of the head"; it was either a precursor of, or appeared concomitantly with *grand mal* patterns. The child would suddenly drop its head, then lift it up again. Series of such nods could sometimes be observed; in a sitting child the head would drop lower and lower until it touched the ground, the child had barely raised its head when a new series of nods forced the head down again. These seizures were accompanied by drooling of saliva. The children seemed unaware of the attacks, although they appeared moody or aggressive.

Approximately 23 percent of the patients seen had shown psychotic states, some of which we observed. These were mostly episodes of frenzy with violent aggressive discharges, which explains the fear people have of *kifafa* patients. Some of these patients wandered off into the wilderness in a dreamlike state. Nobody dared to stop them although they were likely to perish there. The clinical picture of these psychotic episodes closely resembled those classified by French authors as *bouffées délirantes*. (Magnan [1886] cited in Ey 1963:245; Aubin 1939; Collomb 1956, 1965; Collomb and Plas 1958; Ey 1963; Jilek and Jilek-Aall 1970).

A phenomenon which sets the *kifafa* of the Wapogoro apart from epilepsy as known elsewhere is its extraordinarily high family incidence. The sample of pedigrees in Figure 1 will demonstrate this. Through careful enquiries we were able to show that 75 percent of all patients investigated had other family members who suffered from *kifafa* or who had died from this condition. Experience must have taught the Wapogoro that consanguineous kin of *kifafa* patients have a higher risk of begetting children afflicted with the disease, as bride prices are much lower even for healthy girls from *kifafa* families than for those from families without *kifafa*.

Like other tradition-oriented African populations, the Wapogoro have no fear of contagious diseases such as tuberculosis or leprosy. Even when warned of the danger of contagion, they do not easily abide by the regulations aimed at preventing the spread of such diseases. It was the more surprising to see the Wapogoro behave toward *kifafa* as if THAT was a highly contagious condition. The unmerciful way in which *kifafa* sufferers are treated may be explained by the Wapogoro belief that the evil spirit of *kifafa* can leap from a convulsing person to any bystander during an attack. The patient's saliva, feces and urine are considered especially dangerous. This can be fatal to the patient, as nobody dares to come to his assistance if he falls into the fire; hence the extensive burns with which the poor *kifafa*-sufferers came to our attention. As soon as a person has been labeled as having *kifafa*, he becomes a dangerous outcast and is

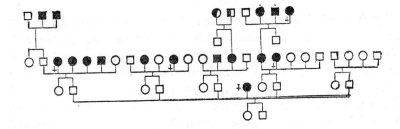

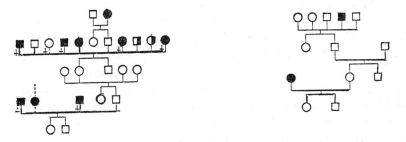

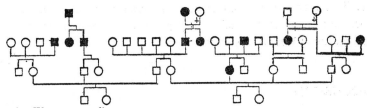

Figure 1. Wapogoro pedigrees

*Key*

□   – healthy male

○   – healthy female

■   – *kifafa* male

●   – *kifafa* female

◨   – mentally defect male, without seizure disorder

◖   – mentally defect, without seizure disorder

†   – deceased

forced to move out to live at some distance from the rest of his family.
Nobody else will use his eating and drinking utensils; he has to fetch his
water from a separate water hole, often far away from the dwellings.
When in a psychotic state, he is brutally beaten and forced into a hole in
the ground where he has to remain with very little water and food until he
regains his senses.

*Kifafa* is looked upon as a disgrace and shame for the entire family and is believed to be caused by witchcraft or to be the punishment for misdeeds of the afflicted himself or of his kin. Parental quarreling might lead to *kifafa* in a child. Lazy, alcoholic, or promiscuous persons, or those who break certain taboos may contract *kifafa* as avenging evil spirits take hold of them. Most sufferers accept the marginal niche and the pariah role reserved for them in Wapogoro society. They become shy, humble, and timid persons who, in mute apathy, have resigned themselves to their fate without hope or complaint, knowing that sooner or later they will succumb either to general infirmity or perish in an attack. A few may seek refuge in another village, but in the whole tribe strangers are viewed with suspicion lest they might spread *kifafa*. In due time, a sudden attack or a severe burn will reveal the illness and the refugee patient has to return to his village or risk being slain by the people he tried to deceive.

The *kifafa* sufferers who receive treatment at the Mahenge Clinic and remain free of attacks for years are looked upon with amazement and respect. Their living conditions have improved and they have regained self-confidence and hope for the future. Requests for further help both from *kifafa* patients and from alarmed elders of the tribe, who report that the disease is on the increase among the younger generation of the Wapogoro, keep reminding us of the urgent need for research into the origin and nature of this tribal illness.


## DISCUSSION

Several conditions which are prevalent in tropical Africa could possibly account for adverse effects on the central nervous system, such as asphyxia due to obstetric mismanagement, severe anemia, infectious diseases, or chronic malnutrition affecting the brain. However, as most of these conditions are present also in neighboring tribes, we have to look for features peculiar to the Wapogoro and their environment which may explain the phenomenon of *kifafa* and its high prevalence in this tribe.

In former days the Wapogoro lived as seminomads in the plains with other Bantu tribes. When war broke out among the tribes some 100 years ago, the Wapogoro, a peace-loving people, fled into the mountains, where they have remained ever since. In the mountains a seminomadic existence is not possible due to the scarcity of arable land. Yet the Wapogoro continued to build temporary dwellings and, following their traditional custom, they cultivated corn and millet only on patches close to their huts, thereby exhausting the soil. Dwellings and fields deteriorated without the people being able to make periodic moves as previously on the plains. Soon the Wapogoro, incapable of adjusting to their new environment, had to live on marginal subsistence levels, with regular annual famine periods. More than the adjacent populations, the Wapogoro are plagued by a combination of malnutrition, avitaminosis, lack of proteins due to protein-deficient plants and scarcity of game, and severe parasitic infestations with anemia. No wonder that they tend to be rather inactive, lacking initiative, and having an unenterprising outlook on life. The neighboring tribes on the plains often make fun of the Wapogoro and call them "lazy corn-eaters"; their young men seldom want to marry Wapogoro girls. "You are a real Wapogoro" is used as a derogatory expression among the people of the plains. These and other historical, geographical, and cultural factors have contributed to make the Wapogoro one of the most isolated populations in East Africa.

As has been mentioned, the Wapogoro have learned through experience that the consanguineous kin of *kifafa* patients as well as the *kifafa* sufferers themselves, have a higher risk of begetting children afflicted with this disease than is the case with couples from healthy families. The fear of marrying someone who could transmit the disease, has lowered the bride-price for afflicted girls and even for apparently healthy girls from *kifafa* families. As the *kifafa* sufferers themselves are at the bottom of the social pyramid and have few means to acquire brides, they tend to marry girls with *kifafa*, or their sisters. This intermarriage pattern, together with the isolation of the Wapogoro tribe and the prevailing tendency toward endogamous marriages in the tribe (Kipengele 1961; Hendle 1912), might well explain the unusually high familial incidence of *kifafa*, as well as the increasing prevalence of this condition among the Wapogoro people.

The Wapogoro are extremely fearful of *kifafa*. They believe that, in a seizure the evil spirit can leap from the afflicted person to bystanders, causing them also to fall ill. The acute anxiety aroused in witnesses of such seizures could easily give rise to spells of psychomotor excitation of the type described in Africans by Collomb (1956, 1965), Gillis (1962), Lambo (1955, 1956, 1960, 1962), Planques and Collomb (1957), and other authors. The question whether *kifafa* might be a hysteriform manifestation has to be considered, therefore, as such an explanation could account for the high prevalence of *kifafa* among the Wapogoro. At our clinic in Mahenge, only those patients who had major burn scars in conjunction with observed seizures of epileptic type, were diagnosed as suffering from bonafide *kifafa*, for the discovery of burn scars in seizure patients in a society where open domestic fires are in common usage, is in itself diagnostic of a chronic convulsive disorder (Gelfand 1957; Orley 1970).

Conclusions about the nature and origin of *kifafa* will have to await further research, in which the following hypotheses should be tested:

1. *Kifafa* is a symptomatic epileptic disorder associated with brain damage resulting from conditions such as neonatal asphyxia due to inexpedient obstetric handling, syphilis, parasitic infestations, toxic enteritis in children, encephalomeningitis of various etiologies, chronic malnutrition and protein deficiency with seasonal exacerbation during annual famine periods. Extensive clinical and laboratory examinations in conjunction with specific ethnographic and nutrition studies would be necessary to test this hypothesis.

2. *Kifafa* is a hereditary form of so-called idiopathic epilepsy. Its unusual frequency among the Wapogoro is due to the marked endogamous patterns in this geographically and socioculturally isolated tribe, with preferential unions between close kinspeople and between the *kifafa* sufferers themselves. The apparent increase in the prevalence of *kifafa* could be explained by the accumulation of neuropathogenic genetic factors in this population. Genetical and kinship system studies, in association with careful neurological and neuropsychological assessments, including electroencephalographic examinations both of the patients and their extended families, would be required.

3. *Kifafa* is a separate disease entity, a progressive systemic illness of the central nervous system, of independent genetic or infectious etiology (the latter is suggested by the fact that the Wapogoro protect themselves against *kifafa* as if it was a contagious condition). *Kifafa* patients show numerous positive neurological signs, often gross neurological defects associated with rapid physical and mental deterioration of a kind not usually seen in "idiopathic" epilepsy. There is also an incidence of transient psychotic episodes in *kifafa* patients higher than found among epileptics elsewhere.

Their sedentary life style, small number, and sociocultural isolation would make the Wapogoro people well suited for investigation in a multi-disciplinary research project involving a team of medical and social scientists.

## REFERENCES

AUBIN, H.
    1939    Introduction à l'étude de la psychiatrie chez les noirs. *Annales de la médecine psychologique* 97:1–29, 181–213.
COLLOMB, H.
    1956    Introduction à la psychiatrie tropicale. *Médecine tropicale* 16:141–151.

1965 Bouffées délirantes en psychiatrie africaine. *Psychopathologie africaine* 1:167–239.

COLLOMB, H., R. PLAS
1958 Les états délirants aigus. *Médecine tropicale* 18:1–6.

ENGELBERGER, A., K. LUSSY
1954 Religiöse Anschauungen und Bräuche bei den Wapogoro. *Anthropos* 49:103–122, 605–626.

EY, H.
1963 *Manuel de psychiatrie*. Paris: Masson.

GELFAND, M.
1957 *The sick African*. Cape Town: Juta.

GILLIS, L. S.
1962 "Observations from South Africa," in *Conference Report, First Pan-African Psychiatric Conference, Abeokuta, Nigeria*. Edited by T. A. Lambo, 236–238. Ibadan, Nigeria: Government Printer.

HENDLE, I.
1912 Brautwerbung und Hochzeit bei den Wapogoro. *Anthropos* 7:252–253.

JILEK, W.
1967 "Mental health and magic beliefs in changing Africa," in *Beiträge zur vergleichenden Psychiatrie: aktuelle Fragen der Psychiatrie und Neurologie*, volume six, part two. Edited by E. Gruenthal and N. Petrilowitsch, 138–154. Basle, New York: Karger.

JILEK, W., L. M. JILEK-AALL
1967 "Psychiatric concepts and conditions in the Wapogoro tribe of Tanganyika," in *Beiträge zur vergleichenden Psychiatrie: aktuelle Fragen der Psychiatrie und Neurologie*, volume five, part one. Edited by E. Gruenthal and N. Petrilowitsch, 205–228. Basle; New York: Karger.

JILEK, W., L. M. JILEK-AALL
1970 Transient psychoses in Africans. *Psychiatria clinica* 3:337-364.

JILEK-AALL, L. M.
1964 Geisteskrankheiten und Epilepsie im tropischen Afrika. *Fortschritte der Neurologie-Psychiatrie* 32:213–259.
1965 Epilepsy in the Wapogoro tribe in Tanganyika. *Acta psychiatrica scandinavica* 41:57–86.

KIPENGELE, N.
1961 "Marriage celebration among Wamatumbi and Wapogoro and its relation to Common Law." Unpublished doctoral dissertation, Rome University.

LAMBO, T. A.
1955 The role of cultural factors in paranoid psychosis among the Yoruba tribe. *Journal of Mental Science* 101:239–265.
1956 Neuropsychiatric observations in the western region of Nigeria. *British Medical Journal* 2:1388–1396.
1960 Further neuropsychiatric observations in Nigeria. *British Medical Journal* 2:1–24.
1962 Malignant anxiety, a syndrome associated with criminal conduct in Africans. *Journal of Mental Science* 108:256–264.

LUSSY, K.
1951   Die Wapogoro, Tanganyika Territory. *Anthropos* 46:431–433.
MURDOCK, G. P.
1959   *Africa, its peoples and their culture history.* New York: McGraw-Hill.
ORLEY, J. H.
1970   *Culture and mental illness, a study from Uganda.* Makerere Institute of Social Research, Kampala. Nairobi, Kenya: East African Publishing House.
PLANQUES, L., H. COLLOMB
1957   Les psychoses des noirs. *Revue Corps Santé Militaire* 13:194–205
SCHOENAKER, S.
1965   *Die ideologischen Hintergründe im Gemeinschaftsleben der Pogoro.* Acta ethnologica et linguistica 7. Oesterreichische Ethnologische Gesellschaft. Vienna.

## COMMENT *by Nancy Rollins*

Regarding the interesting syndrome of *kifafa* reported by Jilek-Aall, is it possible that some of these patients suffer from conversion hysteria? The fugue states, the psychotic episodes, the violence and the long duration of some of the spells are all consistent with the diagnosis of *hysteria major*, manifested by convulsions and dissociated states of consciousness. The atmosphere and terror and social scapegoating surrounding the illness also might contribute to the appearance of the illness as a form of hysterical identification with other patients. Does the native fear of contagion contain a grain of truth?

## REPLY *by Louise Jilek-Aall*

The idea that *kifafa* might be a form of conversion hysteria has been proposed time and again in discussions on this unusual syndrome and its high prevalence rate among the Wapogoro. This possibility was, of course, considered by the author already during her field work in Tanzania (Jilek-Aall 1964).

Several facts render such a possibility highly unlikely:

1.   Hysterical reactions with hyperventilation, fainting spells, convulsions, fugue states ("running into the bush") are well recognized by the Wapogoro and are never confused with *kifafa*. They are treated quite differently in a sophisticated and effective way, e.g. by *ngoma ya sheitani* (Jilek-Aall 1964:222).

2.   Only those patients whose typical seizures were observed by medical staff or who showed conspicuous burns and keloid scars from falling into the domestic fire during an attack were diagnosed as suffering from *kifafa*. Only a deeply unconscious person would sustain the extensive burns, which resulted from falling into the small fire kept burning in the Wapogoro huts, that we saw in the epileptic patients. According to an authority like Gelfand, "the discovery of these scars is often sufficient for a diagnosis of chronic epilepsy" (Gelfand 1957:554) in the context of a history of seizures.

3.   *Kifafa* is a chronic disease process which, in most untreated cases, leads to

mental and physical deterioration and often to death. For the Wapogporo tribesman, *kifafa* is a personal catastrophe, isolating him from normal human intercourse, downgrading his living conditions, and marking him as a permanent social outcast. There is no conceivable secondary gain, but only severe "secondary loss," for him in *kifafa*.

Summing up: *kifafa* is incompatible with any concept of hysteria, traditional or modern.

# REFERENCES

GELFAND, MICHAEL
   1957   *The sick African* (third edition). Cape Town: Juta.

JILEK-AALL, LOUISE
   1964   Geisteskrankheiten und Epilepsie im tropischen Afrika. *Fortschritte der Neurologie-Psychiatrie*, 32:213–259.

*Focus on Mental Health Workers*

# Introduction

Until now work in the field has focused on recipients of mental health care services. Studies have now begun to concentrate on care-givers and systems of care-giving as well. Their arrival is none too soon. As interethnic contacts increase, "modern" mental health workers need to learn how they might be helpful to those from cultural groups other than their own. And as the "modern" technology for care of those few mental patients who are severely impaired spreads about the world, there is yet need for the services of "traditional" healers and their time-proven technologies in the care of the greater number of people with mild to moderate disturbances. "Traditional" or "community" care for some problems may even work more rapidly and effectively than the "modern" or "hospital" care.

In the paper from Guyana, an anthropologist, a psychiatrist, and a native healer review their collaborative efforts in rendering mental health care. Pressed by huge numbers of patients requiring psychiatric services and sparse resources to meet the need, they developed means to enhance their own individual efforts and, by doing so, to enhance the efforts of the others. Each learned from the others, to the ultimate benefit of those needing mental health services.

Ruiz and Langrod, working in a Puerto Rican neighborhood in New York, independently discovered the same *modus operandi* as the former group in Guyana. Faced with great need in a largely Spanish-speaking community, they indentified those who were already serving the mental health needs of the people. Finding spiritual healers already actively involved, they joined efforts with them. Mutual education and inter-consultation resulted, again to the benefit of people experiencing mental health problems. Spiritual healers and middle-class therapists complemented each other, offering a broader range of resources to troubled people than either could do alone.

As with accounts of field ethnographical work, reams have been written on how to do cross-cultural counseling. But the practitioner of either field work or counseling is generally expected to learn as best he can by "jumping in." There exists no technique for teaching this activity, nor any means by which one trying to learn it can be evaluated. Into this vacuum Pedersen brings a training model which may help mental health workers to proceed comfortably and competently in cultures besides their own. Moreover, the model could potentially be adapted to mental health trainees regardless of professional discipline. It may also provide a means by which minority communities can train and evaluate "modern" mental health professionals from ethnic groups besides their own.

From studies of Tungus shamans a half-century ago down to contemporary studies of psychiatrists and other physicians, one finding has been replicated so often as to have become fact (if indeed, it were not a strongly suspected truism from the beginning): both "traditional" and "modern" healers are subject to certain role-specific behaviors and eccentricities. However, such studies have been heir to similar studies among psychiatric patients in that the intrapsychic aspect of the healer's behavior has become an investigative obsession, while the social significance of his behavior has been largely ignored. Sociologist Light now corrects this oversight with his study of psychiatry residents in which he evolves a categorization based on what these physicians do in the clinical setting. Of course, much is inferred regarding the interests and emotional responses of these clinicians; but the emphasis falls on the separate ways in which these practitioners operate in the clinical setting rather than on ways in which they differ from the rest of humankind. It must be added that Light's sample is a limited one based on only one institution which, as indicated by the data, poorly represents the ethnic composition of its community.

The son of a German theologian-scholar-author and himself an academic clinician in American psychiatry, Huessy brings both the insider's experience and the outsider's perspective to his task. He reviews the historical antecedents ("historical evolution" would be too complimentary and too sanguine a term at this point in time) of mental health care in the United States. His overview brings back to our attention that "modern" mental health care has many elements in it which are decidedly "folk" or traditional and, in the sense of the Scientific Method, most unscientific. The paper demonstrates that, in many ways, today's problems in mental health care have in part resulted from decisions made in the past — at which time these decisions appeared to be the right and proper thing to do. Now, though we live in a different world and operate from different premises compared to those when the decisions were made, we live with their consequences. Will we, can we, be any more enlightened today in making decisions which will affect our successors?

# Coalition of a Kali Healer and a Psychiatrist in Guyana, Mediated by an Anthropologist

PHILIP SINGER, ENRIQUE ARANETA, JR., and
JAMIE NAIDOO

An illiterate sugarcane plantation worker and a Kali cult healer worked with a psychiatrist and anthropologist. Over a year's association, the healer successfully modified his own mental illness categories to include dynamic concepts of diagnosis, history taking and patient management. For example, the traditional and limited cultural dream repertoire was expanded, long-range goals discussed, and the traditional role of the healer expanded from passive mediator of supernatural power to active therapist and community social worker. The development of the inter-disciplinary collaboration is traced, several case histories presented, and implications for community psychiatry in emerging countries discussed.

The working relationship among the three men achieved the following: (1) It provided the psychiatrist with the means of learning the cultural patterns, the existing social institutions and organizations along which he might direct his therapy, which must take cognizance of the attitudes of the community to be effective. (2) It provided a possible option for alleviating the desperate problem of psychiatric facilities (only one psychiatrist for the whole country) and was a frantic move to meet emotional needs in the community. (3) It showed a possibility for evolving methods of evaluating techniques of community psychiatry while, at the same time, discovering, testing out, and articulating psychodynamic principles that might be operating in the Kali healing methods, thus affording an invaluable laboratory, already in existence, and calling for no additional responsibility from the psychiatrist. (4) The relationship

The complete article of which this is a summary, appears in *The realm of the extra-human: agents and audiences*. (Edited by A. Bharati. World Anthropology. The Hague: Mouton; 1976.)

also afforded the psychiatrist a chance to introduce Western psychiatric concepts where he felt this might be of help to the healer in integrating Western (allegedly more rational) concepts of dealing with mental disorders into the healer's methods. (5) It gave the psychiatrist a chance to effect those changes in cultural awareness and attitudes which were needed to prepare the community to cope with the anticipated cultural impact of increasing Western infiltration into the socioeconomic structure of the country. (6) The prospect of utilizing the healer's help for specific psychiatric syndromes, in which the anthropologist had reported considerable beneficial results, offered the desired resource for the already impossible work schedule of the psychiatrist. (7) The need to control the operations of the healer, who had no training in the recognition of somatic disorders, made the relationship an urgent humanitarian medical responsibility. (8) The collaboration also offered a social rehabilitation facility which had been nonexistent up to the time of the psychiatrist's involvement with the service. (9) The establishment of a liaison with the leaders of the communities, of which the Kali healers involved were found to be the most influential, enabled the mental health service to evolve into a culture-modifying institution contributing to the allaying of the social ills of the community. (10) With the evolution of the mental health service into a culture-modifying institution through this collaboration, it was hoped that insights could be gained into the preventive measures against mental illness through the elucidation in greater depth of the personal and environmental interrelationships that were predisposed to regression.

# Psychiatrists and Spiritual Healers: Partners in Community Mental Health

PEDRO RUIZ and JOHN LANGROD

Community psychiatry in order to be relevant today must involve all the behavioral sciences in its work. Anthropologists were among the first to study religious and folk beliefs and their relationship to the field of mental health. Psychiatrists have recently become aware of the interrelationship between psychiatry, religion, and the folk healer (Nelson and Torrey 1973). Kiev (1968) describes the role of the *curandero* 'folk healer' among Mexican-Americans, Rogler and Hollingshead (1965) among city dwellers in Puerto Rico.

It is our intention here to compare mental health services offered by spiritual healers with those provided by psychiatrically oriented mental health therapists. In addition, we will illustrate how these differences can create difficulties in the delivery of sound mental health services.

Along these lines, we will share with you our experiences of cultural values among Puerto Rican families and how these values can be used as positive mental health resources in a deprived community. Our experience was obtained by working for several years in a comprehensive mental health center located in an inner-city ghetto whose population is composed predominantly of Spanish-speaking persons, of whom it is estimated 65 percent are Puerto Rican. According to the 1965 census 72.5 percent have not graduated from high school.

## THE PROBLEM

One of the most serious problems we faced in our program was that one-half of our female patients and one-third of the male patients (of nearly

2,000 outpatients who came to the Lincoln Community Mental Health Center during 1968) were visiting mediums and spiritual healers through the *botánicas*[1] and spiritual centers existing within our catchment area while at the same time coming to our clinics. In most instances, the reasons for visiting both the spiritual healer and the mental health center were found to be the same. As this experience is not an unusual one for persons working with Spanish-speaking minorities in the field of mental health, it behooves us to look closely at this problem which appears to create an unnecessary duplication of services.

Our first effort was to understand why this happened. In doing this, we quickly discarded the explanantion prevalent among white professionals, which ascribes this phenomenon to a lack of available medical services. Certainly this was not the cause in our case. After examining this problem in depth, in terms of our clinical experience, we came to the conclusion that people, when deprived of an opportunity to express their inherent traditions and cultural values, turn to magic as a partial resolution of this conflict. Also, along these lines, when persons find themselves in an essentially hostile atmosphere, which deprives them of social and economic achievements, they are likely to utilize to the maximum identification with their own ethnic traditions in order to neutralize the effects of such a repressive environment.

## ESTABLISHING THE PARTNERSHIP

With this in mind, we searched for common pathways between our classical psychiatrically oriented community mental health program[2] and spiritualist centers and *botánicas*. Two years ago this led us to develop a liaison program between these two different models of service delivery. As part of this liaison program, we hired a number of well-known mediums as community mental health workers in our center, at the same time developing for our staff a preservice training program designed to familiarize them with the approaches utilized by folk healers. This preservice training and orientation program is given to all employees of the Lincoln Community Mental Health Center, whether professional or nonprofessional. The program is compulsory and includes classes about cultural values and

[1]   *Botánicas* are spiritualist "pharmacies" in which herbs, statues, and other ritual materials prescribed by cult healers are sold.
[2]   Our program, in contrast to the greater informality of the spiritualist center and *botánicas* is characterized by regular appointments and record keeping; medications are offered by way of prescriptions, and the thinking is scientifically oriented. This is an outpatient program, but inpatient hospitalization is available for those who need it.

traditions of Puerto Ricans and blacks in the United States. Also, seminars are conducted with mediums in which the mental health clinic staff obtains direct experience about the methods mediums use, such as small-group approaches, the utilization of symptoms as positive resources, development of leadership qualities within the community, and the utilization of religious concepts with a view toward developing and maintaining social and cultural identity. At the same time the spiritualists obtain knowledge, through the seminars, of diagnostic techniques and of medical resources for referral and backup. Their ability to utilize these medical resources gives the mediums greater scope in the development of their own community functions.

Among our principal concerns here are symptom formation in mental illness and the methods by which symptoms are utilized in the treatment context.

In general, mediums and spiritual healers see symptoms among their clients, such as hallucinations, not as something to get rid of before any cure can be achieved, but rather as an asset on which it is possible to build the patient's ego strength. This approach is not generally utilized by classical mental health therapists. For instance, a patient coming to a psychiatrist with a complaint of hearing voices is looked upon as severely mentally ill, and all available medical resources are used to stop such symptomatology at once. The spiritualist, on the other hand, would say that the afflicted person possesses spiritual faculties which should be developed further. This becomes a matter of prestige which increases the patient's self-esteem, thus assisting him in his functioning.

Another area of importance is prognosis, which for patients most often seen in ghetto areas is almost always guarded; however, because spiritual healers are much more accepting of the presence of severe symptomatology, a more hopeful picture emerges. We would like therefore to emphasize the function of role fulfillment and expectancy when this happens. This problem is not unique to mental health but applies to all aspects of everyday life and particularly to the urban educational system in the United States, where ghetto children have been labelled "ineducable" and are consigned to vocational programs and often drop out of school.

In terms of nomenclature, or diagnostic nosology, something similar takes place. Hollingshead and Redlich (1958) indicate that lower-class patients are more likely to be diagnosed as psychotic compared to upper- and middle-class patients. While psychiatrists will label patients as psychotic or schizophrenic, our spiritual-healer colleagues call them "possessed" or having "mediumity." Certainly, the latter has less negative connotations, thus making the basic conflict easier to accept and the condition confronted easier to deal with. This beneficial situation is not limited to clients but also extends to their relatives and peers. One frequently sees the psychiatrist dichotomizing between psychotics or schizophrenics and neurotics. This dichotomy, which has built-in negative connotations and prejudices, can result in a less favorable treatment outcome for the psychotic or schizophrenic client. This definitely is the case when the psychiatrist applies his own moral and cultural values to his patients. The mediums and spiritual healers, on the other hand, do not make this differentiation, thus offering greater hope to the severely afflicted client who is in greatest need of receiving confidence in his potential for full recovery and maximum achievement in life.

Another quality distinguishing spiritual healers in their treatment methodology is the deep involvement of others such as *comadres* 'godmothers', *padrinos* 'godfathers', *ahijados* 'godchildren', etc. within the therapeutic milieu. We need not emphasize the importance of the extended family concept within the Hispanic culture.

Finally, we would like to call attention to the opportunities offered by mediums and other spiritual healers for the expression through cult practice of wishes and desires which would not be toerlated by society if expressed directly; in particular, wishes relating to hostility, aggression, and death. This provides clients with a unique way of abreacting and discharging tensions which differs markedly from the techniques utilized by classical therapists who tend to emphasize the role of unconscious factors and do not always take into account the importance of the "here and now" concept within this ethnic group. As Torrey (1972) points out, there is a great deal that Western psychotherapists can learn from "witch doctors." We fully agree.


CONCLUSION

The experience of a mental health ghetto program located in an urban setting illustrates the utilization of spiritual healers as full members of a mental health treatment team. Special emphasis has been placed on the methodology of the spiritual healers in their treatment approach which offers a learning experience to the classical mental health specialist. Narrowing the gaps between the network of indigenous healers and classical middle-class therapists can only result in providing more effective services to the people in the community.

# REFERENCES

HOLLINGSHEAD, A. B., F. C. REDLICH
  1958   *Social class and mental illness.* New York: John Wiley and Sons.
KIEV, A.
  1968   *Curanderismo.* New York: Free Press.
NELSON, S. H., E. F. TORREY
  1973   The religious functions of psychiatry. *American Journal of Orthopsy-chiatry* 43 (3): 362–367.
ROGLER, L. H., A. B. HOLLINGSHEAD
  1965   *Trapped: families and schizophrenia.* New York: John Wiley and Sons.
TORREY, E. F.
  1972   What western psychotherapists can learn from witch doctors. *American Journal of Orthopsychiatry*: 42 (1): 69–76.

# A Model for Training Mental Health Workers in Cross-Cultural Counseling

PAUL PEDERSEN

The constructs of "healthy" and "normal" that guide the delivery of mental health services are not shared by all persons from every culture and may betray the culturally encapsulated counselor to become a tool of his own dominant political, social, or economic values. Ethnocentric notions of adjustment tend to ignore inherent cultural values, allowing the encapsulated counselor to evade reality while maintaining a cocoon of value presuppositions about what is "good" for the counselee. The very data which define the task of counseling can take on a reified meaning in reinforcing modal stereotypes of cultural groups, separating counselors from the social reality of people from other cultures.

## CULTURALLY ENCAPSULATED COUNSELORS

As the counselor faces a lifestyle different from his own for any length of time he goes through a process of acculturation, which may result in cultural assimilation, where the dominant culture enforces its adoption; integration, where the "best" elements of another culture are incorporated; or adaptation, where the individual or group accommodates to the foreign environment. The person undergoing acculturation must first recognize his own style of behavior, attitudes, beliefs, and personal assumptions that will allow him to experience another culture as a means of learning about that culture. Otherwise, the therapist may substitute

The author wants to acknowledge the assistance of Theater Arts students David Cook, Richard Hilger, and Theresa Johnson, who helped train participants in a demonstration of our model, and Richard Theis who directed the videotaping.

his own criteria of desired social effectiveness for alternative criteria more appropriate to a client's environment (Kanfer and Phillips 1970). Bloombaum, Yamamoto, and James (1968) describe ways in which psychotherapists are culturally conditioned in their responses. Other research reveals how cultures either directly or unconsciously condition client responses to suit their theoretical orientation (Bandura, Lipher and Miller 1960; Murray 1956; J. Rogers 1960; Bandura 1961).

Wrenn (1962) described encapsulation as a process causing the counseling profession to disregard cultural variations among clients in a dogmatic adherence to some universal notion of truth, threatening the insecure professional with his own failure to communicate, and dogmatizing a technique-oriented definition of the counseling process. Kagan (1964) and Schwebel (1964) further suggest that counselor education programs may actually be contributing to the encapsulation process, implanting a cultural bias, however implicit, in their curricula.

Helpers who differ most from their helpees, in race and social class, have the greatest difficulty effecting constructive changes, while helpers who are most similar to their helpees in these respects have a greater facility for appropriate helping (Carkhuff and Pierce, 1967). Mitchell (1970) goes so far as to say that most white counselors cannot be part of the solution for a black client since they are so frequently part of the problem. Radical blacks likewise assert that the white mental health worker cannot successfully counsel the "black psyche." Ayres (1970) and Russel (1970) describe an implicit or sometimes explicit bias in the counseling process itself that is frequently perceived as demeaning, debilitating, patronizing, and dehumanizing.

In cross-cultural counseling there is a greater danger of mutual misunderstanding (McFayden and Winokur 1956), less understanding of the other culture's unique problems (Kincaid 1969), a natural hostility that destroys rapport and creates greater negative transference toward the counselor (Vontress 1971).

Thomas (1962) points out the danger of mistaking a client's culturally appropriate negative response for neurotic transference. Ignorance of one another's culture contributes to hostile resistance between the counselor and client. Vontress (1969) describes ways that a counselor's cultural attitudes destroy counseling rapport by inhibiting empathy, ignoring significant aspects of a client's background, misunderstanding a client's language, or violating taboo subjects.

Cultural sensitivity relates to an awareness of indigenous resources within the other culture. Torrey (1970) gives an example of why urban Mexican-Americans fail to utilize modern mental health services, even when they are available. The Westernized systems are irrelevant because they are inaccessible, are inhibited by a language problem, are class bound with the quality of treatment dependent on the individual's class, are culture bound and insensitive to the indigenous world views, and are caste bound relating primarily to the ruling Anglo community because the indigenous alternatives are less popular. Saslow and Harrover (1968), Suchman (1964), Sprang (1965), Bryde (1971), Morales (1970) and Madsen (1969) likewise describe the types of problems and resources unique to the various ethnic groups but frequently overlooked by insensitive counselors. Each lifestyle provides its own structures, rules and mechanisms to cope with aggression and anxiety; and while they may differ from one another, they are able to promote and preserve mental health within that particular community (Mechanic 1969; Glazer and Moynihan 1963).

## CROSS-CULTURAL COUNSELOR TRAINING

Torrey (1971) concludes that there is sufficient evidence from cross-cultural studies of counseling and psychotherapy to raise many questions about our system of selecting, training, and certifying therapists. Stranges and Riccio (1970) found that counselor trainees preferred counselees of the same racial and cultural background. It appears (Gordon 1965) that professional psychologists are currently trained toward the ultimate goal of serving the psychological needs of the middle class. Locke and Lewis (1969) point out specific examples of racism in the training of counselors, while Vontress (1969) calls for more in service and preservice training designed to help counselors examine their attitudes toward the culturally different by exposing them directly to the culture of their clients. There is increasing evidence for professional psychologists that the trained counselor is not prepared to deal with individuals who come from racial, ethnic, or socioeconomic groups whose values, attitudes and general lifestyles are different from his own (Padilla, Boxley, and Wagner 1972). The innovations in counselor training which appear most promising for cross-cultural counseling involve the use of a "microcounseling" model developed by Ivey, Normington, Miller, Morrill, and Haase (1968) for teaching interviewer skills in attending behavior, reflection of feeling, and summarization of feeling (Moreland, Phillips, Ivey, and Lockhart 1970). Microcounseling emphasizes systematically teaching facilitative interviewer behaviors that are applicable to a variety of theoretical orientations bridging the gap between classroom learning and initial applied experience in a program designed to supplement traditional counselor education curricula.

Most applications of microcounseling utilize some form of recording such as videotape for self-confrontation by the trainee. Kagan (personal communication, 1969) has effectively demonstrated how using videotapes of a trainee's counseling session can help to identify and strengthen positive facilitative behaviors and change nonfacilitative behaviors, using the supervisor as a third person who interrogates and debriefs the trainee after the interview. Other studies (Reivich and Geertsma 1969; Watts 1973) indicate that videotaped self-confrontation promotes behavioral change in trainees (Walz and Johnston 1963), schizophrenics (Stroller 1967) and teacher trainees (McDonald and Allen 1967). Salomon and McDonald (1970) concluded that appropriate behavior change was more likely to result when the videotape playback served as a source of information feedback to the trainee by modeling the desired skills.

The use of simulation "role-play" techniques has been increasingly popular in microcounseling counselor training programs (Delaney 1969; Thayer, Peterson, Carr, and Merz 1972; Gysbers and Moore, 1970; Spivack, 1973). The successful use of coached clients in simulated interviews has also been well documented both in therapy and research (Carkhuff and Alexik 1967; Pierce, Carkhuff, and Berenson 1967; Kelz 1966, Heller, Meyers, and Kline 1963; Dustin 1968; Whiteley and Jakubowski 1969; Roark 1969). The simulation of critical incidents has likewise proven its effectiveness in programs of cross-cultural communications (Fiedler, Mitchell, and Triandis 1970; De Crow 1969), teaching skills that parallel those required by counselors.

Counseling can be described as a function of push and pull factors where the counselor seeks fulfillment in being helpful, the counselee seeks to reconcile internalized ambiguity, and the problem, viewed as an active rather than a passive entity, seeks its own survival and increased power over the client. In cross-cultural counseling, this suggests a triad of stress, response to it, and ameliorative intervention, all three of which are potentially subject to being culturally mediated (Draguns and Phillips 1972). Bolman (1968) suggests that at least two therapists, one representing each culture, be used in cross-cultural therapy to provide a bridge between the population being served and the counselor. In this way counseling can both transcend the ethnocentric approach and incorporate the contributions of each culture to the relationship through mutual adaption.

The triad of counselor, counselee, and problem is the basis of a cross-cultural coalition model described in this paper. Triads have been applied to family therapy as illustrations of pathogenic coalitions (Satir, 1964) where the therapist employs mediation and side-taking judiciously to break up and replace pathogenetic relating. Counseling becomes a series of negotiations in which all three parties vie for control. Zuk (1971) describes this approach as a "go-between" process where the therapist catalyzes conflict in a crisis situation that is favorable for change in which all parties can take an active role.

## THE CROSS-CULTURAL COALITION TRAINING MODEL

The cross-cultural coalition training model places three persons in a videotaped microcounseling context to role-play a simulated critical incident problem of cross-cultural counseling. In this modification of the microcounseling model, the counselor role is filled by a counselor trainee; two persons are counselees; and there is an "anti-counselor" or "problem" role-played by a paired team from the same culture as the counselees but different from the counselor's culture. The three-way interaction of counselor and counselee with an "anti-counselor" or person in the problem role is expected to explicate cultural aspects of the problem and resistance to counseling in an open struggle for power between the counselor and anti-counselor more effectively than in a cross-cultural counseling dyad model.

The unique element in this modification is the personified and personalized role of the anti-counselor. The anti-counselor is encouraged to view his best interest as preventing the counselor from coalescing with the counselee towards a "solution" of the problem. The anti-counselor attempts to achieve goals opposite from those of the counselor, seeking to increase the counselee's dependence on the problem. The counselors are encouraged to deal with a counselee much as they would in any normal counselor/counselee dyad. The counselee is encouraged to accept help or guidance from both the counselor and the "anti-counselor" according to which of these two persons seems to offer a more satisfactory alliance. The counselee is then forced to choose between the counselor from another culture or the "anti-counselor" from his or her own culture.

This design assumes that counseling occurs in a force field where the counselor, the counselee, and the problem interact in a constellation of conflicting or complementary goals. Counseling is thus conceptualized as a dynamic interaction of contrary forces in the model of social power theory and in the context of an equilibrium between the counselor in coalition with the counselee on the one hand and the problem or anti-counselor seeking increased disequilibrium, through intensified resistance to counseling, thereby isolating the counselee from alternative sources of help. The distribution and use of power in counselling properly encourages a temporary means-oriented alliance between counselor and counselee as an alternative to the counselee's continued and indeterminate dependence on the problem. A counselor-counselee coalition against the problem becomes the vehicle of effective counseling while ineffective counseling results in a counselee-problem coalition which isolates the counselor.

The controlled conditions of microcounseling allow persons from different cultures to interact on controversial issues, learning from one another as well as from the problem, benefiting from both positive and negative feedback. Inappropriate intervention is made apparent immediately and the "target audience" participate as partners in training their own counselors.

Perhaps the most difficult role to conceptualize is that of the "anti-counselor" or problem as a person. While the strategies of a counselor and the role expectations for a client are familiar to us, the notion of an active, back-talking problem at first seems bizarre and strange. The problem or anti-counselor role develops its own unique strategies.

The role of the problem is distinguished from the role of a person with a problem. The problem role carries an "anti-counselor" function just as the counselor carries an "anti-problem" function in the counseling relationship, thereby polarizing these two roles. The role of the counselee is consequently strengthened as the sought-out partner for a winning coalition with either of the other two participants. In preliminary trials otherwise passive counselor trainees become noticably more aggressive when faced with a third person in the role of an anti-counselor. Persons having tried the role of "anti-counselor" find it difficult at first to empathize with the problem, having associated the problem exclusively with the "enemy" of a counseling relationship. As trainees became more familiar with the problem role, they were able to build on those more attractive and tempting resources an "unresolved" problem offers which contribute to the ambivalence of counselees toward counseling.

The problem's strategy is to contain counseling at a superficial level where he can confuse, distort, distract, discredit, complicate, or otherwise frustrate the counselor. Most problems can make themselves very attractive to clients, not being constricted by rules of consistency and with private "cultural" access to the client. The problem can provide negative feedback that would not be "appropriate" from clients, even in role play, enacting the resistance which would otherwise be symbolically ambiguous.

## A VIDEOTAPE DEMONSTRATION OF THE MODEL

In December, 1972, the University of Minnesota Center for Educational Development and the Department of Radio and Television provided resources for three hours of videotaping fifteen-minute episodes of cross-cultural counseling between persons in the three roles of counselor, counselee and "anti-counselor." The counselor role was played by a series of counselors or counselor trainees at the University of Minnesota. The counselee role and the problem or "anti-counselor" roles were played by a series of paired teams from the same culture, different from the counselor's culture. About twenty-two people were invited to participate in the model. In total, eight triads were videotaped for about fifteen minutes each, although in the final pilot demonstrator videotape only five triads were retained, and parts of these were edited out.

As the participants arrived, they were given a brief written statement of the model describing the three roles. They formed themselves into cross-cultural groups with the counselor being from one culture while the client and anti-counselor were from another different culture. Each team selected a problem with which it felt comfortable and rehearsed role-playing the model for about fifteen or twenty minutes before going on videotape. Participants were matched according to their availability and were given no guidance on choice of problems. Before being video-taped themselves, participants were generally able to view others role-playing the model while being videotaped.

The episodes were videotaped using three cameras. The Department of Radio and Television directed the making of a single mastertape edited from the three cameras and later dubbed from a complete mastertape. After the videotaping each participant was asked to write down his reaction to the experience and how he felt about the model as a training device for cross-cultural counseling.

In the first triad a black female student described difficulty with inter-cultural relationships. The anti-counselor, a black male graduate student in counseling psychology, kept the counselor, a white male graduate student in counseling psychology, on the defensive. The anti-counselor side-tracked, reinterpreted, distracted, and frustrated counseling through a constant flow of soft-spoken interference that prevented the client from hearing the counselor: "The questions you [counselor] ask don't stick in my head as well as what he [anti-counselor] says!" The counselor, by emphasizing content more than feeling, identified with the client as a "black" rather than as an individual, ignoring the problem which consequently took control of the interview.

In the second triad a Latin female student described to a counseling psychologist difficulty in sexual relationships with American males. The anti-counselor, another female Latin counseling student, cued almost every response for the client, hovering like an alter ego conscience over the interview. After seducing the counselor to make an inadvertent sexual advance toward the client the anti-counselor pressed her advantage as a cofemale and fellow countrywoman to keep the counselor off balance. The counselor again ignored the problem of who was allowed to take control, "I [anti-counselor] was the personalized hidden self, out in the open, exposing all the contradictions, value conflicts, fears, expectations....."

In the third triad the American male graduate student in counseling described difficulty in sexual relationship with Latin females, role-playing an interview with a female Latin counselor who was also a graduate student in counseling. The anti-counselor, another American male student, attempted unsuccessfully to shock the counselor with obscenities that, while never verbalized by the client, were readily acknowledged by him as authentic to his situation. The counselor interacted with both the client and anti-counselor, leading the client to separate himself gradually from the problem and ally himself with the counselor toward a more satisfactory solution. The client, a practicing clinical psychologist, reported that objectifying the problem proved to be of considerable help in removing some of the ambiguity from counseling.

In the fourth triad a Chinese graduate student described the incongruence between demands from his fiancée and from his studies to a white, American graduate student. The anti-counselor, a Chinese female graduate student in counseling, related to the client in a matriarchal role as if toward a disobedient son, injected punishing proverbs and pronouncement against counselor and client which forced the client to withdraw visibly from the counseling exchange. The counselor did not get defensive and opposed the anti-counselor directly while admitting his own cultural insensitivity. The counselor's honest self-disclosure helped win over the client to accept continuing assistance.

In the fifth triad a black male graduate student in counseling described problems with racist elements in the curriculum to a white male counseling psychologist faculty member in his own department. The anti-counselor, another black faculty member, emphasized his "brotherhood" with the client and finally succeeded in angering the counselor, who attacked the anti-counselor for his inability to "really help" the client. The counselor relied on rational confrontation while the anti-counselor emphasized emotional feelings. A highly controversial topic was discussed with an open exchange of ideas and feelings that at times required participants to step out of role to defend or attack a point of view within the safety of a microcounseling context.


CONCLUSION

A review of the literature on mental health in different cultures suggests a need for improved in-service as well as preservice training of mental health specialists in the ways cultural differences affect counseling. The counselor needs first of all to recognize unique aspects of a client's culture that contribute to both the problem and the solution. Secondly, the counselor needs to be reminded of ways in which his own culture may help or hinder counseling, preventing his being encapsulated by learned cultural values. Thirdly, working with clients who are most different from himself can expand his counseling capacity for "open mindedness" and "empathic understanding" necessary to effective counseling. Fourth, alternative styles of indigenous conseling can be identified in terms of labeling, coalition formation, fixing an external cause, to lessen ambiguity, liberate clients, and mediate between the client and the problem. Fifth, cross-cultural training models that use role-play simulations of critical incidents in videotaped microcounseling show considerable promise of increasing a participant's skill in cross-cultural communication. Sixth, this paper has attempted to describe a model for training counselors that incorporates the preceding advantages of cross-cultural training in a triad model where the counselor is in a position to establish a cross-cultural coalition with the client against the problem.

The cross-cultural coalition model uses videotaped simulation of cross-cultural counseling interviews between a client, the counselor, and an "anti-counselor" in an attempt to (1) identify the problem more clearly from the client-culture point of view by allowing an "anti-counselor" from that culture to empathize in role with the problem and (2) to rehearse the kinds of specific resistance a counselor from one culture is likely to encounter when dealing with a client from that particular other culture on a specific problem. In order to test the model's effectiveness, a more systematic research project is being designed to compare the cross-cultural coalition model with a cross-cultural dyad training model.

If the cross-cultural coalition model demonstrates its effectiveness in training counselors, it might supplement traditional training in a variety of ways. Nonspecialist counselors and para-professionals in training are being sought out for advice or help but, lacking formal training in counseling, are frequently more dependent on self-taught skills. Even without benefit of understanding the theories of counselor training, the cross-cultural coalition model reinforces those behaviors which produce a counselor-client coalition and punishes behaviors which destroy that coalition. As a supplement to traditional curricula in formal counselor education, the model provides a useful link between didactic theory and practicum experiences in cross-cultural counseling. The model is directed toward both formal classes of preservice training and in-service training programs among persons already working in multicultural populations.

As the model is developed, the types of problems can be selected in a more systematic fashion in a comprehensive and balanced demonstration of authentic critical incidents. The cultural backgrounds of participants can be more carefully controlled to demonstrate the degree to which training in working with one culture or problem can produce skills that generalize to other cultures or problems. The concept of an "anti-counselor" is not limited to the cross-cultural training model described in this paper. The cross-cultural application tests the model under "most power" where cultural differences between counselor and client are most different and where the target skills of this model would be most necessary. The model provides one approach to the critical and urgent task of training mental health professionals to work with clients from other cultures.

## REFERENCES

AGEL, J.
  1971   *The radical therapist.* New York: Balantine Books.
ALLEN, T. W.
  1967   Effectiveness of counselor training as a function of psychological open-
         ness. *Journal of Counseling Psychology* 14:35–40.
AYRES, G.
  1970   "The disadvantaged: an analysis of factors affecting the counselor
         relationship." Paper read at the Minnesota Personnel and Guidance
         Association Mid-Winter Conference, Minneapolis, Minnesota, Feb-
         ruary, 1970.
BANDURA, A.
  1961   Psychotherapy as a learning process. *Psychological Bulletin* 58:143–
         159.
BANDURA, A., D. LIPHER, P. MILLER
  1960   Psychotherapists approach avoidance reactions to patients' expressions
         of hostility. *Journal of Consulting Psychology* 24:1–8.
BARNA, L. M.
  1972   "Intercultural communication," in *Readings in intercultural communi-
         cations.* Edited by D. Hoopes, 119–132. University of Pittsburgh.

BLOOMBAUM, M, J. YAMAMOTO, Q. JAMES
1968    Cultural stereotyping among psychotherapists. *Journal of Consulting and Clinical Psychology* 32(1):99.

BOLMAN, W. M.
1968    Cross cultural psychotherapy. *The American Journal of Psychiatry* 124 (9):1237–1243.

BOWEN, M.
1966 The use of family theory in clinical practice. *Comprehensive Psychiatry* 7:345–374.

BRYDE, J. F.
1971    *Indian students and guidance*. Boston: Houghton Mifflin.

CARKHUFF, R. R., M. ALEXIK
1967    Effect of client depth of self-exploration upon high- and low-functioning counselors. *Journal of Counseling Psychology* 14:350–355.

CARKHUFF, R. R., G. BANKS
1970    Training as a preferred mode of facilitating relations between races and generations. *Journal of Counseling Psychology* 17:413–418.

CARKHUFF, R. R., R. PIERCE
1967    Differential effects of therapist race and social class upon patient depth of self-exploration in the initial clinical interview. *Journal of Consulting Psychology* 31:632–634.

CAUDILL, W., T. Y. LIN
1969    *Mental health research in Asia and the Pacific*. Honolulu: East-West Center Press.

CHENAULT, J.
1968    A proposed model for a humanistic counselor education program. *Counselor Education and Supervision* 8(1):4–11.

COLE, M. B., J. S. BRUNER
1972    Cultural differences and inferences about psychological processes. *American Psychologist* 26:867–876.

CRAWFORD, F. R.
1969    "Variations between Negroes and whites in concepts of mental illness, its treatment and prevalence," in *Changing perspectives in mental illness*. Edited by S. Plog and R. Edgerton. New York: Holt, Rinehart and Winston.

DE CROW, R.
1969    *Cross-cultural interaction skills: A digest of recent training literature.* ERIC Clearinghouse on Adult Education.

DELANEY, D.
1969    Simulation techniques in counselor education: proposal of a unique approach. *Counselor Education and Supervision* 8(3):183–188.

DRAGUNS, J. G.
1971    "Investigations of psychopathology across cultures: issues, findings, directions." Mimeographed manuscript.

DRAGUNS, J. G., L. PHILIPS
1972    *Cultures and psychopathology: the quest for a relationship*. Morristown, New Jersey: General Learning Press.

DUSTIN, E. R.
  1968   "The client as a source of reinforcement in the counseling interview."
         Unpublished doctoral dissertation, University of Minnesota.
FIEDLER, F., T. MITCHELL, H. TRIANDIS
  1970   *The cultural assimilator: an approach to cross-cultural training.* Tech-
         nical report 70–5. Organizational Research Department of Psychology,
         University of Washington.
FLAUGHER, R. L., J. T. CAMPBELL, L. W. PIKE
  1969   *Prediction of job performance for Negro and white medical technicians.*
         Princeton, New Jersey: Educational Testing Service.
FOULDS, M.
  1971   Dogmatism and ability to communicate facilitative conditions during
         counseling. *Counseling Education and Supervision* 2(2):110–114.
FREEBERG, N. E.
  1969   Assessment of disadvantaged adolescents: A different approach to
         research and evaluation measures. *Research Bulletin* (May). Princeton,
         New Jersey: Educational Testing Service.
GIORDANO, J.
  1973   *Ethnicity and mental health: research and recommendations.* New York:
         National Project on Ethnic America of the American Jewish Commit-
         tee.
GLAZER, N., D. MOYNIHAN
  1963   *Beyond the melting pot.* Cambridge: MIT Press.
GORDON, E. W., P. M. SMITH
  1971   "The guidance specialist and the disadvantaged student," in *Guidance
         for education in revolution.* Edited by D. R. Cook. Boston: Allyn and
         Bacon.
GORDON, J.
  1965   Project cause: the federal anti-poverty program and some implications
         of sub-professional training. *American Psychologist* 20:333–343.
GUTTMAN, M. A. J., R. HAASE
  1972   Generalization of micro-counseling skills from training period to ac-
         tual counseling setting. *Counselor Education and Supervision* 12(2):98–
         107.
GYSBERS, N., E. MOORE
  1970   Using simulation techniques in the counseling practicum. *Counselor
         Education and Supervision* 9:277–284.
HAVINGHURST, R. J.
  1971   "Social class factors in coping style and competence." Mimeographed
         manuscript, University of Chicago, Committee on Human Develop-
         ment.
HELLER, K., R. A. MYERS, L. K. KLINE
  1963   Interviewer behavior as a function of standardized client roles. *Journal
         of Consulting Psychology* 27:117–122.
HOLLINGSHEAD, A. B., F. C. RIDLICH
  1958   *Social class and mental illness.* New York: Wiley and Sons.
IVEY, A. E.
  1971   *Microcounseling: innovations in interviewing training.* Springfield, Illi-
         nois: Charles C. Thomas.

IVEY, A. E., C. NORMINGTON, C. MILLER, W. MORRILL, R. HAASE
  1968   Microcounseling and attending behavior: an approach to prepracticum counselor training. *Journal of Counseling Psychology* 15(2):1–12.

KAGAN, N.
  1964   Three dimensions of counseling encapsulation. *Journal of Counseling Psychology* 2(4):361–365.

KANFER, F. H., J. S. PHILLIPS
  1970   *Learning foundations of behavior therapy.* New York: Wiley.

KELZ, J. W.
  1966   The development and evaluation of a measure of counselor effectiveness. *Personnel and Guidance Journal* 45:511–516.

KEMP, C.
  1962   Influence of dogmatism on the training of counselors. *Journal of Counseling Psychology* 9:155–157.

KIEV, A.
  1969   "Transcultural psychiatry: research problems and perspectives," in *Changing perspectives in mental illness.* Edited by S. C. Plog and R. B. Edgerton. New York: Holt, Rinehart and Winston.

KINCAID, M. L.
  1969   Identity and therapy in the Black community. *Personnel and Guidance Journal* 47(9):884–890.

KUPFERER, H. J., T. K. FITZGERALD
  1971   *Culture, society and guidance.* Boston: Houghton Mifflin.

LEUNG, P.
  1973   Comparative effects of training in external and internal concentration on two counseling behaviors. *Journal of Counseling Psychology* 20(3): 227–234.

LEWIS, M. D., J. A. LEWIS
  1970   Relevant training for relevant roles: a model for educating inner city counselors. *Counselor Education and Supervision* 10(1):31–38.

LOCKE, D., S. O. LEWIS
  1969   Racism encountered in counseling. *Counselor Education and Supervision* 9(1):49–60.

MADSEN, W
  1969   "Mexican Americans and Anglo Americans: a comparative study of mental health in Texas," in *Changing perspectives in mental illness.* Edited by S. C. Plog and R. B. Edgerton. New York: Holt, Rinehart and Winston.

MAYESKE, G. W.
  1971   *On the explanation of racial-ethnic group differences in achievement test scores.* Washington, D. C.: U.S. Office of Education.

MC DONALD, E., D. ALLEN
  1967   "Training effects of feedback and modeling procedures on teaching performance." Unpublished report, Stanford University.

MC FAYDEN, M., G. WINOKUR
  1956   Cross-cultural psychotherapy. *Journal of Nervous and Mental Disorders* 123: 369–375.

MECHANIC, D.
   1969   "Illness and cure," in *Poverty and health.* Edited by Kosa, et al. Cambridge: Harvard University Press.
MERCER, J. R.
   1971   "Pluralistic diagnosis in the evaluation of Black and Chicano children: a procedure for taking sociocultural variables into account in clinical assessment." Paper presented at the meetings of the American Psychological Association, Washington, D. C., September 3–7, 1971.
MEZZANO, J.
   1969   A note on dogmatism and counselor effectiveness. *Counselor Education and Supervision* 9(1):64–65.
MIDDLETOWN, R.
   1963   Alienation, race and education. *American Sociological Review* 28: 973–977.
MILLIKAN, K. L., J. J. PATERSON
   1967   Relationship of dogmatism and prejudice to counseling effectiveness. *Counselor Education and Supervision* 6:125–129.
MILLIKAN, K. L.
   1965   Prejudice and counseling effectiveness. *Personnel and Guidance Journal* 43:710–712.
MITCHELL, H.
   1970   The black experience in higher education. *The Counseling Psychologist* 2:30–36.
MORALES, A.
   1970   *The impact of class discrimination and racism on the mental health of Mexican Americans.* Western Interstate Comission for Higher Education, Mexican American Mental Health Issues. Boulder, Colorado: Stanley W. Bancher.
MORELAND, J., J. PHILLIPS, A. IVEY, J. LOCKHART
   1970   "A study of the microtraining paradigm with beginning clinical psychologists." Unpublished paper, University of Massachusetts.
MORROW, D. L.
   1972   Cultural addiction. *Journal of Rehabilitation* 38(3):30–32.
MULIOZZI, A. D..
   1972   "Inter-racial counseling: does it work?" Paper presented at the American Personnel and Guidance Association meeting, Chicago, 1972.
MURPHY, J. M., A. H. LEIGHTON, *editors*
   1965   *Approaches to cross-cultural psychiatry.* Ithaca: Cornell University Press.
MURRAY, E.
   1956   *The content analysis method of studying psychotherapy.* Psychological monographs 70 (13).
NAROLL, R.
   1969   "Cultural determinants and the concept of the sick society," in *Changing perspectives in mental illness.* Edited by S. C. Plog and R. B. Edgerton. New York: Holt, Rinehart and Winston.
OPLER, M.
   1967   *Culture and social psychiatry.* New York: Atherton Press.

PADILLA, E., R. BOXLEY, N. WAGNER
1972   "The desegregation of clinical psychology training." Paper presented at the American Psychological Association meeting, Honolulu.

PARSONS, R., W. E. MC CREARY
1967   Problem and paradox in counselor education. *Counselor Education and Supervision* 6(3):187–190.

PATTERSON, C. H.
1970   President's message: counseling psychology in the 1970's. *The Counseling Psychologist* 3(2):4.

PIERCE, R., R. R. CARKHUFF, B. J. BERENSON
1967   The differential effects of high- and low-functioning counselors upon counselors-in-training. *Journal of Clinical Psychology* 23:212–215.

PULVINO, C. J., P. A. PERRONE
1973   A model for retooling school counselors. *Counselor Education and Supervision* 12(4):308–313.

REIVICH, R., R. GEERTSMA
1969   Observational media and psychotherapy training. *Journal of Nervous and Mental Disorders* 148:310–327.

ROARK, A. E.
1969   The influence of training on counselor response in actual role playing interviews. *Counselor Education and Supervision* 8(4).

ROGERS, C. R.
1965   "The interpersonal relationship: the core of guidance," in *Guidance: an examination.* Edited by R. Moser, R. Carle and C. Kehas. New York: Harcourt, Brace and World.

ROGERS, J.
1960   Operant conditioning in a quasi-therapy setting. *Journal of Abnormal and Social Psychology* 60:247–252.

RUSSEL, R. D.
1970   Black perceptions of guidance. *The Personnel and Guidance Journal* 48:721–729.

RUSSO, R. J., J. W. KETZ, G. HUDSON
1964   Are good counselors open-minded? *Counselor Education and Supervision* 3(2):74–77.

SALOMON, G., F. J. MC DONALD
1970   Pretest and posttest reactions to self-viewing one's teaching performance on videotape. *Journal of Educational Psychology.* 61:280–286.

SASLOW, H. L., M. J. HARROVER
1968   Research on psychological adjustment of Indian youth. *American Journal of Psychiatry* 125(2).

SATIR, V.
1964   *Conjoint family therapy.* Palo Alto, California: Science and Behavior Books.

SCHWEBEL, M.
1964   Ideology and counselor encapsulation. *Journal of Counseling Psychology* 2(4):366–369.

SINCLAIR, A.
    1957    *Field and clinical survey report of the mental health of the indigenes of the territory of Papua and New Guinea, Port Moresby.* Government publication.

SODDY, K., *editor*
    1962    *Cross cultural studies in mental health.* Chicago: Quadrangle Books.

SPIVAK, J. D.
    1973    Critical incidents in counseling: simulated video experiences for training counselors. *Counselors Education and Supervision* 12(4):263–270.

SPRANG, A.
    1965    Counseling the Indian. *Journal of American Indian Education* (October).

STRANGES, R., A. RICCIO
    1970    A counselee preference for counselors: some implications for counselor education. *Counselor Education and Supervision* 10:39–46.

STROLLER, F. M.
    1967    Group psychotherapy on television: an innovation with hospitalized patients. *American Psychologist* 23:158–163.

SUCHMAN, E.
    1964    Sociomedical variations among ethnic groups. *American Journal of Sociology* 70:328–329.

THAYER, L., V. PETERSON, E. CARR, D. MERZ
    1972    Development of a critical incidents videotape. *Journal of Counseling Psychology* 19(3):188–191.

THOMAS, A.
    1962    Pseudo transference reactions due to cultural stereotyping. *American Journal of Orthopsychiatry* 32:894–900.

TORREY, E. F.
    1969    The case for the indigenous therapist. *Archives of General Psychiatry* 20:365–373.
    1970    "The irrelevancy of traditional mental health services for urban Mexican Americans." Paper presented at the American Orthopsychiatric Association.
    1971    *The mind game: witchdoctors and psychiatrists.* New York: Emmerson Hall.

TRENT, R. D.
    1954    The color of the investigator as a variable in experimental research with Negro subjects. *Journal of Social Psychology* 40:281–287.

VONTRESS, C. E.
    1969    Cultural barriers in the counseling relationship. *Personnel and Guidance Journal* 48:11–17.
    1971    Racial differences: impediments to rapport. *Journal of Counseling Psychology* 18(1):7–13.

WALZ, G. R., J. A. JOHNSTON
    1963    Counselors look at themselves on videotape. *Journal of Counseling Psychology* 10 :232–236.

WATTS, A. W.
1961   *Psychotherapy: East and West.* New York: Pantheon Books.

WATTS, M.
1973   Behavior modeling and self devaluation with video-self-confrontation. *Journal of Educational Psychology* 64(2):212–215.

WEIDMAN, H. H.
1969   The self-concept as a crucial link between social sciences and psychiatric theory. *Transcultural Psychiatry Research Review* 6:113–116.

WEIDMAN, H. H., J. N. SUSSEX
1971   Cultural values and ego-functioning in relation to the atypical culture-bound reactive syndromes. *International Journal of Social Psychiatry* 17(2).

WHITELY, J. M., P. A. JAKUBOWSKI
1969   The coached clients as a research and training resource in counseling. *Counselor Education and Supervision* 2:19–29.

WILLIAMS, R. L.
1970   Black pride, academic relevance, and individual achievement. *The Counseling Psychologist* 2:18–22.

WOLF, S. R., R. C. W. HALL
1971   The use of psychodrama to demonstrate transcultural distance in psychotherapy. *Group Psychotherapy and Psychodrama* 24(1):17–23.

WOODS, F. J.
1958   Cultural conditioning and mental health. *Social Casework* 39:327–333.

WRENN, G.
1962   The culturally encapsulated counselor. *Harvard Educational Review* 32(4):444–449.

YAP, P. M.
1969   "The culture-bound reactive syndromes," in *Mental health research in Asia and the Pacific.* Edited by W. Caudill and Y. L. Tsung, 33–53. Honolulu: East-West Center Press.

ZUK, G.
1971   *Family therapy: a triadic based approach.* New York: Behavioral Publications.

# Work Styles Among American Psychiatric Residents

DONALD W. LIGHT, JR.

A minor cultural distinction of "modern" cultures is that psychiatrists control an ever-growing domain of services to the mentally ill. Thus how they approach their work influences the entire character of those services. The problem is to identify different types of psychiatrists and to analyze their impact on mental health services. Although we confine ourselves here to the American scene, the analysis may be useful for students of other societies.

## THE PROBLEMS OF IDEOLOGICAL TYPES

The first serious effort to differentiate between types of psychiatric residents was made by Myron Sharaf and Daniel Levinson (1957). They devised a bipolar attitude scale of Psycho-Sociotherapeutic Ideology consisting of specific items which measured the extent to which a resident was psycho-analytically oriented and the extent to which he favored more social approaches such as group therapy, use of a therapeutic team, structuring the patient's milieu, and the like. Items also probed for the resident's inclination toward somatic types of therapies.

Several years later, Strauss and his colleagues (1964) pointed out that the PSI scale ASSUMES the sociotherapeutic orientation to be the opposite of the psychoanalytic one and that it assumes an orientation toward somatic therapies to be part of the sociotherapeutic perspective. To test these assumptions, they designed three separate scales and found (1) that the first two orientations are not opposites but quite independent and (2) that a somatic ideology correlates negatively with psychoanalytic beliefs

and is independent of a sociotherapeutic orientaton. One might summarize these results by saying that the psychoanalytic and somatic ideologies
are opposites along a psychological-physiological axis and that the
sociotherapeutic ideology is independent of the other two. However, there
was a fly in the ointment: the sociotherapeutic ideology was not clearly
formed in respondents who leaned in this direction, and so this important
type was not well defined.

The reader will already have noticed the political character of this approach to classifying residents. The three ideologies reflect factions in the
profession as a whole, not in new residents, who generally have only vague
ideas about psychiatry (Ehrlich and Sabshin 1964). *This approach of trying
to create scales which slice up the resident's reality according to the ideologies of the day appears to be the central flaw in efforts so far to find out what
kinds of residents enter psychiatry.* For these are not THEIR terms but perspectives brought to them by the researcher. Thus we should not be surprised that neither effort at ideological scaling produced clear results.[1]

The very construction of these scales for distinguishing between types
of residents also highlights the dangers of being taken in by the profession's
ideologies. A good example is Strauss's point that Sharaf's and Levinson's
PSI scale assumes the sociotherapeutic outlook to be opposite to the psychoanalytic one. So far as we know, this was the view which prevailed
among the heavily psychoanalytic staff at Massachusetts Mental Health
Center when Sharaf and Levinson worked there. Moreover, the sociotherapeutic end of their scale was a catchall for anyone NOT strongly committed to psychoanalysis. Without realizing it, perhaps, they constructed
an instrument which reflected the strong psychoanalytic orientation of
the residency where they worked.

Strauss and his colleagues ran into the same problem, suggesting another
pattern of interest — that neither team in the late 1950's and early 1960's
could find a clear pattern of the social approach to psychiatry. In sampling
both an elite and a state hospital (where staff with a social approach were
expected to be found), the Strauss group turned up so few people with
either a sociotherapeutic or a somatic viewpoint that they had to draw
special, biased samples just to test their instruments. This probably reflects
the extent to which the psychoanalytic view gained dominance throughout
psychiatry after World War II. Even people using shock therapy and

---

[1]   On a range of 10 to 70, Sharaf and Levinson got a mean of 54 and a high score of 58.
Because the test was administered in an analytically oriented program, these figures cast
doubt on the validity of the instrument. The revised scales of Strauss' group also appear
to slice reality into jumbled pieces, as evidenced in Ehrlich and Sabshin's study (1964,
especially pages 469–477).

caring for hundreds of patients at a state mental hospital believed in psychoanalytic values and therapeutic approaches. At the same time, psychoanalytic principles became so diffuse (as do the core principles of any group that acquires a wide following) that greatly divergent practices became legitimated in psychoanalytic terms. One might say that psychoanalysis had become, as in *The structure of scientific revolutions* (Kuhn 1962), the new paradigm of psychiatry. Opinions will vary as to whether it is still.

## THREE WORK STYLES AMONG PSYCHIATRISTS

Even if the ideological biases of these measures could be cleared up, it appears that they are not a good way to find out what kinds of psychiatrists make up the psychiatric profession. In my own fieldwork, which was confined to observing residents, I found that the approach of each resident to his work remained quite consistent from the first week to the end. As the resident gained skills and new beliefs about psychiatric work, he essentially incorporated them into his work-style. Moreover, the psychiatric profession requires no more than this. Socialization into psychiatry is less a matter of acquiring new behaviors than of recasting one's behavior and even one's personality into a new interpretative framework, a new language. What psychiatry admires is less that a person act in a certain way than that he know why he acts the way he does in terms of his psychodynamics. Thus, a good typology would eschew ideologies and delineate styles of work.

The kinds of residents described below have not yet been crystalized into scales. They emerged during a study of Massachusetts Mental Health Center, the largest of Harvard's training facilities in psychiatry and one of the largest in the country (Light 1970). Because the processes under investigation were both subtle and continually changing over time, I used ethnographic techniques in combination with focused interviews. Known as a research social scientist, I observed ward activities, staff meetings, and case conferences as I worked with residents. More important for a study of socialization, I had continued access to individual supervision, group supervision, "feelings meetings" (where a small group of residents share their frustrations, hopes, and diasppointments), and the sensitivity group for residents. Few senior psychiatrists have access to these settings and, to my knowledge, no outside investigator of professional training in psychiatry has drawn upon them.

In this range of settings I used mainly participant observation as a way of recording actual behavior and natural conversations. Like the residents, I would arrive every weekday by 8:30 A.M. and leave by 6:00 P.M., sometimes staying for night duty as well. Thus, in more than a year I spent about 3,000 hours observing. This meant that I came to know many residents well, and I could constantly interweave observation with questions about their sense of specific actions. Thus hypotheses could be continually tested and refined. Once a pattern emerged I would move to another location where other residents were presumably doing the same thing to see if the pattern persisted. In this manner one could accumulate a body of data on observed phenomena and their meaning to participants that were addressed to emergent themes.

The Center admitted about twenty-five residents each year. Because many third-year residents moved to special programs in other locations, about sixty residents worked at this clinic and hospital of 225 beds. At the time (1967–1969), the residents were overwhelmingly white males with an average of one woman and fewer than one Negro per cohort. Three-quarters came from Jewish homes, and 90 percent grew up in a city or suburb. While these are not unusual figures for elite programs in psychiatry, the materials are confined to one program at one point in time. Moreover, though the data are qualitatively hard (firsthand, behavioral) they are quantitatively soft (no controls, no scales) so that what follows are hypotheses for further research.

In the fieldwork and interviews, three quite distinct work styles became evident: the therapeutic, the managerial, and the cognitive. THERAPEUTIC PSYCHIATRISTS want very much to help their patients. Ideologically they are open-minded and eclectic. They will employ whatever techniques promise results. They are not usually committed to psychoanalysis before they begin, but if they come to believe that psychoanalysis works — and many are channeled into thinking so — then they will incorporate it into their therapy. These are the residents who suffer the most anxiety and who experience the transition from medicine to psychiatry most intensively. As a group, they loved medical school and internship. They always wanted to be doctors, friendly family doctors. Because they attended sophisticated medical schools in the era of modern medicine, they realized that family doctors went the way of roadside towns. "I couldn't go the boondocks," said one resident. Eighty percent of them are from Jewish, metropolitan homes. They could have become general practitioners in the suburbs, but they thought the work would be dull and would lack prestige. In addition, many said that at some point in the final years of medical school, "I realized that I would much rather talk to this patient about her kid than her kidney."

MANAGERIAL PSYCHIATRISTS share many background traits with therapeutic residents. They wanted to become doctors, they enjoyed medical
school and internship, and now they want to get patients better. However,
their work style is quite different. They do not become nearly so emotional
about their patients, and from the start they prefer administrative techniques of therapy. On the hospitalized patients, they use restrictions, drugs,
ECT, perhaps behavioral therapy, and they organize a therapeutic milieu
for a patient, with nurses and attendants. In short, they manage their
patients. Emotionally, they are less expressive, less (apparently) neurotic.
In their second and third years, they tend to become administrators or to
choose some instrumental form of psychiatry such as community psychiatry. Given the analytic tone of the program, they may still go into psychoanalysis and even attend the Psychoanalytic Institute, but they speak of
the decision in terms of connections, power, and "the right thing to do."
They also gain satisfaction from simply organizing and running things.
Unlike the therapeutic residents, they do not become emotionally involved
in identifying with certain psychiatrists.

COGNITIVE PSYCHIATRISTS distinguish themselves by approaching
patients as cases which illuminate theoretical aspects of the psyche. Often
they decided very early to become psychiatrists. Many of these residents
hated medical school and internship. They suffered through them in order
to reach their life's goal, psychoanalytic psychiatry. As a result, they incorporated less of the medical model and entered psychiatry NOT expecting to cure patients. In addition, they have read and talked psychoanalysis
over the years so that they do not find it frustratingly vague. Therefore,
they do not suffer the initial anxiety which other residents experience.

They approach their patients cognitively, less to cure them or to understand them as persons than to understand their intrapsychic dynamics.
Seemingly unaware of it, they talk about their patients as case studies in
psychoanalytic theory and are very intellectual. Unlike the other residents,
they do not resist early suggestions of countertransference, and they can
easily talk about their neurotic tendencies. Their greatest and most terrify-
ing moment comes when they apply to the Psychoanalytic Institute, a
moment beautifully described by Sharaf and Levinson (1964). They feel as
if their whole life, their worth as a person, is being judged. In the balance
rest their careers, and after all those hateful years of premed courses,
medical school and internship, some do not make it.

Space does not allow an examination of how each kind of resident goes
through his training, but the descriptions above give some indication.
Most common at Massachusetts Mental Health Center were the therapeutic residents of whom David Viscott, in *The making of a psychiatrist* (1972),

is an articulate example. They constituted half or even two-thirds of the cohorts observed. Unlike the breezy Dr. Viscott, they experienced a larger and more painful transformation from medical to psychiatry than did the other two types. Supervisors called their initial desires to cure patients "rescue fantasies." As they found their medicine training of marginal use and their patients did not respond well, they slid down to a first-year depression which has been widely noted (Bucher, et al. 1969; Light 1970; Sharaf and Levinson 1964; Bucher 1965; Blum and Rosenberg 1968; Halleck and Woods 1962; Merklin and Little 1967). They pulled out of this nadir by refocusing on mastering the therapeutic hour, something which their analytic colleagues had been doing all along and which the managerial types did with more marginal interest. Thus they reimmersed themselves in helping patients with their problems but in a way which protected them from great disappointment.

As the descriptions indicate, the three types of residents do not imply what kind of ideology each will embrace. Rather, they are a first attempt to distinguish ways in which emerging psychiatrists approach their patients and their work. Each type has important consequences for professional training and patient care. First, these work styles are well-established parts of residents' personalities. Therefore, effective training would capitalize on the strengths of each rather than train all psychiatrists the same way and thereby allow certain work styles to reemerge untrained. But good training would also recognize the blind spots of each style and work to overcome them. Second, the profession should respect the skills of all three styles and provide careers for each. This has not always been the case in the past. Finally, mental health services would improve if a system were devised whereby patients were assigned to therapists whose skills and approach matched their needs.

## REFERENCES

BLUM, A. J., L. ROSENBERG
  1968   Some problems involved in professionalizing social interaction: the case of psychotherapeutic training. *Journal of Health and Social Behavior* 9:72–85.
BUCHER, R.
  1965   The psychiatric residency and professional socialization. *Journal of Health and Social Behavior* 6:197–206.
BUCHER, R., J. STELLING, P. DOMMERMUTH
  1969   Implications of prior socialization for residency programs in psychiatry. *Archives of General Psychiatry* 20:395–402.

EHRLICH, D., M. SABSHIN
1964 A study of sociotherapeutically oriented psychiatrists. *American Journal of Orthopsychiatry* 34:469–480.

HALLECK, S. L., S. M. WOODS
1962 Emotional problems of psychiatric residents. *Psychiatry* 25:339–346.

KUHN, T.
1962 *The structure of scientific revolutions*. Chicago: University of Chicago Press.

LIGHT, D. W., JR.
1970 "The socialization and training of psychiatrists." Doctoral dissertation, Brandeis University.

MERKLIN, L., JR., R. B. LITTLE
1967 Beginning psychiatry training program. *American Journal of Psychiatry* 124:193–197.

SHARAF, M. R., D. L. LEVINSON
1957 "Patterns of ideology and professional role-definition among psychiatric residents," in *The patient and the mental hospital*. Edited by M. Greenblatt, D. J. Levinson, and R. H. Williams, 263–285. Glencoe: Free Press.
1964 The quest for omnipotence in professional training. *Psychiatry* 27: 135–149.

STRAUSS, A., L. SCHATZMAN, R. BUCHER, *et al*
1964 *Psychiatric ideologies and institutions*, chapter four. Glencoe: Free Press.

UNGERLEIDER, J. T.
1965 That most difficult year. *American Journal of Psychiatry* 122:542–545.

VISCOTT, D.
1972 *The making of a psychiatrist*. New York: Anchor.

# Historical Antecedents of
# Mental Health Dilemmas in America

H. R. HUESSY

## INTRODUCTION

The clients of mental health programs need therapies designed to deal with problems on at least three levels: the medical level, the psychological level and the social level. Problems at any of these levels can produce secondary problems at other levels. This is but a restatement of the old adage that we must always treat the whole patient. Why is it, then, that today we face such major difficulties in implementing this generally accepted statement?

I would like to sketch out some developments in the history of the mental health movement which I believe have contributed to our dilemma, summarize our present dilemma, and explore opportunities for new developments in the domain of social therapies.

## ORIGINS OF AMERICAN PSYCHIATRY: 1900–1940

Psychiatry began as the field of medicine dealing with illnesses of the mind. It dealt with schizophrenia, manic depressive illness, other depressions, chronic brain syndromes, central nervous system syphilis, senile dementia and postalcoholic psychosis. The goal of early psychiatry was the treatment of illnesses with assumed medical disturbances.

This early emphasis gradually changed. Two developments occurred. First, psychiatrists had few medical tools to help their patients and began to develop psychological and social methods to help their organically ill patients. The second development occurred because workers in mental hospitals, seeing that many of their patients had had difficulties in childhood, began to have hopes that if these emotional disorders could be treated in childhood, the children might not become adult mental patients; and thus the child guidance movement was started. As they studied their child clients, they had no leads to any underlying organic pathology except genetics, but they were impressed by the psychological and social aspects. Psychological and social treatment methods began to be used exclusively in treating children. The hoped-for prevention of adult mental illness was never achieved.

Both developments shared the emphasis on psychological and social approaches and this in turn led to the creation of two new professional groups: the clinical psychologists and the psychiatric social worker. The concept of the team approach, involving psychiatrist, psychologist and social worker in a joint effort, grew from these experiences and in retrospect this was very sound. It recognized that both diagnosis and therapy had to simultaneously involve the medical, psychological, and social level of functioning.

Unfortunately, there was little medical treatment the psychiatrist could contribute, so he became a "higher-level" psychologist or social worker and role confusion became rampant. He became the supervisor of all psychological and social therapy. The psychiatrist, without specific medical therapies to contribute, still operated under the influence of his medical training: a specific treatment for a specific illness. Thus, he was led to use psychological and social therapies as though they were specific therapies. This led to a huge literature on techniques of psychological and social therapy, without addressing the question of the types of problems they should be used for or the results of the undertaking. Because there were few medical therapies, medical diagnosis was seen as unimportant, and causal thinking on the psychological and social level was substituted.

Social therapy appears to improve the ability of individuals and groups to cope with any stress. However, it is nonspecific in terms of the stress being coped with. Social therapy is helpful to anyone with an illness, a problem or some other underlying stress. Psychology developed specific therapies only with the burgeoning of behavior modification techniques. Various techniques of individual psychotherapy dominated its therapeutic activities before that.

With the additional stimulus of psychoanalytic theory, even more enthusiasm for the possibility of prevention and treatment through psychological and social as opposed to organic methods was generated.

IMPACT OF WAR ON AMERICAN PSYCHIATRY: 1941–1952

When World War II came along, a primarily psychological treatment program was set up for military casualties. It was dominated by the medical concept of a specific illness to be treated with a specific therapy. But, as had already been learned in World War I, psychiatric casualties in a war situation consisted primarily of situational stress reactions and did not imply a specific defect in the individual. Medical or psychological treatments were inappropriate as the use of these treatments presupposed a specific defect. The psychological treatment program used was geared to treat specific defects with specific therapies, and it was a complete fiasco with less than 10 percent of the casualties returning to duty. Until this became obvious no one bothered to read the descriptions of the psychiatrists' experiences in World War I. Had they done so they could have prevented this disaster.

Toward the end of World War II and during the interval preceding the Korean War, a new treatment system was built on the ideas of social psychiatry. This was a nonspecific social treatment program for temporary social disorders due to acute stress. Under this program, 70 percent of the casualties were back fighting with their comrades within forty-eight hours. The soldiers who had been successfully treated had a rate of future breakdown which was the same as for the soldiers who had never had a breakdown. This further supported the view that acute situational stress reactions should not be confused with specific illnesses.

I believe this experience of our military emphasizes two important points. First, that good intentions in mental health still can lead to disastrous consequences, and second, that when a therapy conceived on the basis of a medical model (specific defect plus permanent pathology) is applied to what is a disturbance due to causes in the social sphere (acute stress plus temporary reaction), you get disastrous results. The success in Korea was due to the fact that a system of social therapy had been developed for a temporary disorder due to social stress.

The war had turned hundreds of physicians into psychiatrists who came home enthusiastic about the possibilities of psychiatry. They had been trained for the early specific psychological treatment program which was based on psychoanalytic concepts and emphasized intense abreactions and personality reconstruction. They were unaware of its failure. It was these men who dominated academic psychiatry in the postwar years. This is why academic psychiatry continued to be dominated by the concepts of specific therapies for specific illnesses applied in the social sphere and that treatment programs should be based on etiology rather than on diagnosis. Much energy was devoted to turning the nonspecific psychological and social therapies into specific therapies. Rosen's "direct analysis" of schizophrenia was accepted because it fulfilled this goal. Horwitz et al. (1958) later showed that it had been a complete fabrication.

## PSYCHOPHARMACOLOGY ERA BEGINS: 1953

When drug therapy for psychoses became available in 1953, some of these psychoanalytic academicians were strongly opposed. They felt drugs would prevent the resolution of the patient's "underlying" problems. Only psychological therapies should be used for supposedly psychological illnesses. Their theories postulated specific incomplete or pathological experiences as causes for different psychological illnesses, and their therapies were attempts to undo or therapeutically relive these experiences. Their goal was specific therapy based on causes. That organic pathology could be caused by psychological or social factors everyone could accept and thus agree that the organic pathology must be treated for its own sake. And when an elderly lady returns with her third bout of pneumonia, it certainly behooves us to do something about her unheated apartment and her lack of adequate blankets. But we must still treat her pneumonia. When a disorder is on the psychological or social level we tend to deny that the organism has been changed by the etiological agents and will need treatment even if the etiological agents are eliminated. Instead, the etiological agents are attacked and the organism is expected to return to normalcy by itself.

## PSYCHIATRY AS PANACEA: 1960's

Other returning psychiatrists took up work in state mental hospitals and through their enthusiasm obtained greatly increased budgets for public mental health programs, with the implied promise that not only would we treat the mentally ill more successfully, but also we would prevent other people from becoming mentally ill. This expansion created many new jobs for clinical psychologists and psychiatric social workers. But the work with the mentally ill was undramatic and unsuccessful, and, as a compensation for this, the domain of mental health was continually expanded, in the name of preventing mental illness, to include marital problems, problems of delinquency and crime, job problems, career problems, and retirement problems. In a word, besides dealing with organic and psychological problems, psychiatrists were dealing with more and more social problems. There was little evidence to substantiate the notion that these disorders in the social sphere were precursors of major mental illness. And it was for this new group of patients who were not "ill" according to the old criteria, that the new therapeutic methods of psychoanalysis, client-centered therapy, group and family therapy, Gestalt therapy and transactional analysis were developed. All these therapies tried to supply professionally what people were losing through social change.

Under the pressure of rapid expansion, the indigenous paraprofessionals were added to the staff. They were added because of a very real shortage of trained professionals for the growing community mental health services and also because middle-class mental health professionals seemed unable to relate effectively with clients from minority or poverty groups.

These paraprofessionals were often working with clients who seemed to suffer from the deficits of inadequate social organization in an industrial society. But, because they were working under the aegis of a medically oriented program which supposedly was addressing itself to the prevention of major mental illness, they tended to apply the organic or the psychological model to these social problems and to think in terms of treatment and cure. Individual therapy, group therapy, family therapy, Gestalt therapy, transactional analysis and sensitivity training all were applied in attempts to find ways of helping patients overcome social problems. Unfortunately, while the immediate results seemed very promising, follow-up studies were more disappointing. If their clients' problems were a response to inadequate social structure, it is, of course, difficult to see how any temporary therapeutic intervention could make a difference in the long run. If they were basically healthy individuals with only minor hang-ups, the results looked good, but other data indicated that these problems tend to subside, even without treatment.

The lumping of all clients with medical, psychological and social problems into one therapeutic bucket led to bad consequences for all. Thomas Szasz is the champion of the view that most psychiatric illness is a purely social phenomenon. He sees no rationale for medical therapies with psychiatric patients. But there are clients who need medical or psychological treatment who are not getting it because social therapists see all disturbance as socially caused and treat it on purely social levels. At the other extreme, people with exclusively psychological or social problems are getting medical treatment by some physicians who see all problems as related to organic causes. Clients with either medical or social problems are treated by psychological means if cared for by a a behavioral psychologist. The treatment obtained by a particular patient is determined by the professional orientation of his therapist rather than by the illness from which he suffers. When quality control is attempted, the technical quality of the treatment is judged, not the relevance of the treatment to the patient's needs. The severely ill psychiatric patient usually needs therapy at all three levels simultaneously.

The mental health professions developed groups of narrowly overspecialized therapists, each of which conceived of all illnesses exclusively in terms of its own particular methodology and level of operation. A caricature of their attitude would be "We have a wonderful treatment. It is good for everybody."

## DISCUSSION

The social healer in primitive societies does not share this need for exclusiveness. Both in Nigeria and among the Navajos, native healers have been happy to add specific medical therapies to their psychological and social therapy resources, fully aware that they had been unsuccessful in their treatment of severe organic illnesses. These native healers, without benefit and burden of our theoretical labors, have used the principles of social psychiatry for millennia.

Many mental health workers feel that medical treatment should be employed only when they can convince themselves that there may be underlying organic causes. For instance, for children with minimal brain dysfunction many doctors will not prescribe the stimulant medications which often help dramatically unless they can find some neurological signs or a history of a major insult to the nervous system. There is no evidence that the etiology has the slightest effect on the results that these medications may achieve. The drugs affect specific symptoms. The etiology of the problem is unknown, but there is a medical therapy which very successfully can deal with some of the symptoms. There are also psychological and social means of helping these children. The evidence indicates that the best results are achieved when all three methods are used simultaneously. Follow-up studies of these treatments should determine the therapy of choice. Too many workers in the field have this need for exclusiveness and will only use their own particular method of treatment. They tend to believe that a problem at any of the three levels must have both its cause and its therapy on the same level. But a social problem can cause an ulcer, and a brain tumor may present as a social problem.

At the other extreme of the patient spectrum is a person from a disorganized urban community who is unable to function because of the lack of social organization. His symptoms are a response to inadequacies of the environment. Is community mental health the proper aegis for providing help to these clients? Are mental health workers qualified to be therapists of the community?

There is a tendency to blame the dominance of the medical model for some of our problems in the field of mental health. The medical model is appropriate for dealing with illness. It is not appropriate for dealing with social problems or with temporary responses to stress. Many of today's therapists have never dealt with psychotic individuals, and they are the ones who think that their therapies would cure these sick patients if only the psychiatrist and his medical model would get out of the way. These therapists, untrained in diagnosis, have never learned to distinguish the ill from individuals with temporary adjustment problems. For clients suffering from inadequacies of social organization, the medical model does not apply and social therapy cannot eliminate the deficiencies in social organization which caused the problem in the beginning. A temporary friend paid for by mental health funds will never be the same as a real friend. An artificially created therapeutic community in a hospital ward can never replace needed social organization outside. If the client's difficulty is due to inadequacies in the social organization of an industrialized society, then new social organizations must be created. "Temporary therapies" will not do. This problem has caused community health programs to become involved in trying to change society. Its professionals were not trained for this task and it has presented them with the dilemma of having to bite the hand that fed them when they played the role of social revolutionary.

During my work in college mental health, I saw many students in need of a wise man. Their problem was at a high social level. Seeing a psychiatrist forced them into a patient role, to view themselves as sick. To make the concerned student into a sick patient can have negative consequences.

In planning social therapy we must specify: (1) Are we helping someone to return to a previous level of functioning after a major illness? (2) Are we trying to teach some new behaviors? (3) Are we trying to compensate for lacking social organization? (4) Are we trying to help basically healthy individuals through a period of temporary stress?

Many psychotherapists have become aware that for many of their patients the ongoing interest and concern that they showed was the essential ingredient of their therapy. This led to attempts to utilize nonprofessionals for such supportive relationships. Perhaps a nonprofessional volunteer relationship could do more than a professional one. The goal was to make the relationship as genuine and natural as possible and to overcome the limitations of professionalism. These limitations will be discussed later.

In the days of the child guidance movement, the big-brother organization was begun to bring to needy problem boys relationships with successful adult males who were not professional therapists. During the 1950's, we began to develop the use of college student volunteers as big brothers and big sisters. Use of college students had the advantage of having a normal termination due to graduation from college, which the original big brother movement did not provide. The local businessman could not terminate his friendship without making the child feel rejected. Many mental hospitals began to experiment with the use of volunteers both for various kinds of activities and for relationship purposes. In Cambridge, Massachusetts, a halfway house was manned by college student volunteers. All of these programs were built on the individual personal qualities of the volunteers.

In the urban community mental health field, indigenous paraprofessionals were developed. These individuals' relationships with their clients were to approximate more closely genuine social interactions than any relationships with professionals could. Soon even the indigenous paraprofessionals became professionalized and developed the same problems in relating to their clients: a professional relationship is a limited relationship.

This posed a problem. All these programs were attempts to respond to the feeling that many of the clients of the mental health movement needed genuine relationships or a role in a social organization rather than professional therapy. Who could fulfill such needs?

Specific treatments at all levels require that someone with sufficient knowledge decide when they should be used. They are dependent on adequate professional knowledge and depend little on the personal involvement of the therapist. Nonspecific social therapies depend heavily on the personal involvement of the therapist and require little professional knowledge. Professionalization limits effective nonspecific social therapy. Professionalism is essential for the proper application, but not necessarily execution, of specific medical and psychological therapies.

If a majority of the clients of mental health programs suffer from the deficits in our social structure, then near-permanent social structures must be created to help them. Many present-day communes are attempts to create these structures. In order to utilize these and to create other new resources, we must learn to diagnose our clients' problems on at least three levels: medical, psychological and social. The experts on each of these three levels must be able to accept that the patient lives on each of these three levels simultaneously and that treatment or replacement interventions may be indicated on more than one level at a time. The social level may have to be divided further into the level of everyday living, the level of meaningful relationships and the level of commitment to some cause or ideal.

We will have to learn to separate etiology from treatment. The psychological arena during this century has been heavily dominated by thinking which led to designs of treatment on the basis of postulated etiology. This model does not apply on the medical level and there is little reason to believe that it would apply any more on the psychological or social level. An understanding of causes is important for prevention but not for treatment. We can treat the slovenly personal habits of the chronic patient by psychological means without having to pay much attention to their origin. We can treat the acute symptoms of the schizophrenic by medical means despite our general lack of knowledge as to the etiology of the condition. Therapies which are justified on the basis of causes should always be suspect, because the only justification for therapeutic intervention is that it produces improvement.

## RECOMMENDATIONS

We must meet the growing need for deprofessionalized social therapy. Experience suggests that no one can maintain committed interaction with the chronically ill on an indefinitely full-time basis. We have learned to deal with this in two ways: part-time involvement like student-volunteer big brothers and sisters or time-limited full commitment. At Spring Lake Ranch, a therapeutic community, young people come for three months to a year. They can give of themselves fully because they know their commitment will end. A social therapeutic institution needs long-term staff for stability and direction, and short-term staff for committed service. Spring Lake Ranch is a therapeutic institution, yet its workers are not therapists. In fact, we continually work to keep them from becoming therapists. The workers are there to find themselves, not to cure others. The paradox of this kind of social therapy is the utilization of genuine nonprofessional human interactions for therapeutic ends. Such an undertaking cannot be institutionalized, i.e. professionalized, and remain effective.

## QUESTIONS FOR SOCIAL SCIENCE

What can anthropology, from its studies of tribal and agricultural societies, tell us about the necessary ingredients for viable new social structures or alternate ways of filling social roles in our present-day industrial life? Are there principles which would help my friends at Spring Lake Ranch? Can anthropologists help us to delineate the differences between social-therapeutic endeavors, endeavors for social enrichment, endeavors for social change, and the creation of new social structures? Are there examples of specific social therapies which would help us go beyond the individualized application of the principles of social psychiatry? Is the assumption that tribal and agricultural societies are more supportive and less stressful a valid one? Are there aspects to various rites of passage which could be adapted to our society?

Crisis intervention is the latest psychiatric pet. Should social crises be handled by a psychiatrist or is this another example of role confusion?

Psychiatry, rooted in the study of illness, needs the help of anthropologists. It needs their help in returning to the healer's role and in giving up the mantle of the all-wise.

## REFERENCES

DABROWSKI, D.
1964   *Positive disintegration.* Boston: Little, Brown.

GRUENBERG, E. M., H. B. SNOW, C. L. BENNETT
1969   Preventing the social breakdown syndrome. *Social Psychiatry* 47. The Association for Research in Nervous and Mental Disease.

HARRIS, T. A.
1969   *I'm O.K. –you're O.K.* New York: Harper and Row.

HAUSMAN, W., D. MC K. RIOCH
1967   Military psychiatry: a prototype of social and preventive psychiatry in the United States. *Archives of General Psychiatry* 16 (June):727–739.

HORWITZ, W. A., P. POLATIN, L. C. KOLB, P. H. HOCH
1958   A study of cases of schizophrenia treated by "direct analysis." *The American Journal of Psychiatry* 114 (9):780–783.

HUESSY, H. R.
1957   Planning a mental health program for a rural area. *The Milbank Memorial Fund Quarterly*, 66–81.
1966a  "Middlebury College mental health program," in *Mental health with limited resources.* Edited by H. R. Huessy. New York: Grune and Stratton.

1966b "Spring Lake Ranch — the pioneer halfway house," in *Mental Health with limited resources*. Edited by H. R. Huessy. New York: Grune and Stratton.

1969   Beyond the half-way house. *The International Journal of Social Psychiatry* 15 (3):235–239.

HUESSY, H. R., C. D. MARSHALL, R. A. GENDRON
1973   Five hundred children followed from Grade 2 through Grade 5 for the prevalence of behavior disorder. *Acta Paedopsychiatrica* 39 (fascicule 11):301–309.

MITCHELL, W. E.
1966   "The use of college student volunteers in the out-patient treatment of troubled children," in *Mental health with limited resources*. Edited by H. R. Huessy. New York: Grune and Stratton.

PARAD, H. J.
1965   *Crisis intervention: selected readings*. New York: Family Service Association of America.

## COMMENT *by Nancy Rollins, M.D.*

H. R. Huessy showed in his paper how psychiatric disorders can exist with the primary etiology on the organic, psychological, or social level. Inappropriate applications of the medical model led to confusion because it was assumed that treatment should be etiological, directed to the same level as the etiology of the disturbance. Huessy demonstrated, with several examples including schizophrenia and social disintegration, that regardless of etiology therapy must be conducted at several different levels simultaneously. I would add that the distinction between the etiology and the pathophysiology and/or pathopsychology of a given disorder is a useful one in refining our diagnostic thinking and deciding at which level or levels to intervene.

Huessy's paper points up the need to restore the respectability of diagnosis in the field of psychiatry in order to avoid serious error in therapeutic management of our patients. One specific clinical point I found instructive is that phobias can become worse in depressed patients. A careful diagnostic assessment of the depression as well as the phobia might lead to the decision to intervene at the physiological level first with an antidepressant rather than the intrapsychic level with individual psychotherapy. Another of his clinical points is the need to distinguish between an acute, reversible stress reaction and the beginning of a serious psychiatric disturbance. While I acknowledge the importance of this differential diagnosis, in practice it may initially be difficult or impossible.

In his discussion of social therapy, Huessy distinguished between social rehabilitation after a severe illness, supplying missed social experience, promoting more adaptive social behaviors, and compensating for lacking social organization. He correctly saw that some patients who seek psychiatric help do not need medicine or a professional psychotherapeutic relationship but rather real nonprofessional interpersonal relationships, a constructive social role to fulfill, an opportunity to serve and to be needed, a simplification of the expected set of social roles for one individual, or even a new and healthier social organization in which to live and function. My own thinking about the influence of the social sphere on the individual has led me to distinguish between the microsocial level of small groups, such as the nuclear family, and the macro-social level, including the restricted one of the nation or a sociopolitical system, and the broader one of the epoch, including the characteristics of a post-industrialized society. I agree with Huessy's implication that a psychiatrist can diagnose the probable levels of effective intervention with an individual but he cannot be expected to become the architect of a new social order. He might, as consultant along with the anthropologist, have some contribution to make to "complementary programming," e.g. matching the needs of two different groups in society. As an astute diagnostician, he can also help individuals and society as a whole to relinquish unrealistic expectations of therapeutic interven-tion at all levels.

SECTION FOUR

*Prevention of Mental Disorder*

# *Introduction*

The concept of "mental health" maintenance gained increasing attention as the term "mental illness" was falling into disrepute. Mental health is not a new abstraction, however. The idea that mental health might be maintained (and, by implication, that mental illness might be prevented) goes back a half century in the United States. It gained new currency as public health methods came to be applied to mental health problems after World War II. ("Primary prevention" comes from public health and refers to the intervention of disorder before it appears, as exemplified by smallpox immunization.)

Early attempts at prevention were based on prevalent psychiatric theory of the time: namely, that if children with problems could receive adequate attention early enough, they would grow to be "well" adults. Not only was the method inordinately expensive and limited to a small segment of the population, but children so identified and treated were much MORE apt to require psychiatric care subsequently than were their untreated peers. So ended the foray of clinicians into this difficult area.

Later studies by social scientists and epidemiologist did point to factors that could be expected to precipitate mental health problems in a society. These included earthquakes, unemployment, loss of a spouse. Alas, such factors tended to occur at the whim of God, politics, the social system.

But hold a moment — the social SYSTEM! Perhaps general systems theory (à la von Bertalanffy) could provide a partial answer to this goal of mental health maintenance. The last few years have witnessed heated discussions in beerhalls and editorial pages over "sick" societies, how to "cure" them, how systems analysis might be used to effect change. As the cultural relativism stance is reviewed, people even dare to speak (in both the abstract and the concrete) about cultures detrimental to mental health and those supportive of it.

In the midst of this controversy, Dubreuil and Wittkower examine the evidence and take a stand. While acknowledging that this is a legitimate ground for the investigative efforts of social scientists and clinicians, they aver that social scientists and clinicians are far from the final answer — or even tentative answers, for that matter.

Unlike those who approach primary prevention from a pan-societal perspective, Rosenblatt, Walsh, and Jackson address a specific, delimited problem current in many societies today: the surviving spouse. Especially where extended families do not function as the norm, the surviving spouse encounters major morbidity and mortality in the months following a mate's death. Employing a careful cross-cultural method, the authors sift out those factors which they believe may assist surviving spouses to get on with their lives.

These two papers can be summarized by stating that perhaps our efforts at studying primary prevention would be better served by emulating the careful artistry of Rosenblatt, Walsh, and Jackson's carefully delimited investigation, rather than imitating the gross strokes of the global analyst.

# Primary Prevention: A Combined Psychiatric-Anthropological Appraisal

GUY DUBREUIL and ERIC D. WITTKOWER

The thesis that both psychiatry and anthropology were and continue to be cultural and even political products of Occidental societies has been well documented by many authors (Alexander and Selesnick 1966; Bastide 1971; Ellenberger 1970; Foucault 1972; Harris 1968; Kiev 1968, 1972). Therefore it is necessary to approach primary prevention not only as a scientific, professional, and technical enterprise, but also as a phenomenon arising from and leading to cultural, social, and even political trends and values.

What is primary prevention? Most definitions given by psychiatrists emphasize the negative aspects of sociocultural factors in relation to mental illness; the following is typical: "By definition, primary prevention programs in psychiatry are designed to lower the rate of onset of emotional disorder in the community by counteracting the stressful or potentially harmful social conditions which produce mental illness, and by prompt intervention when such conditions exist" (Visotsky 1967). As this definition indicates, the borderline between primary and secondary prevention is not always sharply drawn. It is agreed that both forms of prevention require the cooperation of psychiatrists with different social scientists and practitioners. As Barnouw (1963), Caudill (1953), Kluckhohn (1944), La Barre (1958), Wallace (1967), and many other anthropologists demonstrate, a wide range of anthropological studies is directly or indirectly related to medicine, psychiatry, psychology, and prevention.

The growing interface between anthropology and psychiatry raises a number of scientific, professional, ethical, and ideological questions. Do psychiatrists and anthropologists have coherent and clearly defined guidelines (theoretical, social, cultural, or ideological) by which they can engage in an enlightened policy of prevention of mental illness? This question raises these fundamental issues: (1) What is to be learned from the past development of psychiatry and anthropology with respect to contemporary interests in problems of mental illness and prevention? (2) What are the cultural and scientific bases of our present knowledge of the relation between mental health and sociocultural factors? (3) How can we apply this knowledge to primary prevention with a reasonable degree of certainty? (4) With due regard to our scientific and ideological orientations, who should do what with regard to prevention?

## HISTORICAL BACKGROUND

*Psychiatry*

A comparative historical essay (Dubreuil and Wittkower 1972) has shown how psychiatric and anthropological theories have been influenced by political and ideological trends. The same applies to primary prevention.

During the European Middle Ages, "primary prevention" amounted to religious rituals against demons, other malevolent spirits, and witches. The confinement in family cellars or attics of individuals considered marginal and insane as well as those who had no opportunity to find cathartic outlets in crusades, wars, or heretic movements could also be considered as a type of primary prevention based on fear of contagion, imprisonment, or torture. The latter part of the eighteenth century witnessed the triumph of an organic and genetic approach to mental illness, criminality, and even poverty. This trend led most psychiatrists to a somewhat nihilistic attitude toward prevention. In such a context, primary prevention per se could not exist, unless we accept encouragement to work or to engage in foreign wars or expeditions as preventive measures.

At the end of the nineteenth and the beginning of the twentieth century, the advent of psychoanalysis reflected the need to alleviate guilt feelings and to unmask the contradictions between Puritan education, religious world view, and the rising ideology of individual self-enhancement. Quite rapidly, especially in the United States, psychiatry and psychology were offered as sciences able to provide principles for enhancing individual autonomy and for a more efficiently functioning society. For many psychoanalysts, primary prevention boiled down to diatribes against specific institutions, customs, and cultural values. However, to many psychiatrists, who could well be considered the precursors of social psychiatry, it became obvious that such diatribes and piecemeal changes would never succeed in improving the mental health of the population at large. For instance, Halliday (1948) and Alexander (1942) concluded that the society itself was sick. Fromm (1941, 1956) went further: following some of Marx's ideas, he advocated profound, if not revolutionary, economic and political transformations that he believed could result in improved mental health. In brief, primary prevention required political involvement of psychiatrists. This view is now shared by a growing number of young psychiatrists and social scientists.

*Anthropology*

Similar considerations could apply to anthropological perspectives. However, the case of this discipline is more ambiguous. Even now, the majority of anthropologists idealize their science as a fundamental one. For instance, Lévi-Strauss (1954) said that "the anthropologist is the astronomer of social sciences." However, as Diamond (1970) noted, evolutionary schemes developed by the first anthropologists of the end of the nineteenth century were actually "prospective" in nature. Most evolutionists of that period accepted the dogma of the superiority of the Occidental world, but the idea of primary prevention was certainly implicit in many of their writings, especially in relation to continued social progress and a better social organization (Terray 1972).

Bastide (1971) stated that social evolutionism raised one fundamental question that has concerned many philosophers and anthropologists up to the present time, a question that is most pertinent to primary prevention and applied anthropology. If our "primitive brothers" are retarded at lower stages of civilization, is it not our duty to help them to attain the superior level of Euro-American societies? Some thinkers, such as de Gobineau (1853), argued that this humanitarian endeavor was unnecessary, impossible, or even dangerous. Obviously, the white colonial masters who needed new territories and cheap labor were quick to prove to themselves and, for a time, to the state and to the church that the primitives had been created to serve them and that only hard work and harsh discipline were efficient measures of "primary prevention." Those who attributed their backwardness to external factors, such as tropical conditions that were conducive to disease, proposed measures to improve the milieu. They thought that the disappearance of diseases such as malaria would automatically give an impetus to cultural progress. Others, among them Lévy-Bruhl (1927, 1928), before his dramatic retraction (1949), attributed cultural retardation to moral, psychological, and mental traits (e.g. excessive sensuality or prelogical mentality) that supposedly impeded superior mental functions. The solution consisted, therefore, in fostering changes in the hearts and minds of the savages. Despite changes of terminology, those three trends still persist.

The triumph of cultural relativism among North American anthropologists did not bring significant changes in this regard. The human value of exotic cultures was loudly proclaimed by anthropologists who insisted that all possible efforts should be made to help them to survive in their pristine cultural purity. However, these same anthropologists went and lived among "their primitives," collected their artifacts for Western museums, and introduced them to Western techniques and ideas. Some even wrote textbooks with a final chapter suggesting "good" techniques to foster "positive" changes among primitives (Herskovits 1948; Kluckhohn 1949).

British anthropologists were perhaps more cynical or, if one prefers, more lucid. For instance, Malinowski (1929) stated that theoretical anthropology could and should serve colonial administrators. In England, ethnographic training was offered to future colonial administrators. Indeed, knowledge of the actual functioning of primitive societies became more useful than understanding their history. Functionalism was therefore eminently practical.

In this general context, primary prevention amounted to a set of techniques (1) to improve the living conditions of the native, (2) to change the values of primitives in order to induce them to accept white superiority, and (3) to devise methods of avoiding the traumatic effects of interracial contacts. As Bastide (1971) has noted, applied anthropology (and its primary prevention aspects) necessarily implies asymmetric relations. This, together with the realization that their actions have always remained relatively innocuous, has engendered sentiments of despair, resignation, or revolt among a growing number of anthropologists.

Nowadays, many anthropologists realize that piecemeal measures are of little avail and they are considering the introduction of more radical means of action. This trend has established new links between anthropology and psychiatry, cemented by the agreement that the mad, the poor, and the exploited primitives are victims of the Occidental social order and prophets of a new world (Cooper 1967; Deleuze and Guattari 1972; Jaulin 1970; Laing 1967; Marcuse 1955).

## MENTAL HEALTH AND SOCIOCULTURAL FACTORS

In the last few decades, many changes, both theoretical and methodolog-ical, have diversified the fields of psychiatry and anthropology. The development of social, cultural, community, and transcultural psychiatry has opened new areas of research and prevention. Growing anthropolo-gical interest in the fields of ethnomedicine, ethnopsychiatry, ethnosocio-logy, and "anthropotherapy" (Brameld 1965) has also made applied anthropologists more aware of the manifold aspects and consequences of their practices. However, the general ethos of psychiatry and an-thropology still needs to be scrutinized in order to see how it affects conceptions of sociocultural factors in relation to mental health and prevention.

We suggest here that these new developments contain contradictions similar to those summarized in the preceding section. On the one hand, it is assumed that intimate (emic) knowledge of human groups will help to promote positive changes in families, communities, and societies at large, and that these changes will lead to a decrease in mental illness, delinquency, criminality, and violence. Evolution toward a "better society" continues to be the basic assumption and goal. On the other hand, a somewhat alarmist attitude seems to pervade not only psychiatric and anthropological circles, but also groups of humanists, philosophers, and scientists who offer gloomy predictions about the future of the world. They often advocate a return to more authentic (primitive) communities.

In this general context, which is, of course, not limited to Occidental societies, it is surprising that many psychiatrists emphasize the negative sociocultural factors affecting mental health. Furthermore, the upper strata of society seem to have realized that this focus could be useful in keeping society in good order. The perception of social and political threats by the bourgeoisie influences the types of scientific research that are subsidized (for example, investigations of the causes of violence, criminality, and, tangentially, mental illness). Positive aspects of some types of rebellion and violence are likely to be disregarded. Bienen (1968:8) wrote: "Perhaps what has been considered a legitimate field of study depends, in part, on what is considered a legitimate form of social action."

Most anthropologists, at least until very recently, have emphasized the positive factors of culture. They have noted positive social and psy-chological functions for many phenomena that psychiatrists would consider pathological, including trance and possession (Bastide 1972; Herskovits 1937; Lee 1968; Leiris 1958; Métraux 1958; and many others), witchcraft (Evans-Pritchard 1937; Fortune 1932), and aggression (Chagnon 1968). This somewhat unilateral conception of culture is now changing. Research in acculturation, in culture and personality, and in psychiatric anthropology has led many anthropologists to insist that some negative aspects of culture and especially of culture contacts exist (Jaulin 19070; Leiris 1969).

*Sociocultural Factors Generally Perceived as Negative*

It is agreed that mental illness is found in all human societies, that the rates of mental illness are higher in some societies than in others, and that certain cultures predispose their members to specific psychopathological patterns. The data available lead to the inevitable conclusion that culture per se, taken in its broadest sense, is a universal source of psychological tensions and conflicts.

Much has been written about specific sociocultural stresses that are likely to have negative effects on mental health (Leighton and Hughes 1961; Wallace 1961, 1967; Wittkower and Dubreuil 1971; Guthrie 1973; Kiev 1972; Yap 1969). Some of these stress factors concern cultural content: excessive numbers and intensity of taboos, excessive strength of some values, cultural discontinuities (Benedict 1949), dysfunctional role replacement (Wallace 1961), excessive exposure of individuals to simultaneous statuses, role deprivation, culture-bound systems of sentiments, and basic personality structure. Others pertain to social organization: anomie, rigidity of structures, and minority status. Still other factors concern different types of sociocultural change and acculturation. It has also been claimed that because of the complexity of stimuli impinging on their members, complex societies are more pathogenic than are simpler societies, and that cultures that encourage their members to use mind-damaging drugs are more pathogenic than are cultures that discourage such usage.

No conclusive evidence exists that any of these factors in isolation or in combination increases the rate of mental disorder in a given culture. For instance, in the case of sociocultural change, it is almost impossible to pinpoint the specific effects of the many different factors involved, all of which are intricately interrelated (Murphy 1961). However, some suggestive evidence exists. Fortes and Mayer (1966) studied an African tribe that had been confronted with the need for major social adjustments; they reported a marked increase in mental disorders over the rate that had obtained ten years earlier. In a neighboring tribe that did not have these adjustment problems, the rate of psychoses had remained low. Caudill (1963) showed that in traditional Japanese culture, eldest sons who shoulder heavy responsibility are overrepresented among schizophrenic patients.

More evidence relating specific sociocultural factors to mental illness could be added. However, to make their harmful effects convincing, it is necessary (1) to consider their functions in relation to the total fabric of culture and social organization, and (2) to demonstrate the psychodynamics involved. For instance, it has been suggested that the *bouffée délirante* (a short-duration psychotic episode) is more common in some African societies than in Western countries. According to Collomb (1967), this phenomenon could be attributed to the following personality characteristics exhibited by many Africans: a weak ego structure, brittle ego-defense mechanisms, and a tendency to massive regression in response to stress. These characteristics could stem partly from particular child-training practices and from the dependence of individuals on kinship and other groups. The frequency of the Latah reaction (a disorder characterized by echolalia and echopraxia) in Javanese servants has been attributed to their ambivalent submissiveness to their colonial masters in bygone days and to a regression to infantile imitativeness imposed on children by their parents (Wittkower and Murphy n.d.). Only case studies and/or therapeutic experiences with sufferers from the disorders could verify these hypotheses.

## Positive Sociocultural Factors Affecting Mental Health

Most available data seem to indicate that, except in traumatic situations (brutal conquest, genocide, ethnocide, ecological tragedy, etc.), the so-called negative sociocultural factors are or tend to be counterpoised by sociocultural mechanisms. Depending on how these factors are viewed and on the ideological or political perspective adopted, the functions of specific cultural traits can be considered either positive or negative. For example, British social anthropologists, among them Gluckman (1960, 1963, 1965 [ed.], Leach (1954, 1966), and Turner (1957), have emphasized that conflict and structural contradictions are inherent in certain types of non-Occidental societies. They have shown how these societies adopt specific social and cultural strategies to alleviate the potentially negative effects of these factors and/or to integrate them positively in a dynamic sociocultural system.

These strategies, which vary from one society to another, could be considered spontaneous mechanisms of primary prevention. They are summarized below in five broad clusters:

1. The first cluster is the broadest in scope: it is culture per se. As a whole, cultures and subcultures can be represented as protective shelters against natural dangers, social anarchy, and psychological isolation. More positively, they can be viewed as familiar landscapes where human problems and their solutions are laid out according to a specific social order and world view that give meaning to human life and behavior, and even to suffering, frustration, and death. In every society, most individuals, in the course of growing up, internalize a sociocultural map of this landscape. However, as Wallace (1961) noted no individual possesses in his mind the exact duplicate of this sociocultural map. All individuals do not share the same comprehension of their culture nor the same feelings with respect to social interactions. Thus, one of the positive functions of culture is to synchronize individual differences. In this very general sense, culture per se is a set of mechanisms of prevention of mental disease.

2. The second cultural cluster comprises specific mechanisms that alleviate the negative effects of tensions arising from the constraints imposed on individuals by social rules and inequalities. For example, Barry, Child, and Bacon (1959) demonstrate a correlation between child-training practices and types of subsistence economies. It would seem that each culture provides particular techniques of learning and internal control in relation to its ecological adaptation and its tension-induced values.

3. A third aspect of the preventive functions of culture consists of a wide variety of mechanisms that serve as emotional outlets. Most cultures provide for "cathartic strategies" (Wallace 1961:191) — periodic carnivals, feasts, games, and rituals in which such diverse techniques as intoxication, torture, dance, or trance are practiced. In this cluster should be included all rituals that temporarily reverse or destroy the social order, either through symbolic processes or through the creation of marginal groups of countercultures. These symbolic processes are well illustrated in Turner's description (1957) of "status reversal rituals" and in Bateson's description (1936) of the Naven rituals of the Iatmul in New Guinea, whereby the rich and powerful are humiliated by the poor and humble. Such devices "cleanse society of its structually engendered 'sins' and what hippies might call 'hang-ups' " (Turner 1969:185). Hippy groups furnish us with a good example of a cathartic counterculture in which "existence" through spontaneity, ecstasy, and sexual freedom represents purity in opposition to the dullness of culturally sanctioned behavior.

4.   All cultures not only recognize abnormality, marginality, and crime, but also contrive appropriate techniques and specialists for curing, isolating, or killing individuals perceived as sick, marginal, or guilty (Kiev 1964). The cleavage among different types of healers in the assessment of insanity is not as large as is generally believed (Torrey 1972). They are likely to agree that a person is mentally ill if his behavior is grossly disturbing to others, if he is unable to function in various spheres for psychological reasons, and if he suffers severe psychological stress. Furthermore, as Hughes (1963) and a growing number of psychiatrists and anthropologists have noted, different therapeutic techniques used in different cultures often produce similar beneficial results. Obviously, this cluster refers more specifically to secondary prevention. However, almost universally, the so-called witch doctors have a wide gamut of activities in many cultural spheres that are directly or indirectly related to primary prevention. This also applies to psychiatrists of the Occidental world.

5.   The fifth cluster concerns ideology in relation to socioeconomic organization and political control and leadership. In small, simple tribes where there is little social differentiation, at least in terms of access to economic goods, contradictions between levels of society are at a minimum. Among these groups, beliefs are generally flexible enough to adapt to small economic and social changes. In most cases, the traditional or sporadic leadership that prevails in these societies succeeds in resolving conflicts. Often, members reach unanimous decisions when problems present themselves. In more complex tribes, social mechanisms temporarily or periodically erase structural contradictions and conflicts: in this way they contribute to the perpetuation of the social structure or to social innovations.

In general, in nonindustrialized and noncolonialized societies, ideology, which in many cases merges with a religious system, positively supports most activities. It would seem reasonable to conclude that ideology has positive effects on mental health when it symbolizes a socioeconomic order that is gratifying to most members of a group. In such a case, it stimulates and channels individual motivations so that conflicts and structural contradictions are toned down and some frustrations are accepted as necessary or even positive ingredients of life.

Yet these positive aspects should not be overemphasized. For instance, claims made by psychiatrists in China, Israel, and the Soviet Union that a strong "positive" ideology would eliminate mental illness have not been substantiated (Kiev 1968). However positive its effect on mental health, apparently no ideology, especially in complex societies, can operate without simplifying, distorting, and contradicting the actual inter-actions that occur in a society (Dunn and Dunn 1967; Monteil 1957). When an ideology distorts the socioeconomic reality to the point where it fails to mask a lack of reciprocity between ethnic or social groups, confusion and resentment must result. We could term this a conspira-torial ideology, consciously or unconsciously entertained in order to keep the elites in power. In such cases, negative functions should prevail and primary prevention would be of almost no avail because it would require a complete reorganization of the society.

In many cases, ideology and political organization are linked to the influence of strong leaders. Theoretically, mature members of a nation can do without powerful leadership. But when a group or nation is in distress, as in the course of war, segregation, persecution, or fear of some catastrophe, charismatic leadership tends to arise. In some instan-ces, it can have positive functions insofar as it acts as an emotional catalyst for curing society of its dysfunctional contradictions, inertias, useless survivals, or anarchic patterns of change. Nevertheless, many examples might be given where charismatic leadership has so hyper-trophied some ideological trends that human tragedies or sterile messianic ventures have been precipitated. The case of Nazi Germany immediately comes to mind, as do numerous revivalist movements that prevailed among minority groups (Lanternari 1963).

Obviously, strong leadership involves many dangers for human socie-ties. Nevertheless, it might be hypothesized that most groups and nations seek or need strong leaders either as father substitutes or as idealized incarnations of moral and ideological models, especially during crises. In the same hypothetical vein, it could be suggested that, with the possible exception of simple societies, "fatherless" nations (Doi 1973) are apt to experience what some would consider chaos: contradictory values, counterideologies, countercultural subgroups. In this context, primary prevention amounts to a Sisyphean endeavor, for neither psychiatrists nor anthropologists can create mature and strong leaders, nor can they alone change an all-pervading cultural confusion.

## IDEOLOGY, SCIENCE AND PRIMARY PREVENTION

How can we apply our present knowledge to primary prevention with a reasonable degree of certainty? If we carefully analyze the literature dealing with this subject, we cannot fail to be bewildered by the contra-dictory interpretations given the same data. These contradictions can be attributed to (1) the weakness of methodological tools of research; (2) the complexity of phenomena under scrutiny; (3) ill-defined orientations that confront psychiatric anthropology, especially in the field of primary prevention; (4) contemporary divergent social changes and experiments in Occidental and colonialized societies; and (5) personal and professional influences that these changes and experiments exert on anthropologists and psychiatrists.

When psychiatrists preached against what they considered to be harmful from a psychoanalytical perspective they entered the social scene as actors already "programmed" by the cultural machine (Ingleby 1970). Their diatribes against taboos and frustrating customs and their homilies for individual self-realization were dictated by a latent cultural program that already contained a codification of norms and ideals. Psychiatry thus translated into a scientific and professional language and praxis ideas and values that had remained more or less latent in the culture. Psychiatry also devised therapeutic and preventive techniques in accordance with cultural trends and elaborated theories coincident with these trends. The time has now come for psychiatrists as well as anthropologists to realize that they are protagonists. They must earn their living, enhance their social prestige, cultivate their self-esteem, and retain their feeling of social usefulness. They should therefore recognize that their theories, methods, and practices are cultural products of their society. For psychiatrists, as Pouillon (1970) noted, the universal triangle created by the sickness, the patient, and the doctor varies from society to society. The relationship between anthropologists, culture, and human beings studied in the field are analogous. Lévi-Strauss (1966) states that anthropologists should transform their most intimate subjectivity into means of objective experience; psychiatrists should do so as well. Consequently, both groups should constantly engage in some degree of self-analysis with regard to their social statuses and their personal participation in different institutions, in order to develop a more refined sociology of knowledge and action. This process might increase their feelings of uncertainty or confusion, but it might be more productive than current tendencies to simplify for the sake of intellectual and emotional, social and political security.

However, it would be quite unrealistic to advocate the eradication of ideology from these disciplines, although many believe that ideology is the enemy of objectivity. Ideology universally impregnates all social and individual activities and beliefs. This issue is especially relevant to primary prevention, which is necessarily based on cultural representations of what is and what ought to be normality. This is indeed a tricky issue, because for most people ideology seldom reaches the level of consciousness. Psychiatrists, for example, have often proposed preventive measures that were in fact rooted in their own moral values. In 1911, Bleuler wrote: "The avoidance of masturbation, of disappointment in love, of strain or frights are recommendations which can be made with a clear conscience because these are things which should be avoided under all circumstances." Why? Some contemporary essays, following Reich (1927, 1932), contradict these assertions. Bowlby's platform (1956) against maternal deprivation had positive consequences in children's hospitals but spread anxiety among mothers who thought that any sporadic maternal deprivation would kill their children emotionally. According to Mead (1954), whose reactions were not devoid of ideological overtones, Bowlby's warnings smacked of a disguised antifeminism: keep your women at home.

Many of Freud's attitudes also reflected an ideological perception of life and society: "The moment one inquires about the sense or value of life... one is sick, since objectively neither of them has any existence. In doing so, one is admitting a surplus of unsatisfied libido" (Freud quoted by Jones 1957 III; 465). Should we conclude that the general disenchantment of the young and their constant questioning about the value of life reflect individual psychopathological patterns? Obviously, Freud, who was aware of Marx's writings, had taken a different ideological stand. Freud's attitude should also be compared with that of Ellenberger (1973) on "creative illness," which has been illustrated by Erikson's biography (1958) of Martin Luther and even by Jones's biography (1957) of Freud. Similar considerations could be added about deviants and marginals, who are often considered mentally ill and socially dangerous but whose social functions may be viewed in many cases as positive in relation to social change and innovation.

Such contradictory judgments and debatable interpretations of scientific findings have had a direct impact on primary prevention. This impact is now stronger and potentially more dangerous for the following reasons: (1) The breakdown of traditions, coupled with anxieties produced by migrations, rapid technological and social changes, cultural pluralism, ideological contradictions, and disguised colonialism, has made more people search for guidance from different specialists, especially psychiatrists. (2) Since the past century, as Zola (1972) has well demonstrated, medicine (and, we should add, social science) has become more deeply involved in the management of society. For instance, the medical treatment of deviants, although it is undoubtedly humanitarian and medically defensible, tends to depoliticize deviance. (3) This involvement of psychiatrists and social scientists has already contributed to certain socio-cultural changes. For instance, new methods of child training and education as well as therapeutic techniques that foster individualism have been diffused. However, whereas it was originally imagined that these methods would foster mental health through a selective eradication of customs and beliefs deemed psychologically harmful, it now appears that the changes thus induced have radiated throughout many other sectors of culture and social organization, without lessening the level of anxiety and hostility (Freud 1966). Some would even affirm that these changes have been negative. Be this as it may, certainly the changes have not promoted a smoother functioning of the traditional social fabric.

This is even more certain with respect to psychiatry and applied anthropology in non-Occidental cultures. These induced changes may even have contributed to the emergence of countercultures and marginal groups protesting structural inequalities and contradictions, and to an increase in mental illness. Psychiatrists alone do not appear able to evaluate the rather distressing fact, familiar to anthropologists, that planned or unplanned changes occurring in one cultural cluster are liable to affect the whole culture in ways that are very difficult to predict. This raises the problem of the competence and status of each discipline with regard to primary prevention.

## CONCLUSION: RESPECTIVE COMPETENCE AND ROLES OF PSYCHIATRISTS AND ANTHROPOLOGISTS

Anthropologists and psychiatrists are simultaneously inside and outside their own culture. They are inside because, like all other members of their society, they have internalized their native culture. But they are also outsiders because, like witch doctors who use natural and supernatural elements for or against individuals and groups, they are prompted by their professional training and probably their motivations to manipulate intimate psychological and cultural fibers. These practices tend to produce an attitude that Lévi-Strauss has called DISTANCIATION, implying a certain estrangement from the cultural norms and values of their own society.

Because of this ambivalent status, the objectivity and usefulness of anthropology and psychiatry will probably remain questionable in the eyes of the general population and most political authorities. This might constitute one of the strongest incentives for their practioners to search for objective knowledge, questioning their own ideological standpoints, their personal motivations, and their actual usefulness. This self-analysis should convince them that they must not become "hidden preachers" who smuggle in ethical prescriptions under the guise of scientific understanding (Roazen 1968:293). This should also lead them to resist the tendency to give hasty explanations which could serve to satisfy their patients' and the public's quest for certainty but which might raise hopes that are unlikely to materialize. "Medicalizing" and "anthropologizing" of communities or societies might just produce such effects. They must remember that they are "reluctant revolutionaries," "revolutionary surrogates" (Leupold-Lowenthal 1972), reactionary technocrats, ivory tower scientists, or what have you. No professional ethical code of conduct will ever change such personal and ideological orientations.

This personal and collective consideration of their competence, their social status, and their ideological tenets should also help to solve the delicate and sometimes explosive problem of cooperation among anthropologists, psychiatrists, and other scientists or practitioners engaged in primary prevention. Many models for a good working relationship have been proposed (Pattison 1967). However, should psychiatrists not limit themselves to dealing with mentally ill individuals, to determining which specific factors (physiological, situational, familial, social, cultural, etc.) have pathogenic effects and then to transmitting to social scientists their hypotheses and conclusions? Should anthropologists, on the basis of their ethnographic techniques, not limit themselves to describing and analyzing so-called supraindividual phenomena (forms of social organization, cultural patterns) and then to informing psychiatrists of their interpretations of positive and negative functions of sociocultural factors? In order to counterpoise the recurrent insistence on the negative aspects of some social phenomena (e.g. violence), should they not also orient their research and reflections toward the positive contributions of these phenomena to society and to "progress"?

Affirmative answers to the previous questions would at least imply that no specialist would trespass the frontiers of his own scientific and professional competence. However, primary prevention requires more than scientific competence and more than give-and-take between relatively closed circles of human scientists. Action research and concrete interdisciplinary action for change are *de facto* ingredients of primary prevention. This is indeed the area where much confusion exists at present, largely for the following reasons: (1) it involves interdisciplinary teams composed of differently motivated and trained individuals; (2) it fosters ideological and professional clashes; (3) it is generally restricted to small, underprivileged neighborhoods or regions whose plight depends more on political and financial decisions than on piecemeal preventive measures.

Two prerequisites underlie efficient primary prevention: (1) Interdisciplinary teams should not be thrown together in a haphazard fashion, as is generally done; rather, they should result from specific teaching and training programs directly related to primary prevention. Such programs are almost nonexistent, unless one considers the few joint training programs in psychiatric anthropology and transcultural psychiatry as embryonic models (Jeffress 1968/1969; Wintrob 1972). (2) The second prerequisite, should it be politically possible, would be the screening by psychiatrists and social scientists of political and technocratic personnel whose tasks are to improve living conditions and allocate financial resources for programs of primary prevention.

Another solution would be the personal involvement of psychiatrists and anthropologists in politics. This solution has been adopted in a few cases but has not resulted in social and political improvement. Examples are François Duvalier, a medical doctor and student of ethnology, and Jacques Soustelle, a well-known ethnologist, whose political role in Algeria met with failure. However, anthropologists and psychiatrists certainly have the ability and perhaps the duty to advise governments on problems related to primary prevention. As for becoming official government advisors, they themselves must decide not only on the basis of their competence, but also on the basis of ethical codes and ideological stands.

In conclusion, at present it appears that little can be done on a large scale by psychiatrists and anthropologists regarding primary prevention, though the field of secondary prevention, along the lines taken by Leighton (1959) and Caplan (1964), is wide open for the activities of both.

## REFERENCES

ALEXANDER, F.
   1942   *The age of unreason: a study of the irrational forces in social life.* Philadelphia: J. B. Lippincott.
ALEXANDER, F., S. T. SELESNICK
   1966   *The history of psychiatry.* New York: Harper and Row.
BARNOUW, V.
   1963   *Culture and personality.* Homewood, Illinois: Dorsey Press.
BARRY, H., I. L. CHILD, M. BACON
   1959   The relation of child training to subsistence economy. *American Anthropologist* 61:51-63.

BASTIDE, R.
1971   *Anthropologie appliquée*. Paris: Flammarion.
1972   *Le rêve, la transe et la folie*. Paris: Nouvelle Bibliothèque Scientifique, Flammarion.

BATESON, G.
1936   *Naven*. Stanford: Stanford University Press.

BENEDICT, R.
1949   "Continuities and discontinuities in cultural conditioning," in *Personality in nature, society and culture*. Edited by C. Kluckhohn and H. A. Murray, 414–423. New York: Knopf.

BIENEN, H.
1968   *Violence and social change*. Chicago: University of Chicago Press.

BLEULER, E.
1911   *Dementia praecox*. New York: International Universities Press. (Reprinted 1950.)

BOWLBY, J.
1956   Maternal care and mental health. *British Journal of Medical Psychology* 29:211–247. (Originally published in 1950 in Geneva.)

BRAMELD, THEODORE
1965   *The use of explosive ideas in education*. Pittsburgh: University of Pittsburgh Press.

CAPLAN, G.
1964   *Principles of preventive psychiatry*. New York: Basic Books.

CAUDILL, W.
1953   "Applied anthropology in medicine," in *Anthropology today*. Edited by A. L. Kroeber, 771–806 Chicago: University of Chicago Press.
1963   Social background and sibling rank among Japanese psychiatric patients. *Transcultural Psychiatric Research Review* (15):20–22.

CHAGNON, N. A.
1968   "Yanomamö social organization and warfare," in *War: the anthropology of armed conflict and aggression*. Edited by M. Fried, M. Harris, and R. Murphy, 109–159. New York: Natural History Press.

COLLOMB, H.
1967   Les bouffées délirantes en psychiatrie africaine. *Psychopathologie Africaine* 1:167–239.

COOPER, DAVID G.
1967   *Psychiatry and anti-psychiatry*. London: Tavistock.

DE GOBINEAU, J. A., COMTE
1853   *Sur l'inégalité des races humaines*. Paris: Nouvel Office d'Editions. (Reprinted 1963.)

DELEUZE, G., F. GUATTARI
1972   *Capitalisme et schizophrénie: l'anti-oedipe*. Paris: Les Editions de Minuit.

DIAMOND, S.
1970   A revolutionary discipline. *Critical Anthropology* 1:3–13.

DOI, TEAKEO
1973   *The anatomy of dependence*. Tokyo: Kodansha International.

DUBREUIL, G., E. D. WITTKOWER
  1976   "Psychiatric anthropology: a historical perspective." *Psychiatry 2.*
         39:130–141.

DUNN, S. P., E. DUNN
  1967   Soviet regime and native culture in Central Asia and Kazakhstan.
         *Current Anthropology* (3):147–184.

ELLENBERGER, H. F.
  1970   *The discovery of the unconscious: the history and evolution of dynamic
         psychiatry.* New York: Basic Books.
  1973   Freud in perspective: a conversation with Henri F. Ellenberger.
         Interview by J. Mousseau. *Psychology Today* 6 (10):50–60.

ERIKSON, E.
  1958   *Young man Luther.* New York: W. W. Norton.

EVANS-PRITCHARD, E. E.
  1937   *Witchcraft, oracles and magic among the Azande.* Oxford: Clarendon
         Press.

FORTES, M., D. MAYER
  1966   Yenkaner's psychosis and social change among the Tallensi of
         northern Gahana. *Cahiers d'Études Africaines* 6:5–40.

FORTUNE, R.
  1932   *The sorcerers of Dobu.* New York: Dutton.

FOUCAULT, M.
  1972   *Histoire de la folie à l'âge classique.* Paris: Gallimard.

FREUD, A.
  1966   *Normality and pathology in children.* London: Hogarth Press and the
         Institute of Psycho-Analysis.

FROMM, E.
  1941   *Escape from freedom.* New York: Rinehart.
  1956   *The sane society.* London: Routledge and Kegan Paul.

GLUCKMAN, M.
  1960   *Custom and conflict in Africa.* Oxford: Blackwell.
  1963   *Order and rebellion in tribal Africa.* New York: Free Press.
  1965   *Politics, law and ritual in tribal society.* Oxford: Blackwell.

GLUCKMAN, M., *editor*
  1965   *Political sysems and the distribution of power.* Association of Social
         Anthropologists Monograph 2. London: Tavistock.

GUTHRIE, G. M.
  1973   *Culture and mental disorder.* Addison-Wesley Module in Anthropol-
         ogy 39:1–26. Reading, Massachusetts: Addison-Wesley.

HALLIDAY, J. L.
  1948   *Psychosocial medicine: a study of the sick society.* New York: W. W.
         Norton.

HARRIS, M.
  1968   *The rise of anthropological theory: a history of theories of culture.*
         New York: Thomas Y. Crowell.

HERSKOVITS, M. J.
  1937   *Life in a Haitian valley.* New York: Knopf.
  1948   *Man and his works.* New York: Knopf.

HUGHES, C. C.
    1963   "Public health in non-literate societies," in *Man's image in medicine and anthropology*. Edited by I. Galdston, 157–233. New York: International Universities Press.

INGLEBY, D.
    1970   Ideology and the human sciences. *Human Context* 2:159–187.

JAULIN, R.
    1970   *La paix blanche: introduction á l'ethnocide.* Paris: Editions du Seuil.

JEFFRESS, J. E.
    1968/1969   Training in transcultural psychiatry in the United States. *International Journal of Social Psychiatry* 15:69–72.

JONES, E.
    1957   *Sigmund Freud.* New York: Basic Books.

KIEV, A.
    1964   *Magic, faith and healing: studies in primitive psychiatry today.* New York: Free Press.
    1972   *Transcultural psychiatry.* New York: Free Press.

KIEV, A., editor
    1968   *Psychiatry in the communist world.* New York: Science House.

KLUCKHOHN, C.
    1944   "The influence of psychiatry on anthropology in America during the past one hundred years," in *One hundred years of American psychiatry*. Edited by J. K. Hall, G. Zilboorg, and H. A. Bunker, 589–617.
    1949   *Mirror for man.* New York: McGraw-Hill.

LA BARRE, W.
    1958   The influence of Freud on anthropology. *American Imago* 15:275–328.

LANTERNARI, V.
    1963   *The religions of the oppressed.* New York: Knopf.

LAING, R. D.
    1967   *The politics of experience and the bird of paradise.* London: Penguin.

LEACH, E.
    1954   *Political systems of Highland Burma.* Boston: Beacon Press.
    1966   *Rethinking anthropology.* London: Athlone Press.

LEE, R. B.
    1968   "The sociology of Kung Bushman trance performances," in *Trance and possession states*. Edited by R. B. Prince, 35–54. Montreal: R. M. Bucke Memorial Society.

LEIGHTON, A. H.
    1959   *My name is legion.* New York: Basic Books.

LEIGHTON, A. H., J. M. HUGHES
    1961   Culture as causative of mental disorder. *Milbank Memorial Fund Quarterly* 39:446–488.

LEIRIS, M.
    1958   La possession et ses aspects théatraux chez les ethiopiens de Gondar. *L'homme; cahiers d'ethnologie, de géographie et de linguistique*, second series. Paris: Plon.
    1969   "L'ethnographe devant le colonialisme," in *Cinq études d'ethnologie*. Edited by M. Leiris, 83–112. Paris: Editions Gonthier.

LEUPOLD-LOWENTHAL, H.
1972    "The impossible profession: the social position and social responsibility of psychoanalysis today." Mimeographed manuscript, Canadian Psychoanalytic Society, Montreal.

LÉVI-STRAUSS, C.
1954    "Place de l'anthropologie dans les sciences sociales et problèmes posés par son enseignement," in *Les sciences sociales dans l'enseignment supérieur*, 102–133. Paris: United Nations Educational, Scientific and Cultural Organization.
1966    The scope of anthropology. *Current Anthropology* 7 (2):112–123

LÉVY-BRUHL, L.
1927    *L'âme primitive*. Paris: Librairie Félix Alcan.
1928    *Les fonctions mentales*. Paris: Librairie Félix Alcan.
1949    *Les carnets de Lucien Lévy-Bruhl*. Preface by M. Leenhardt Paris: Presses Universitaires de France.

MALINOWSKI, B.
1929    Practical anthropology. *Africa* 2:22–38.

MARCUSE, H.
1955    *Eros and civilization: a philosophical inquiry into Freud*. New York: Random House.

MEAD, M.
1954    Some theoretical considerations on the problem of mother-child separation. *American Journal of Orthopsychiatry* 24:471–483.

MÉTRAUX, A.
1958    *Le vaudou haitien*. Paris: Gallimard.

MONTEIL, V.
1957    *Les musulmans soviétiques*. Paris: Editions du Seuil.

MURPHY, H. B. M.
1961    Social change and mental health. *Milbank Memorial Fund Quarterly* 39:385–445.

PATTISON, E. M.
1967    Psychiatry and anthropology: three models for a working relationship. *Social Psychiatry* 2 (4):174–179

POUILLON, J.
1970    Malade et médecin: le même et/ou l'autre? (Remarques ethnologiques.) *Nouvelle Revue de Psychanalyse* 1:77–98.

REICH, W.
1927    *Die Funktion des Orgasmus*. Leipzig: Internationaler Psychoanalytischer Verlag.
1932    *Der Einbruch der Sexualmoraly*. Berlin: Sexpol.

ROAZEN. P.
1968    *Freud: political and social thought*. New York: Knopf.

TERRAY, E.
1972    *Le marxisme devant les sociétés "primitives."* Paris: François Maspero.

TORREY, E. F.
1972    *The mind game: witchdoctors and psychiatrists*. New York: Emerson Hall.

TURNER, V.
1957    *Schism and continuity in an African society: a study of Ndembu*

*village life.* Manchester: Manchester University Press.

1969   *The ritual process: structure and anti-structure.* Chicago: Aldine.

VISOTSKY, H. M.

1967   "Community psychiatry, II: Intervention," in *Comprehensive textbook of psychiatry.* Edited by A. M. Freedman and H. I. Kaplan, 1499–1516. Baltimore: Williams and Wilkins.

WALLACE, A. F. C.

1961   *Culture and personality.* New York: Random House.

1967   "Anthropology and psychiatry," in *Comprehensive textbook of psychiatry.* Edited by A. M. Freedman and H. I. Kaplan, 195–201. Baltimore: Williams and Wilkins.

WINTROB, R.

1972   "Transcultural psychiatry: a personal view of the current scene." Paper presented at the American Anthropological Association meeting in Toronto, November, 1972, at the symposium "Psychiatric Anthropology: Past, Present and Future."

WITTKOWER, E. D., G. DUBREUIL

1971   "Reflections on the interface between psychiatry and anthropology," in *The interface between psychiatry and anthropology.* Edited by I. Galdston, 1–27. New York: Brunner/Mazel.

WITTKOWER, E. D., H. M. M. MURPHY

n.d.   Crosscultural psychiatry. Unpublished manuscript.

YAP, POW MENG

1969   "The culture-bound reactive syndrome," in *Mental health research in Asia and the Pacific.* Edited by W. Caudill and Tsung-yi Lin, 33–53. Honolulu: East-West Center Press.

ZOLA, I. K.

1972   Medicine as an institution of social control. *Sociological Review* 20 (4):487–504.

## COMMENT *by Nancy Rollins, M. D.*

Dubreuil and Wittkower pose three questions, each deserving development in depth as separate themes: the effect of sociocultural factors on mental health, our capacity to influence social systems to foster health, and our ideological orientation as it relates to other prevailing trends. The authors have made some provocative and interesting points which I would like to discuss from my vantage point as an American psychiatrist who had the opportunity to gain perspective on American culture through studying child psychiatry in the Soviet Union in some detail. I attempted to look back into my own culture in a preliminary analysis of how psychoanalytic constructs dovetail with deeply held values in the United States such as individualism, rebelliousness, and free speech.

The preventive functions of the psychiatrist place the profession in a serious dilemma. Our own culture-bound value systems largely determine what preventive measures we advocate and, as Dubreuil and Wittkower pointed out, our efforts will have unforeseen consequences. For example, the lifting of social, religious, and sexual prohibitions has led to a trend among young people to lack self-discipline, motivation to be productive, and the capacity to work cooperatively in groups. Even this statement, I am aware, reveals my bias to admire achievement.

But the psychiatrist can ill afford to cop out and refuse his role as consultant in preventive measures for the community. So let me suggest we look at the collectivist values of Russian society and consider how these values may prevent decompensation. Phyllis Greenacre used the term "collective alternates" in discussing the psychology of gifted people. From early childhood, she said, the very talented have a love affair with the world so that object relations extend beyond the nuclear family. Perhaps something similar operates when socialist societies function at their best. Young children from the beginning are taught to relate to other collectives besides the nuclear family. This may become a source of strength under the stress of separation and social upheaval.

The Soviet curtailment of individual autonomy has a hidden positive aspect. Collectivist values require behavioral conformity and limitation of personal freedom to travel, to dissent outwardly, etc. But there is a vast inner space which becomes highly developed in the consciousness of the Russian people. Solzhenitsyn's novel, *A day in the life of Ivan Denisovich*, depicts a free mind in a Siberian prison. I sense a craving for collectivism and a sense of belonging to a greater cause in American young people. One small group rebelled by cutting sugar cane for Castro in Cuba. They returned praising the austerity, the hard work, and particularly the sense of collective effort toward a common goal.

# Breaking Ties with Deceased Spouse

PAUL C. ROSENBLATT, R. PATRICIA WALSH and
DOUGLAS A. JACKSON

In many societies there are death customs which either eliminate reminders of or increase psychological distance from a deceased spouse.
These customs include destroying, giving away, or temporarily putting
aside personal property of the deceased, observing a taboo on the name
of the deceased, changing residence, and fearing the spouse's ghost. Of
what use are these customs? We believe these customs serve to break ties
with the deceased spouse and, as a consequence, facilitate the establishment of a new relationship in which the pattern of rights and obligations
resembles the one in the marriage that was ended by the spouse's death.
Such tie breaking would be especially useful if the new relationship is between people who formerly had to inhibit marital response to one another,
that is, between people who formerly knew one another and who did not
have a marital relationship.

Reminders of a deceased spouse may stimulate responses that are likely
to interfere with a new marital or quasi-marital relationship. Consider a
widower living in the dwelling he shared with his deceased wife and surrounded by her possessions. If activities such as sharing a meal or having
sexual relations with some other woman were improper and inhibited in
this setting before his wife's death, they will continue to be more difficult
to practice than if the setting were changed. Further, the familiar setting
will remind the man of previously well-learned behavior specific to the
marriage ended by the death or motivate him to engage in such behavior,
such as perhaps a routine morning conversation or a going-to-sleep

The complete article, of which this is a summary, appears in *The realm of the extra-
human: agents and audiences.* (Edited by A. Bharati. World Anthropology. The Hague:
Mouton; 1976.)

routine that requires the presence of the deceased wife. Such residual dispositions may block resumption of a normal, productive life by promoting grief and denial. We believe that spouse-specific response patterns cued by reminders of the spouse are modal cross-culturally. Hence, we believe a common condition of bereavement around the world is that something resembling marriage to a new person is difficult in the presence of reminders of the previous marriage.

From a cue-conditioning perspective the disposition to respond in a manner inconsistent with a new marital relationship would be reduced by eliminating cues to respond as one did while the spouse was still alive and by learning new responses to the old cues. Thus, both removing the wife's personal possessions and changing one's feelings about her through fear of her ghost will reduce old response dispositions.

In addition, others in the environment of the widow or widower will retain response dispositions toward the widow or widower that are cued by reminders of the deceased person and make it difficult for the surviving spouse to enter a new marital routine with someone else. For these other people it will also be easier to accept a new marital relationship of the widow or widower if reminders of the deceased are reduced and if psychological distance from the deceased is increased by such devices as the fear of the deceased's ghost.

Our results suggest that remarriage in the urban areas of the United States and Europe could be facilitated by a customary disposal of the personal property of the deceased, change of residence, and name taboo. It seems unlikely that the fear of the deceased's ghost could become customary. If surviving spouses in the urban United States and Europe continue to be left on their own about moving, disposing of personal property of the deceased, and treating the memories of and past relationship with the deceased, we can expect remarriage for them to be difficult. Moreover, without the force of custom behind the tie-breaking acts, the acts may seem to be selfish, frivolous, or disrespectful to the dead. Thus, the acts are potentially of use, but are unlikely to be widely used if they are left as mere options, advocated by counsellors and the popular literature, for dealing with bereavement.

# SECTION FIVE

*New Theoretical Directions*

# Introduction

Studies in anthropology and mental health have served mostly to validate hypotheses generated in other fields either of anthropology or mental health. Such hypotheses have then been subjected to cross-cultural method to see whether they were culture-specific or more general. Rarely have any new hypotheses of note been developed in the field of anthropology and mental health. Generally also, investigators have been ethnic Euroamericans who, armed with Euroamerican theories, have sought to validate these theories in non-Euroamerican societies.

You will note that in this section the non-Euroamerican worm has turned. Two Sioux-American investigators, Trimble and Medicine, and the Chinese-American anthropologist, Hsu, bring a massive argumentative *tour de force* against that psychological darling of the last half-century: personality theory. Not only do they indict it as having little predictive or pragmatic value. They proceed to condemn its use as a major rationale for health care systems and educational systems, since these systems have often proven to be detrimental to so many non-Euroamerican people (and to some Euroamericans as well) in the United States. Their arguments are logical, moral, pressing, and cannot be ignored.

Nor are these authors satisfied with limiting themselves to criticism only. Hsu stresses that our focus should be on interpersonal relations (which can be observed, on which at least two persons can reflect, etc.) rather than on one person's intrapsychic events (which are less liable to validation and replication, which are less directly related to our contemporary social problems, etc.). The Trimble-Medicine team emphasizes the ecological setting within which each behavioral bit occurs. These two papers require the careful attention of all of us who are so thoroughly ingrained with notions such as "attitude," "motivation," "superego," and "narcissism" that these terms have become reified into the same order of reality as the sunset or the family pet.

Jilek's paper requires an agile mind also, but in a different direction. He weaves a common thread through such diverse elements as drumming, altered states of consciousness, electroencephalographic events, religious ritual, psychological therapies, and life-style change. Omitting little more than the kitchen sink, he deftly uses an extensive literature to build a linking theory between events at the psychobiological, behavioral, and social levels. As a case to assist our understanding, he presents data on Canadian Indian spirit dancing; but one could as readily use data from "canned" music in a dentist's office or the electrosleep therapy currently favored by Soviet neuropsychiatrists. The important feature is that linkages have been sought between various kinds of abstraction, linkages which cross our traditional disciplinary lines. With more such linked theories, our various disciplines may yet contribute to each other and learn from each other – again, to the benefit of humankind.

# Rethinking Our Premises

FRANCIS L. K. HSU

I.   We need to revise the Western monolithic view of man and his problems. Some of us are finally realizing that many native drugs, remedies, beliefs, and practices may have a great deal of validity – or may be just as good or bad as Western ones. For example, the United States Department of Health, Education, and Welfare recently gave a grant to a Navajo medicine man to instruct students in Navajo medicine! The situation reminds me of China in the 1930's in contrast to China today. In the late 1930's I was a medical social worker in the Peking Union Medical College Hospital; this was once sponsored by the Rockefeller Foundation; it later became the Anti-Imperialist Medical College and Hospital and is now Capital Medical College and Hospital, (where James Reston of the *New York Times* recently had his appendix removed). The Western doctors in that hospital were very antagonistic to traditional Chinese medical practices, but the Western-trained Chinese doctors there were even more bigoted about it. A Chinese patient customarily approached doctors and medicine avidly: if one doctor did not give him quick results, he thought nothing of trying another doctor or some herbal medicine or remedies that his neighbor's brother-in-law had recommended. If that still did not cure him, he might have decided to try witch doctors or simply return to the hospital and the first doctor — just to see what would happen. "When sick, scramble for cures" ran a common Chinese proverb. But this used to precipitate such crises between the Western-trained Chinese doctors and the patients that I, the poor social worker, spent most of my time trying to make peace. Believe me, it was hard work. The doctor was convinced that the patient was malicious, while the patient did not see why the doctor was so strange, bull-headed, and unreasonable. But since 1949 China has promoted and ensured peaceful coexistence and cooperation between those trained in Western medicine and those versed in traditional practices.

II.    Having recognized the pitfalls and inadequacy of this Western mono-lithic approach to social and individual problems, let us state, once again, that the most important factor affecting human behavior, not only social but also antisocial, in health and illness, is the individual in relation to his fellow human beings, not the individual-individual. This is true whether we think of the matter in terms of development (and therefore emphasize parent-child interaction) or whether we think in terms of con-figuration (and therefore emphasize the social situations and cultural contexts of all adults).

I know little about the biological or the physiological side of man, but it is clear that interpersonal relationships affect biological developments (e.g. infants who have had little physical contact with adults do not grow well) and determine many forms of physical infirmities (e.g. psychoso-matic illness).

Western indivudualism is stuck with the concept of personality. I think the term "personality" should be banished from our scientific vocabulary. Instead, we should concentrate on the interpersonal nexus as a distinct entity for study. For this I have formulated the theory of psychosocial homeostasis (PSH) (Hsu 1971). This theory runs counter to the prevail-ing trend in which premises rooted in Western individualism predominate.

I have observed that the stronger the emphasis on individualism, the greater the avoidance of the interpersonal nexus and the greater the belief in the efficacy of external defenses or inner biological remedies.[1] The popularity of Maharishi and other Hindu promoters of transcendental meditation is one more expression of the same escape from the interper-sonal nexus.

Consequently, however sophisticated our investigations and the cures or preventive measures they may suggest, they inevitably suffer from the intellectual myopia of their designers and executors. Some of our scien-tific investigations are not unlike counting, classifying, and computerizing pebbles on the beach to determine the causes of the rising and ebbing

---

[1]    The Center for the Study and Reduction of Violence in California recently concluded that riots are not caused by social conditions but by a group of people with "low violence thresholds." The people with such low thresholds are male, youthful, black, and slum dwellers. The solution is to operate on the brain or to give drugs, which will remove the danger of violence. These treatments have already been tried on certain criminals in California (*Chicago Sun-Times* 1973b).

of tides. And the blind faith on the part of many in sophisticated communications, protection, and research procedures is quite comparable to premodern man's reliance on intensified ritual activities to allay his fears and solve his problems. The two are not only analogous but are also rooted in the same psychological basis. Neither kind of exercise has anything to do with reality.

III.   If this sounds too absurd, consider our approach to violence or drug abuse. Air piracy is surely a major form of violence. In an hour-long television program on hijacking by the Columbia Broadcasting System in October, 1972, Dr. David G. Hubbard, a psychiatrist who is the director of the Aberrant Behavior Center in Dallas, Texas, and who has served as a consultant both to federal prisons and to the United States Federal Aviation Administration, gave his conclusions after interviewing forty-eight culprits in jail. He said that these men are schizophrenic paranoiacs. They are suffering from a sense of failure, e.g. failure with women, and inadequate masculinity; they have dreams of glory forever and are interested in death but do not wish to die by their own hands. They consider any of the following outcomes of their actions as success: (1) touching the $100,000 (or whatever amount), even if they lose it five minutes later; (2) death after causing death of others; (3) landing in a foreign jail after having forced the plane to land where they command; and (4) even taking the plane from its authorized ramp.

Given this kind of approach, it is natural that our major attempts to prevent air piracy have been in the form of detection (electronic devices, search of passengers before boarding, personality profiles, etc.), force (sky marshals, sealing the rear exits of planes, guards and fences around airports, etc.), and attempts to eliminate sanctuaries for hijacked planes (agreement with Cuba). The astonishing thing is that Dr. Hubbard, after concluding that "the hijacker is unique, he should be treated as such" (Hubbard 1972), now admits that an estimated eight million Americans have the psychiatric syndrome he describes. Add to this the hundreds of thousands who bought sweatshirts bearing the sentiment "D. B. Cooper, where are you?"[2] and countless others who have helped transform songs eulogizing these criminal exploits into financial successes, and we must come up with considerably more than eight million potential air pirates with whom we have to contend.

---

[2]   The first successful hijacker who got away with $ 200,000 by parachuting out of a Northwest Orient plane gave his name as D. B. Cooper.

Is it not unrealistic to think that we can successfully deal with such a large number of potential air pirates in the population by electronic detection and guards? Is it not time for us to see why so many potential air pirates exist in such an affluent society?

Because they, too, are confined by the traditional Western line of thinking about social problems (I do mean "traditional" — Westerners usually relegate the patterns of thinking in other cultures to the category of "traditional," while equating, openly or implicitly, Western and American ways with "modern"), it is not unnatural that America's foremost university researchers who are concerned with the air piracy problem are as intellectually myopic as some clinicians and the general public. Thus, a professor of psychology from Wisconsin, also appearing on the television program mentioned above, concluded that good news-reporting of air piracy cases stimulates more hijacking. I do not dispute the notion that news reporting of "how to" may have some escalating effects in all areas of crime. People looking for success without regard for social consequences are bound to seek lessons for the perfect crime. What appalls me is the low level on which our scientific talent and support are focused.

However disrespectful it may seem to compare the dignified work of our eminent scholars with the opinion of a suburban Chicago police chief after a rash of murders (especially of women and children) in 1972, their similarity strikes me with some force. The working "theory" of the suburban Chicago police is that heavy and continuous rains drive some unbalanced individuals berserk, hence the high frequency of murders.

If we examine our prevailing approaches to drug abuse, we find the same picture: detection and punishment of the pushers, explanation of the pitfalls of addiction to our young, and treatment of addicts by physical and psychological means. But we see little about the more fundamental causes of the persistence and spread of the problem, which surely must be found in the conditions of a society that generates so many pushers and especially users. For example, under the impact of the West, China had a drug problem for more than half a century. But Western scientists studying the drug problem have so far not even noted that Chinese drug addicts were mostly adults and the old, while their American counterparts today are predominantly the young. They have also failed to note that although China before 1949 was plagued by hundreds of thousands of opium and other drug addicts, there was no Chinese movement for the use of drugs as a pathway to truth. There simply were no Chinese Timothy Learys and his followers. Surely these differences say something about the systems, not the individuals, as causes.

IV. This same culture-bound myopia has prevented our prominent social and clinical scientists from coming to grips with most other problems, from alienation to the bloody carnage on our highways, from religious and racial tensions to juvenile delinquency, from the sagging morale of Detroit automobile workers to stealing in the supermarkets. We may stop air piracy by the most thorough airport security system in operation, but creative Americans will undoubtedly find other antisocial areas in which to exercise their talents.[3] Antisocial acts seem to outpace our defensive, curative, or preventive methods and techniques. Perhaps it is this seemingly hopeless picture that prompted Billy Graham, our modern Rasputin, to revert to barbarism and offer castration of the rapist as a method for stopping sexual assault on women. "That would stop him pretty quick," he said (*Chicago Sun-Times* 1973a). In other eras a king or tribal chief might punish a pickpocket by chopping off his hands. These premodern lords also must have said something like "That would stop him pretty quick." What is ironic in Graham's proposal is how well it served as a public confession of the failure of his own crusades to date.

Billy Graham shares one thing with our clinicians and social scientists: he and they are firmly wedded to the Western sacred cow of individualism. Consequently, they look to the individual himself for the basic sources of his greater achievements and for the deep roots of his worst troubles.

V. With reference to any of the mental health problems, there are two broad kinds of research questions: (a) which social systems with what cultural characteristics are likely to produce more suicides, drug abuse, crimes, or mental aberrations? (b) In a high- or low-crime society, which

---

[3] After being indicted for embezzling $ 100,000 of government funds intended for the poor, former Chicago Alderman Fred Hubbard gave a hero's interview in jail to a television reporter. Among other things, Hubbard pronounced his life-long policy in this way: "Whenever I see something I want, I just take it." Hubbard's words were nearly identical to those of Juan Gonzales, a Puerto Rican youth in Harlem, expressing his admiration for Napoleon and Hitler: "I admire a person who, when he wants something, he goes after it. Me, I don't do it. I don't do it" (Mayerson 1965:105). Later Hubbard was given an extremely light sentence — one year in prison — from which he would be eligible for parole after serving three months. But many others do not merely lament as did Juan Gonzales, "Me, I don't do it. I don't do it." Arthur Bremer, the convicted would-be assassin of ex-presidential candidate George Wallace, leaves little doubt that he wanted instant fame by killing Richard Nixon or George Wallace (he did not care whom) to fulfill the grandiose delusions of a lonely nobody "who tried to cure his impotence." He has since achieved his goal of instant fame, with some profit as well, for part of his diary was published in *Harper's Magazine* with the notation: "Copyright 1972 by Arthur H. Bremer and Harper's Magazine Press" (Bremer 1973:52). Does anyone believe that arrest and incarceration of such offenders will eliminate the problems they represent?

individuals are likely to commit a crime (or suicide or whatever) and which individual experiences lead to that act?

We have tended so far to deal mainly with part of the second question but not at all with the first. This is also true of the papers in this volume, although a number of interesting points have been raised. Iga's paper (this volume) shows lack of intimacy and heightened narcissism as causes of suicide on the part of two of Japan's foremost literary figures: Kawabata and Mishima. McKinney (this volume) presents overwhelming evidence on the link between social isolation and learned helplessness in animals. Although I am skeptical about the wisdom of generalizing from animal to human behavior, I agree that his results may have some bearing on human development at the early infantile stages.

Elsewhere, however, Schaefer (1976) has suggested some possible answers to the first question: What kinds of social systems with what cultural characteristics are likely to intensify the problem of drinking? Schaefer concludes that

...in societies where people believe that the spirits of their dead ancestor take on the form of unpredictable, arbitrarily harmful, malicious and capricious beings, they tend to drink excessively and brawl when drunk.... [Furthermore,] people in societies where families tend to be dominated by father-son interaction as opposed to any other simple nuclear dyadic dominance pattern, tend to abstain from excessive drunkenness.

These two conclusions are interrelated. People whose kinship situation is orderly and predictable tend to believe that their departed ancestors are predictable, succoring, and noncapricious. Such people tend to drink more moderately than others.

The lack of concern with the latter type of problem is apparently the general trend in American psychology today. In a recent article Nathan Caplan and Stephen D. Nelson, two psychologists at the University of Michigan, report the results of their analysis of six months of issues of the 1970 *Psychological Abstracts* 44 (1–6) plus the semiannual index. They found that there exists

...a person-centered preoccupation and causal attribution bias in psychological research which, when applied to social problems, favors explanations in terms of the personal characteristics of those experiencing the problem, while disregarding the possible influence of external forces (Caplan and Nelson 1973:209).

VI.   In spite of Watergate and the declining United States dollar, the attraction of American achievements for the rest of the world is still great today. I have tried to sound a note of caution, so that our intellectual sisters and brothers from other parts of the world can watch for the dangers of intellectual Uncle Tomism, the risk of being overly impressed by the individualist model of man even when making intercultural endeavors.

## REFERENCES

BREMER, ARTHUR H.
1973  "An assassin's diary." *Harper's Magazine* (January): 52-66.
CAPLAN, NATHAN, STEPHEN D. NELSON
1973  On being useful: the nature and consequences of psychological research on social problems. *American Psychologist* (March):199-211.
*Chicago Sun-Times*
1973a Article about Billy Graham. March 22.
1973b Article on violence. August 27.
HSU, FRANCIS L. K.
1971  Psychosocial homeostasis and *Jen:* conceptual tools for advancing psychological anthropology. *American Anthropologist* 73:23–44.
HUBBARD, DAVID G.
1972  Interview. *Life* (August 11).
MAYERSON, CHARLOTTE LEON
1965  *Two blocks apart.* New York: Holt, Rinehart and Winston.
SCHAEFER, JAMES
1976  "Drunkenness and culture stress: a holo-cultural test," in *Cross-cultural approaches to the study of alcohol: an interdisciplinary perspective.* Edited by M. W. Everett, J. O. Waddell, and D. B. Heath, 287–322. World Anthropology. The Hague: Mouton.

# Development of Theoretical Models and Levels of Interpretation in Mental Health

JOSEPH E. TRIMBLE and BEATRICE MEDICINE

A plethora of research has focused on the mental health, social pathology, and psychopathology of American Indians. Most research offers interpretations as to the causes of a variety of emotional and behavioral disturbances. Conjointly with theory, interpretations are offered as to why the particular problem under investigation should persist within the individual or group. Yet the papers offer little in the way of substantive and systematic recommendations or solutions for the diagnosed problems. Moreover, they ignore the question of whether the problems are worthy of a solution from the perspective of the native people themselves. State and federal governments, private foundations and organizations, and church-related institutions are aimed at resolving problems of Indian mental health, yet the problems still remain. A cursory examination of the social indicators indicative of mental health in any Indian community would indeed support this contention.

It is time for a reassessment of what has been done. Social scientists cannot continue to compile volumes of pragmatic, descriptive, and interpretative research without an ultimate objective. An objective of applied science is to offer practical solutions to problems. Such problems may be conceived not only by the scientific community but by the very people involved with them. A point has to be reached where solutions must

The senior author wishes to express his gratitude to Dr. John M. Steele and the late Professor William R. Hood for their assistance in developing and refining the Ecosystems Analysis Model which appears in this manuscript. As our adviser in graduate school in 1968 at the University of Oklahoma, Professor Hood was extremely instrumental in providing the type of atmosphere so necessary to develop and pursue a concept such as is offered herein.

supplement understanding. At present, it seems that research alone has been the outstanding feature of the focus on American Indian mental health. This calls for a revision in a basic conceptualization of the research model and the types of data analysis that are or have been used, as well as their subsequent utilization.

Our purpose here is to reassess research on mental health processes occurring among American Indians. The inquiry will further clarify the kinds of research that have been done. Finally, we call for the use and implementation of an alternative perspective, one that may assist the researcher and practitioner in sorting through the maze of information and, hopefully, provide these persons with a viable alternative for problem solving.

## THEORETICAL MODELS IN RESEARCH

One's inferences and observations reach the point of acting as blinders, which force the observer to view only those aspects of the physical facts that fit the confines of the theory, and eliminate others. Implicit in the development of any theory is the existence of some basic model or paradigm. That model is the foundation upon which any theoretician will base and subsequently test his assumptions. The theoretician may be unconscious of the model. Advocates of a particular theory may be totally ignorant of a model, yet skilled in the utilization and implementation of the theory. Up to the present, two basic models, discussed below, have directed and guided the theoretical interpretations of mental health studies of American Indians.

## SELF-ACTION MODEL

Aristotle is credited with initiating a system of thought that maintains that there exist things which completely and, hence, necessarily possess being; that these continue eternally in action (under their own power) and continue in some particular action essential to them in which they are engaged. Anything, human or otherwise, in the process of interacting of itself or upon or within itself is involved in some form of self-action. The action itself is the locus of evaluation, and analysis is the act itself linked to a causal relationship with some basic innate or biologically controlled predisposition. The character of this elementary stage of thought, self-action, can be clearly established with a multitude of past and present illustrations. All were competent in themselves as factual, theoretical reports in their times without suspicion of the way in which later generations would reduce them to simpleminded guesswork.

One line of thinking that has resulted in research in the field of mental health is the application of the principles of psychoanalysis. Psychoanalysis approaches the understanding of behavior from a self-action perspective. The sole locus of interpretation in this theory is the "being" of the mind. For many anthropologists seeking explanations of emotional disturbance and mental imbalance, a probing of the dynamics of the personality within the individual seemed the most logical step. Because much of the early work centered around uncovering aspects indicative of one's personality, it appeared to be an attempt to get inside the individual and to pull out certain concepts that fit a rather general pervasive theory of human behavior.

If one were to operate from this particular approach, that is, breaking down the components of the personality into interconnecting subcomponents, then of necessity one would have to resort to a specific theoretical approach. Nadel (1951) suggests that if one desired to study the mental makeup of a person, then one should use only those tests and related methodological techniques used by psychologists. If a person wished to define cultural patterns strictly in terms of resulting psychological agencies, an examination of them must take place as well, IN the individual. This contention is supported by Kardiner's suggestion (1939) and subsequent demonstration that the root of the analysis was the personality and that once this was interpreted or understood, the investigator then proceeded to relate the development of the individual personality along some sociocultural dimension. First, the personality had to be understood. Kardiner attempted to understand an individual in a cultural context, but from an almost strictly psychoanalytic approach.

The dominant theory of early psychology was influenced strongly by psychoanalysis; thus, psychoanalysis became the leading theory in the field of mental health research. An alternative was to examine the dysfunctioning personality from an organic perspective, but that generally was relegated to those who searched for biological, causal relationships. However, most culturally oriented social scientists were looking for the functional causes of behavior rather than the organic. Wallace (1958) suggests synthesizing the organic with the psychosocial approach, but emphasizes more an understanding of the organic process of mental health rather than the functional.

As early as 1932, an appeal was made to anthropologists by Seligman "to study more deeply than has hitherto been the common practice the ideas... that lie behind the beliefs and customs which we, as anthropologists, are accustomed to describe" (Seligman 1932:227). Seligman suggests that the works of Freud and Jung are important for anthropologists because of the many psychological problems that confront them in their research. Specifically, anthropological problems "...lie for the most part not in the sphere of cognition, but in the sphere of motive and emotion" (Seligman 1932:195). Kardiner (1939) defines this view as a phonogenetic perspective in which a person is a "by-product of a biological force." It is common, therefore, to find investigators looking for that particular force that drives the individual into some form of behavior.

Kardiner is probably the individual most responsible for developing a technique based on "psychodynamic analysis" and applying it in analyzing different cultures. He referred to it as "an exercise in pathology" (Kardiner 1945). In keeping with the tenets of the self-action model, Kardiner stresses that one must follow very definite steps in analyzing the personality of any cultural group. The following appear to be steps that he suggests one should follow:

1. Standardizing the reactions of adult neurotic patterns in Western culture to specific institutions.

2. Identifying the institutions which apparently are the causes of neurotic reactions and thus are important causal elements of frustration for "normal" persons in Western culture.

3. Identifying the reactions of groups exposed to similar institutional frustrations in any culture (see Singer 1961).

Seligman's recommendations and Kardiner's developments heavily influenced mental health research on the American Indian. Much of the early work was an effort to substantiate and verify the operation of certain psychoanalytic processes. The Oedipal myth studies, in particular, implied a ubiquitous existence of the phenomenon in all people and thus prompted many verbal attacks, albeit nonscientific, against those who denied its existence. As an example, Roheim (1950:176–191), attacked those who denied the universality of the Oedipal myth and implied that those who were denying it were denying its existence in themselves (see Malinowski 1927).

The main argument in Kardiner's camp is a simple one. By analyzing the processes within a person one comes to an understanding of both the person and his culture because the cultural process is also viewed as an outgrowth of an innate predisposition. This view has generated much emphasis on the interpretations and has indeed dominated the literature (See Kaplan 1961).

Hartmann, et al. (1951) and Wilbur and Muensterberger (1951) have developed very logical defenses for the use of psychoanalysis in understanding cultural behavior, particularly psychopathological behavior. Of course, the development of the theory of psychoanalysis was founded on an understanding of the emotionally disturbed, and from this point received its emphasis. Subsequently, anyone using this theory would, almost of necessity, find and locate the causes if not even the psychopathological behavior itself. The theory predicts that anyone who deviates from the basic tenets of the theory would be "abnormal."

Initially psychoanalysis was a nonempirical, nonscientific theory, but advocates of psychoanalysis wanted to objectify and hence develop empirical methods to substantiate the many postulates and theorems. Because of this they had to develop methodological techniques that would both fit within the purview of the theory and at the same time be considered empirical.

A basic technique of psychoanalysis is dream analysis. This technique rests on the assumption that residing in the unconscious dimension of the individual are repressed experiences which rarely emerge to a conscious level. By looking for cues in the dreamwork of the individual the investigator seeks to find the causes of these experiences. The majority of psychoanalysts began with the assumption that dreams represent unfilled needs. Anthropologists and other social scientists practically accepted this assumption *in toto*. Furthermore, anthropologists insisted that such an approach could be applied readily to all cultures (Lincoln 1935). Some social scientists even suggested that dreams indicated that certain American Indian tribes employed a kind of psychoanalytic approach themselves (Toffelmier and Luomala 1936; Wallace 1958). In the main, these writers suggest that the tribes themselves use a somewhat psychoanalytic approach in interpreting the dreams and certain forms of deviant behavior as being abnormal. The use of dream analysis is seriously questioned by many scientists as nonempirical and at best a quasi-empirical approach to data gathering, particularly because many of them were interpreted by nonmembers of the cultural group under study.

Dream analysis was not the only method of data gathering and theory substantiation. If one developed a theory to explain certain psychological constructs, consideration must be given to the development of instrumentation to measure the concepts that purportedly exist within the individual. The case is true for practically all theories of personality, psychoanalysis notwithstanding. Hence, certain mental tests and in turn an implicit application of the extension of the self-action model were developed by psychoanalysts to investigate certain elements thought to be capable of being measured.

The Rorschach Ink Blot test is the most notable of the psychoanalytically based tests and it has been used extensively by a number of investigators. Boyer, et al. (1965) found in their Rorschach protocols that certain Apache groups differed in their personality traits. They attempted to attribute these differences to the process of acculturation by implying that a form of mental imbalance of psychic energy existed "in" those who were not quite acculturated. Wallace (1952) attempted to determine the existence of a "modal personality" of a Tuscarora Indian community, where the strength of the existence of modality was based on the "average" Rorschach response of the respondents. Kaplan (1954), in an effort to substantiate the claim that "modal personalities" of the American Indian varied from tribe to tribe and group to group, obtained Rorschach protocols from four different, but geographically adjacent, cultural groups – Zuñi and Navajo Indians, Mormons, and Spanish-Americans. He relates, "large areas of personality vary without respect to cultural influence." In each of these studies, the interpretation of the protocols and the personalities was from a psychoanalytic perspective – a self-action perspective!

The Minnesota Multiphasic Personality Inventory (MMPI) is another instrument whose interpretation lies within the purview of psychoanalysis. This instrument has been widely used among American Indians. Herreid and Herreid (1966) found that native Alaskans were seen to be more emotionally disturbed on certain dimensions of MMPI scales when compared with nonnative Alaskans. Bryde (1966:10) administered the MMPI to certain Oglala Sioux age groups and reported, "On each of these measures the total group revealed greater personality disruptions. Notable among the more meaningful variables were feelings of rejection, repression, anxiety and a tendency to withdraw." In both studies it is apparent that the conclusions and findings were nothing short of negative responses; negative, that is, from their particular perspective and level of interpretation. Never, it seems, have trained persons from these native groups been consulted in the interpretation of these results.

Neither of these instruments has been standardized on the populations on which they were applied. Nonstandardization makes sense only because the theory from which they work assumes a universality of human behavior. Clearly, the instruments will uncover certain abnormal responses in one culture just as they will find alternative kinds of normal responses in another culture for comparable and similar reasons. Perhaps this is why these instruments have received almost universal acceptance as being of unquestioned validity.

In addition to the instrumentation developed for psychoanalysis, "analysis" is often used to interpret specific deviant behavioral patterns for which psychoanalysis has no explanation. An example is the study of the *piblotoq* hysteria of Eskimos by Brill (1913). Utilizing psychoanalytic techniques Brill offered an explanation for the causes underlying this supposed strange form of behavior, even though he never visited the group. He obtained most of his information from the writings of explorers. Gussow (1960) agreed with Brill's interpretation. He added a further dimension by concluding that the Eskimo engages in this form of behavior to express frustration and a lack of love. Many disagree with this interpretation (cf. Wallace 1958).

Another form of unusual behavior found among the Cree is referred to as the *wiitiko* psychosis. It has been the source of much investigation. Landes' work (1938) best exemplifies the use of psychoanalysis to interpret this very specialized form of psychotic behavior.

The use of psychoanalysis for interpreting deviant behavior does not stop with specific behavioral patterns. Certain writers have emphasized abnormal development among Indian children. In most instances references have been made to unresolved sexual impulses resulting in a disharmony of the personality (Weinberg 1952). Levy (1935) analyzed sibling rivalry among primitive groups and argued that abnormal patterns occur because of the children's jealousy of one another. Alexander and Anderson (1957) found that the perceptual patterns of Northern Cheyenne children generally demonstrated emotional deprivation. Erikson (1939, 1963) offered interpretations, suggesting that certain Sioux children have poor anal and oral development periods which affect a "normal" adaptation to formal education. Erikson associated the development of this frustration with the traditional Sioux custom of binding the child in a cradle board. The frustration manifested itself in the form of long-lasting aggression.

Psychoanalysis is not the only theory used, however much it pervades the literature. Individuals who resort to the use of self-theory, that is, the explanation of some deviant behavior as a result of an imbalance in the self-concept of an individual, are also using a self-action approach.

Usually when one employs the word "self," its use is synonymous with the concept of personality. Any attempt to study the self either as a stable or unstable form from either an eclectic or specific theory of the self is making reference to behavior as the final source of evaluation. Such terms as "poor self-concept," "poor self-adjustment," or "self-disorganization" allude to an emotional "self-balance" in the self-action model. Saslow and Harrover (1968) found that Indian youth who struggled with self-identity are usually led to behavioral difficulties as a result of poor reality testing. Others who have studied the self-concept of American Indians tended to place the locus of evaluation on the self-concept, preferring to offer some kind of imbalance or irregularity in the self-process as an interpretation that seemed to be at odds with what they construed as being indicative of one's "normal self." Very often this "normal self" is not the "normalcy" defined by the particular native American group.

Perhaps the most damaging and insulting to the Indian are studies that use no theory at all, but still stay within the confines of the self-action model. These studies conventionally allude to each process as "poor ego development," or "unresolved childhood identity problems," "self-conflict," etc. Representative is the work of Saindon (1933) who went to the extreme to conclude that "The Indian is a big child," and that the "Indian has quite a liking for these abnormal mental experiences." While Saindon's article may not be empirical it most assuredly is appalling, insulting, and nonscientific.

More recent approaches have attempted to break away from traditional approaches of studying deviant behavior among North American Indians. Wallace (1972) makes a strong appeal to focus more attention on "biogenic causes." Convincing as is his recommendation, it is the same self-action model, only fancied up with more contemporary theory in neurology and physiology. In fact, the focus on internal physiological systems offers as little as did the psychoanalytic theorists. The language may be more precise, the internal organic causes may be more factual or empirical, but the locus of evaluation is essentially the same. While seeking an explanation and appealing to some imbalance or metabolic irregularity within the individual, it reports little that goes on externally.

Apparently, when the physicists dropped "animism" out of physical reports the effect was not to produce a comparable trend in organic and behavioral fields, but the reverse. All of the entities that once had inhabited portions of matter seemingly took flight to new residences mostly in or at the human body, particularly the human brain. The commonplace "soul" of the middle ages blossomed into the overstrained and morbid "psyche" of the last century. The "mind" as "actor," still in use in present-day psychologies, anthropologies, and sociologies is the old self-action "soul" with its immortality stripped off. "Mind" or "mental" as a preliminary word in casual phrasing is a sound word in need of investigation. "Mind," "faculty," "IQ," or "self" as an actor in charge of behavior is a charlatan. "Brain," as a substitute for mind behaving is equally absurd. Such words insert a name in place of a problem and label it fact. The modern derivative of soul or mind is tautological. "The living behaving organism is present. To add a mind to them is to try and double them up. It is double-talk and double talk doubles no fact" (Dewey and Bentley 1949:132).

For the American Indian "mind" or "mental" is a phrase which has meaning, and as such, has organizing and/or characterizing qualities in the "native world view." It is not a substance but a process that transacts with the world. It is not held as a distinct, separate entity but an integral part of the total configuration of one's life space.


## INTERACTION MODEL

Except for those emphasizing a biogenic or self-theorist's approach, most psychoanalytic interpretation of the behavior of native groups has been abandoned, partly due to the influx and contribution of cultural anthropologists and sociologists appealing more to an investigation of those elements that are contained in the individual's environment. Let it be said that the self-action approach has led many investigators of the mental health of American Indians to an impasse, and we cannot continue to study the individual as an isolated, independent being, separate from everything else.

Psychologists have long recognized this tacit assumption. The early behaviorists of the twentieth century advocated the study of what some referred to as "the empty organism" and stressed an investigation of the observable variables and stimuli that existed in one's immediate environment. Proponents of operant conditioning stress the response-reinforcement contingencies that occur outside individuals. They make no attempt to imply processes located within the individual.

Thus, psychologists concerned with the objective study of the behavior of organisms shifted the locus of evaluation from inside the individual to the outside and, in many instances, it was completely outside. It is hardly the self-action model as it is expressed in this paper. Dewey and Bently (1949) refer to this approach as the interaction model, where a thing is viewed as balanced against another thing in a causal interconnection. Instead of attempting to infer the kinds of operations that exist within the organism the emphasis is shifted over to viewing how the interchanges between the organism and environment affect each other.

Many anthropologists and sociologists were quick to adopt this model, and they appeared to use it to provide them with additional sources of information about what went on in the person. In sociology, the model is very strongly in force and is almost implicitly accepted by all, even to the extent of arguing on the conceptualization of social interaction itself. According to one proponent, Wilson (1970), a sociologist,

...the term action may be used to refer to behavior that is meaningful to the actor. Actions do not occur in isolation but rather are linked to each other as one actor responds to and anticipates the actions of others and this is so even when an act occurs in solitude. Any particular action then is part of a process of interaction involving several actors responding to each others actions.

Wilson continues:

Thus complex social phenomena are seen as tentative arrangements of interactions among individual actors. The process of interaction is at the logical core of sociological interests even though for some purposes it is less implicit.

Hare (1962) offers a similar definition, but places stronger emphasis on group influences on individual behavior. He states "social interaction is seen as a compromise between the inputs from man's BIOLOGICAL NATURE and PERSONALITY... and ROLE, CULTURE, and ENVIRONMENT." The criteria necessary to predict aspects of social interaction, according to Hare, would be the individual's biological nature or, conversely, knowledge of group behavior can lead to the prediction of an individual member. Each, then, could be measured INDEPENDENTLY of the other. The categorical system of Hare's analysis of social interaction is presented in Table 1.

Table 1.   Hare's analysis of social interaction

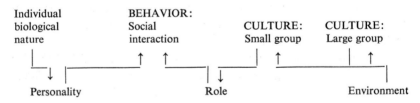

| Individual biological nature | BEHAVIOR: Social interaction | CULTURE: Small group | CULTURE: Large group |
| --- | --- | --- | --- |
| Personality | Role | | Environment |

Hare's system is indicative of much of the work of sociologists, particularly the segments to the right of the word "behavior." Many social psychologists attempt to integrate the segments on both sides, shifting the emphasis of their concern from the individual to the environment and back again.

In like manner, anthropologists' adoption of an interaction perspective led some to offer methodological alternatives as safeguards. Goodenough (1970) makes a distinction between the two kinds of methodological interaction approaches that he sees in operation in anthropological research. He refers to them conventionally as EMIC and ETIC. He defines the former as one in which the investigator makes distinctions which are demonstrably meaningful and significant for competent users of the system under investigation, and the latter as one where the investigator bases his conclusion upon a distinction (typically drawn from cross-cultural psychology) whose meaningfulness for a particular system of users has not been demonstrated and whose significance within the system is therefore open to question.

The concepts of emic and etic have served to clarify the interpretations of ethnological data. However, some researchers have attempted to operate from one of the approaches only to find that they were working from the alternative dimension. A number have been concerned with the emic dimensions as seen by the native peoples themselves, but their data have been misread and subsequently misconstrued.

For example, *heyoka*, a Teton Lakota term in the Siouan language, can be interpreted to refer to certain contrary (but fleeting) behavioral patterns which might be manifest in an individual's behavior at a certain time. Some non-Lakota researchers have equated *heyoka* with "clown," or mentally disturbed beings. The latter interpretation has resulted in a small number of misinterpretations, and has subsequently led to an etic distortion of an emic phrase.

A further example can be found in certain Lakota descriptions of specific behavioral patterns. Within the Lakota framework for "normalcy," the term *winkté* is seen as a nonjudgmental phrase pointing to homosexual behavior, which was part of the rejection of the warrior role by Lakota males. Typically, it was an aspect of the vision quest or subsequent dreams which were interpreted by medicine men to allow this type of "deviant" behavior, but not seen as a form of deviancy from the Lakota view of "person." Further illustrations of this point could include misinterpretations of the sense of propriety for the person – space allocation, self-alienation, linguistic terminology, and other cognitive and affective processes, which are part of the perceptual framework for the Lakota personality. Many of these nuances have native categories inherent in the Lakota language but tend to take on etic dimensions when translated.

For some time certain anthropologists have realized the need for drawing inferences from the native personality of an individual by placing an emphasis on the person's cultural system. Specifically, Opler (1956) suggested that one should look for sources of mental illness in the cultural processes of native groups. Kluckhohn (1954:3-4) related,

"...anthropology can bet high upon the significance of cultural factors for understanding and explanation" by emphasizing the study of personality variables within a cultural framework. Honigmann (1954:3) suggested that "the student of culture and personality studies should study what happens to personality by virtue of an individual's membership in enduring groups whose members follow special standardized ways of acting and thinking."

More recently Hsu (1972:6) defined culture-and-personality research as that which "deals with human behavior primarily in terms of the ideas which form the basis of the interrelationship between the individual and his society"; and "we may take it for granted that there is some connection between the make-up of a culture and the particular personality of human carriers (Nadel 1951:405)."

It would be safe to say that the theoretical positions of Opler, Kluckhohn, Honigmann, and Hsu have had as strong an effect on the studies of mental health of American Indian groups as did those of researchers who advocated using a self-action perspective.

The introduction of the culture-and-personality approach has brought forth a number of problems. In particular, the use of concepts such as "personality" and "psychopathology" on a cross-cultural basis has placed many investigators in a quandary. The search for normal and deviant patterns introduced the question of what is "normal" and "abnormal" and became an integral segment within the cultural frame of reference. Few researchers sensed a concern for the relevance of cultural systems and the support they give to specific behavioral patterns.

The cross-cultural analysis of deviant behavior has led to disastrous consequences for certain subjects as is specifically evidenced in Jewell's report (1952) of a wrongly diagnosed instance of psychosis in a Navajo male. Anthropologists are alert to the functional values of some mental or behavioral distortions but somehow there is little concern for the issue. It seems that much of the research stresses isolating those cultural patterns and factors that are conducive to the production of deviant behavior, and overlooks the value the behavior in question may have in the native group as viewed by the native peoples themselves.

Despite the apparent disadvantages of using ethnocentric interpretations of cross-cultural behavior, many reputable researchers have fallen prey to its subtleties even though they tried to avoid doing so. Honigmann and Honigmann (1953) studied the child-rearing patterns of the Great Whale River Eskimos. They maintain that because the parents had difficulty controlling hostile behavior in the young this led to emotional disturbances in adulthood. Honigmann (1949) also reported that denial of the existence of emotional behavior and reduction of tension in the Kaska society produced a fear of love. He admits that in his culture such a manifestation of behavior is considered abnormal, whereas among the Kaska it is considered normal. He adds, "Psychiatrically, however, the person is disturbed." Honigmann obviously cannot shake the chains of ethnocentric and theoretical bias. His interpretation reflects bias despite his insistence on avoiding it.

As an example of a more formidable stance on relativism, J. E. Levy's study (1965) of suicidal behavior among the Navajo is quite illustrative. Levy regarded the suicidal patterns of the Navajo as aggressive in nature, aimed at a spouse and relatives, growing primarily out of a Navajo's tendency to withdraw from a situation to avoid attention. Levy attributed suicidal behavior to the way the Navajo deals with his problems on a day-to-day basis — a practice not condemned by Navajos, but indeed very much accepted (i.e. withdrawal to avoid attention). Levy's interpretation viewed the suicidal behavior as positively functional rather than negatively, as it would be construed in the dominant society.

Native groups have developed a system of classifying and categorizing different forms of behavior that fit very closely within their world view and the view they have of themselves as people. The classificatory system of personality is as much a part of the total world view as is a description of tribal origins. Analyzing a certain segment from another world view or theory serves only to distort the intrinsic value of the group's interpretation of the segment — treating the segment from another view serves not only to distort and disrupt the behavior in question but can well set off a chain reaction that could disrupt the person's total world view. For example, Dakota concepts of mental health, *tà–un* [being in a state of well-being] are markedly different and seemingly more adaptive. The concept of *tà–un* appears to allow for certain categories of action and action states within the individual, which are more flexible than are permitted within the concept of mental health in the dominant society.

*Tà–un*, as an orientation, has a strong foundation in the Dakota's perception of individual autonomy and decision making. Thus, behavior seen as abnormal by a non-Dakota, (e.g. homosexuality or *winkté*) was historically an institutionalized behavioral role and much of the tolerance for this particular "deviancy" persists in modern reservation life. Furthermore, the process commonly referred to as alienation, *ešna-un* [wishing to be alone] is seen as achieved isolation, and the withdrawal from the social group is respected. Interestingly, however, some Dakota young adults often use psychological terms derived from the dominant society to maintain individual decision making. The statement,

"I can't go to college because I have a low I.Q.," from a young Dakota male is one example. Thus, Dakota people are quick to recognize different personality dimensions within their own group, despite the fact that *Lakota-ča* [being a Lakota, Dakota, or Sioux] is seen as a quality which is an overriding factor in the Dakota socialization processes.

Cultural relativism as a concern and a method still remains, as indicated by Devereaux (1956). He and others are well behind those psychologists who are beginning to question the whole issue of psychiatric nosology and diagnosis as well as psychotherapeutic techniques. Szasz, a psychiatrist-analyst (1961), holds that mental illness is a myth, and he may well be right. After all, many of the psychiatric labels attached to native groups are self-action, medical terms, designed explicitly to explain deviant behavior in terms of an illness or disease. Can one cure mental illness as one cures the disease? Psychologists are saying that even this question is wrong. Social psychologists are asking: if you "cure" the culture do you subsequently "cure" the illness?

Numerous studies have focused on American Indian students attending government educational institutions. The majority of the studies are from the interactional perspective and indicate that attendance at these schools produces forms of deviant behavior. Many authors lay the blame on the process of acculturation, mobility patterns, changing frames of reference, and on the actual institution of education itself (Hoyt 1962; Krush, et al. 1965; Macgregor 1946; Sasaki 1960). For the most part the writers suggest that the dominant cultural environment is simply too disruptive and threatening to the Indian child. Despite the nature of the findings and the attempts to analyze and pinpoint the problems of Indian youths in these institutions, the behavior of the student and the interpretations of the researchers persist. The observed and analyzed behavior may well be a reaction against the very thing that is being imposed upon the student, and this reaction may well be within the limits of the way the culture instructs him to act against some sort of imposition being forced upon him.

The interaction model tends to generate more theory now that anthropologists have been collaborating with psychologists and sociologists under the guise of "psychological anthropology." The production and utilization of other measurement devices to support the various alternative hypotheses have increased, yet some workers persist in using MMPI, Rorschach, and TAT protocols. The influx of instrumentation designed to get inside the person's head substantiates the view that the studies of environmental influences have been inconclusive. Instead of the causes of mental imbalance being self-generated, those working from the interaction model are trying to attribute the causes to other factors. The instruments apparently directed the researcher's aim, with the multitude of environmental variables being the target. Once the environmental cause is located, an attempt is made to tie it in with a psychological process tapped by the instrument. Taken together, both are viewed as the cause of the mental imbalance.

Many of the instruments used are not necessarily tied to any specific psychosocial, cultural theory of personality. The Cornell Index is an example. Martin, et al. (1968) used the Cornell Index to substantiate not only the existence of psychiatric problems, but also to verify certain sociopsychological theories of psychological problems among northeastern Oklahoma Indians. They found that 25 percent of the Indian subjects were psychiatrically impaired. One wonders if the native groups in that region would have found the same percentage using their own criterion.

Apparently there exists a feedback loop in the use of the interaction model, with one camp supplying the other with the findings and the other developing instruments or devices to substantiate and justify empirically the observations and hypotheses of those who appear to be working closer with the cultural group. A sharing of the findings is a welcome sign. But the model from which they work may well be out of step with this approach. Wilson (1970) makes a very weak plea for the inclusion of interpretation rather than the descriptive approach of the framework into the interactional model. He states that:

...by dropping the assumption of a culturally established consensus represented by a shared system of symbols that can be taken for granted by the investigator, the interpretative perspective makes available for increased documentary interpretation itself. In these times it is clear that ethnomethodology and interpretative sociology are not a competitive enterprise whereas one "cause" of the other each deliberately spends interest in what is taken as problematic by the other (Wilson 1970:707).

Yet this seems insufficient. As individuals continue to work from the same model they continue to perpetuate the same behavioral descriptions, dressed up with new interpretations.

## SOCIAL PATHOLOGY AND THE INTERACTION MODEL

Within the past twenty-five years a substantial number of studies has been published on the subject of alcoholism and suicide among Indian groups. Instead of attempting to discern the conditions and patterns of behavior indicative of classic psychiatric nosologies (e.g. neuroses, psychoses, etc.) the effort has been directed at more isolated behavioral patterns where stress and pathological behavior, plus some environmental conditions, appear to be causally related.

A majority of the studies are directed at describing the use of alcohol by various Indian groups, with the major focus on the various patterns of drinking and the degree to which drinking is accepted. Most of the reports suggest that the groups accept and sanction drinking, despite the apparent high incidence of alcoholism (Lemert 1958; Berreman 1956; Curley 1967; Hurt and Brown 1965; Dozier 1966; Ferguson 1968; Kuttner and Lorinez 1967; Honigmann and Honigmann 1965; Devereaux 1948). Some have traced the historical development of drinking among certain tribes and how the group learned how to drink (Honigmann and Honigmann 1965). Lurie (1971:325) went so far as to state that heavy drinking was a reaction against the conditions imposed upon certain tribes by state and federal governments. She states that "getting drunk remains a very Indian thing to do when all else fails to maintain the Indian-white boundary." Honigmann and Honigmann (1965) reported similar findings among Indians living in or around predominantly white communities. One thing remains clear from these initial descriptions: a considerable amount of variation exists in the drinking patterns from group to group, within groups, and within individuals (Westermeyer 1972).

Social scientists offer various psychodynamic explanations of drinking and intoxication of specific Indian groups. Whittaker (1963) attempts to tie in a specific psychodynamic explanation with cultural factors among the Standing Rock Sioux. Mohatt (1972) especially pinpointed the need for drinking as caused by a frustrated desire to experience personal power among the Teton Sioux. Lurie (1971) suggests that Indians drink periodically to reduce tension, as a response to a doubly frustrating life situation, which leads to an excuse for overt aggression. These explanations run close to those of Horton (1943) who stressed that alcoholism in other cultures was an acceptable way of resolving dilemmas growing out of a combination of intense anxiety and frustration created by dominant culture contact.

In keeping with the self-action component of the interaction model a few have offered physiological and metabolic explanations for alcoholic abuse. Kunitz, et al. (1969) suggest that Navajos are genetically more susceptible to cirrhosis of the liver than non-Indians. In a comprehensive investigation of metabolic reactions and changes invoked by alcohol among Indians, Hood (1972) related that "the rate of assimilation and metabolism determines to a large extent how intoxicated a person gets on a given amount of alcohol in unit time." Some of his findings suggest that the Indians' metabolic constitution is such that it processes alcohol at a greater rate than that of Caucasians.

At a sociocultural level of analysis (the other component of the interaction model) several researchers have attributed the cause of alcoholism to acculturation, denial of legitimate means of achievement, anomie, and effective means of social control of the individual (Graves 1967; Dozier 1966; Hamer 1965). Saslow (1972) suggests that the perpetuation of drinking patterns of Indians may well lie in the model that Indian parents set for the children and that drinking patterns which turn into habits may be learned. The general conclusion from these studies strongly suggests that drinking patterns are learned and call for more research from a theoretical perspective of social learning.

Levy and Kunitz (1971) and J. E. Levy (1965) suggest that the unpleasant conditions of Indian reservations are sufficient cause for alcoholism. The social climate of the reservation provides for deviant forms of behavior that are generated by the group itself. These forms may be rejected by the dominant social system as forms of social pathology but considered as acceptable behavioral patterns on the reservation. Thus while recreational drinking may lead to such behaviors as suicide and homicide, it is, in itself, both tolerated and accepted. The question of the relative functional value of social pathologies is equally significant as that of the more dramatic forms of psychopathology.

The use of the interaction model poses many questions. Is it theoretically sound to emphasize the organism or environment and to observe the interaction process, shifting back and forth between the two? Is it methodologically sound to attempt to infer prophecies from some standardized instrument not standardized on the group under investigation? Should a theory untested on a cultural group be applied to the group to grasp an understanding of the mental health of the individual? Should social scientists continue to resort to the use of a language indicative of an outmoded model? Will something come along to knock the personalism out of self-action and interaction models of theory building?

An awakening to the weakness of the belief in the self-action and interactional models seems to be gaining ground. Murdock (1971) suggests that descriptive ethnography in certain social scientific theories has failed in an attempt to come to an understanding of differing cultural groups and differing forms of behavior. As an admission of both his own guilt and the failure of others he relates:

I therefore feel no hesitation in rejecting the validity and futility of the entire bulk of ethnological theory, [including] the bulk of my own work, which derives from the reified concept of either social or cultural systems and in consigning it to the realms of mythology rather than science (Murdock 1971:20).

Murdock calls for radical surgery in the field of ethnology, particularly claiming that it must rid itself of theories and assumptions inconsistent with the findings of contemporary psychology, especially those segments of existing theory which depend on mythological concepts of cultural and social systems. In other words, Murdock is calling for discarding the models of self-action and interaction and shifting entirely the locus of evaluation. If he is calling for the dissection of anthropological theory and methodology he is also at the same time calling for a dissection in the area of mental health research, particularly as it plays on or pertains to interpretation of deviant behavior of American Indians.

Geertz (1968:20) likewise calls for a revision of this sort of evaluation and contends that social scientists must give up their view of people as "layers." Geertz referred to this as the "stratigraphic" approach, where science studies people as though they were layers of processes and subsequently views them as a composite of levels. Geertz states:

As one analyzes man one peels off layer after layer. Each such layer being complete and irreducible in itself revealing another quite different sort of layer underneath. Strip off motley forms of culture and one finds structural and functional irregularities of social organization. Peel off these in turn and one finds underlying psychological factors... pull off psychological factors and what is left but biological foundations.

Like Murdock, Geertz recognizes the rigidity with which methodological approaches and theory can lock one into localizing one's efforts in explaining behavior. The end products both claim results in nothing less than a metaphorical investigation of human behavior which is certainly not science. Geertz, as an alternative, recommends that humanity be defined not by an appeal to some innate predisposition or some "actual behavior alone" but rather as a link between the way the former is transformed into the latter. He states, "It is man's career, in its characteristic source, that we can discern, however dimly, his nature." In short, he is suggesting that the development and growth of a person be studied as a result of the simultaneous influence of internal and external processes. The only way the two can be separated is by abstracting one from the other. They cannot, however, be studied independently of each other.

The criticisms of using the self-action model are partly applicable to the interaction model because one of the inherent components is the organism itself. The organism is still acting of itself in the interaction approach, but social systems and culture are seen as influential vicissitudes and hence are separate from the organism.

From a conceptual framework, the implicit assumption of separating the individual from culture has created some confusion. Social scientists argue over which of the two has more influence on the nature of persons. Some hold that social phenomena result from the individual's innate predispositions, while others stress the possibility that the individual is simply a recipient of culture. Others hold that certain processes "push" the individual while others suggest that certain "external" factors "pull" the person. Each, of course, results in behavior. Both views are one-sided and are really still altered modification of the self-action model (see Sherif and Sherif 1969).

It should be obvious that the social scientist, in attempting to study the intricacies of a person's nature, cannot separate the observer from what is being observed. Social scientists must disavow any approach which implies that an individual acts on an environment or the environment acts on a person. Each one acts through the other. Dewey and Bentley (1949:132) state: "The interactional treatment entered [social science] inquiry just about the time it was being removed from its basic position by the physical sciences from which it was copied." It is apparent that the treatment is still intact. Yet the criticisms of its utility value are increasing primarily due to the rising number of researchable issues that for some reason do not fit the parameters of the interaction approach. An alternative approach must be developed.

## THE ECOSYTEMS ANALYSIS MATRIX – AN ALTERNATIVE MODEL

What, then, are we to do with this confusing array of biomedical, psychological, historical, social, and cultural variables that are relevant to issues concerning American Indians and mental health? It almost seems that there are far too many "answers" rather than approaches. How are we to organize and make sense of, interrelate, and use this wealth of data despite the view of Murdock that it is presently metaphorical. We believe a beginning can be made by using a comprehensive ecological approach and systems analysis technique.

The partial, theoretical perspective for this technique is derived from the more contemporary concerns with the field of general ecology. The word "ecology," as such, was originally developed by Haeckel in 1866 to refer to the general relationship between organisms and their environments. For the greater part of the twentieth century "ecology" was concentrated in the biological sciences, where the concern was primarily with plants and lower-order animals (see Woodbury 1954). Man, as an element of concern within the discipline, entered in the 1930's, which subsequently led to a fragmentation of the discipline's elements (see Theodorson 1961). More recently, however, human ecology has emerged as a recognizable and creditable concern and has been included in the general field of ecology. The pervasiveness of the field can be seen in the fact that it has come to represent a broad area with its focus on comprehensive attacks of large-scale problems. Phillipson (1966:1) relates:

Ecology is that branch of science which deals with the relationship between living things and their physical environment together with all the other living organisms within it. Organisms and the physical environment in which they exist form what for convenience, is termed an ecosystem.

It is this latter term, ecosystem, that offers the essential perspective for the alternative model.

The study and investigation of an ecosystem suggest that it cannot be studied by any one discipline or METHODOLOGY alone, but rather it requires an interdisciplinary coordinated effort. Participation and concerted involvement must come from the physical, biological, psychological, and sociocultural disciplines complete with their methodological and statistical perspectives developed to study phenomena. It would seem that orienting knowledge in this undertaking would, in a word, be overwhelming. Hood (1968:1) relates, "However overwhelming the task, there seems to be little argument today about the necessity for comprehensive attacks on the component problems of the 'ecological crisis'."

One convenient way to set the perspective of an interdisciplinary effort would be to establish *a priori* an appropriate "level of integration." This level would define the parameters or limitations of the system to be investigated. The philosophical rationale for this orientation has already been established (see Egler 1942; Reiss 1954; Dobzhansky 1963; Buckley 1968). Riply and Buechner (1967) offer a most concise discussion of the concept as it relates to any ecosystem. They state:

Biological entities... represent levels of integration in which the whole is more than the sum of its parts. A population... [is an] attribute that emerge[s] at the population level of integration through the interactions of the individual members. By integrating the population... with all other kinds of living organisms and the nonliving, or physical components... a more complex level of organization emerges, to which the term ECOSYSTEM has been applied. An ecosystem, or ecological system, functions as an interacting whole in nature. A single cell and its microenvironment, whether free-living or part of a tissue system, may be conceptualized as an ecosystem. ...Tissues, organs, organisms, populations of organisms of a single kind, interspecific populations of plants or animals and biocommunities constitute biological entities at levels of increasing complexity; each can be considered an ecosystem if the total environment is added as an integral part of the system (Riply and Buechner 1967:1193–1194).

Odum (1969) offers a more succinct definition of ecosystem or ecological system. It is "a unit of biological organization made up of all of the organisms in a given area [that is, 'community'] interacting with the physical environment so that a flow of energy leads to characteristic trophic structure and material cycles within the system."

The appropriateness of a level of integration doesn't provide one with much difficulty nor does the task of setting that level. What does appear troublesome is deciding on how inclusive and comprehensive the level should be. Moreover, a component of the level may be included for which there may not exist a research methodology or an exact way to assess or measure its relationship or significance within the system. If that is the case, then the researchers must decide either to eliminate the component at the risk of losing the effect it may be having on the system or develop an appropriate methodology and assessment scheme, again at the risk of not knowing the subtle impact this in itself would have on the system or component.

The inclusion of the word "system" within "ecosystem" offers an appropriate means of control of the parameters. A system, according to Scott (1967:27), is defined as "a set of components with identifiable attributes, among which relationships persist over a period of time." One can expect little difficulty in defining the limits of a system at a biological or political level. The difficulty arises when one attempts the definition with subcultures or subgroups within a more general system such as an indigenous tribe or an ethnic community. Tascano (1964) and Deutsch (1964) suggest a possible method by approaching the system from what they refer to as a "transaction flow" theory. Essentially, they suggest, through an elaborate procedure, interfacing one system with another. The parameters of the interfacing process would produce a more limiting definition of the system itself.

To develop an alternative model it would appear that the most logical step would be to integrate the orientation of the ecological approach, the methodology of systems analysis and the level of integration technique together with the primary embodiments of transaction flow theory.

The integration of these concepts presents itself with a partial approach to resolving the problems of any ecosystem analysis. An initial step can be taken by separating the total body of variables into two mutually exclusive and exhaustive categories, namely "environmental factors" and "human activities." Taken together they would form a two-dimensional matrix and would resemble the "Map of Culture" developed by Hall (1959). By doing this, every possible combination of human and environmental variables can be assigned to a single cell within a matrix. The categories within each set must be exhaustive enough to include the total class of variables within that cell. This step would reduce considerably the hazard of noninclusiveness of some attribute of the categories and thus contribute to comprehensiveness.

There are many possible sets of categories that could be utilized and it is this very problem that proved an initial stumbling block in developing an alternative model.[1]

Hall (1959) developed a convenient set of ten categories for classifying human categories. These categories form the columns of the matrix and are labeled appropriately "Human Activities" (see Figure 1). Woodbury (1954) developed a comparable set of categories for classifying the other axis of the two-dimensional matrix, "Environmental Factors" which, when added to the matrix, form the rows (see Figure 1).

Taking these two categories together and ordering them in matrix form an 8 by 10 matrix emerges which can be conceived as a generalized model of any ecosystem involving humans-plus-environment.

However, this is just a model of the ecosystem itself; it makes no provision for handling the multidisciplinary efforts required in studying the system or assessing its impact on the system under investigation. A major hazard in ecosystems analysis is in conceiving the total system too narrowly. The investigators themselves and their intrusion into the system under investigation must become an integral part of the total system's conception. All must be conceptually attuned to the interrelationships of data gathering. Furthermore, the interrelations of specialists representing various science areas and of the data they produce must

---

[1]   In the spring of 1968, the late William R. Hood, then visiting Professor of Psychology at the University of Oklahoma and John M. Steele and Joseph E. Trimble (then doctoral candidates), struggled with this problem. The credit for developing and pursuing this line of thinking belongs solely with Dr. Hood. Hood and Steele continued to explore the matrix from a 'systems' perspective, making refinements along the way while Trimble explored the theoretical applications. Hood, together with Steele and Trimble continued to explore the development and implications of the model until his untimely death in the fall of 1972. Much of the earlier material in this section was developed by him and explored at varying levels (see Hood 1968, 1969, 1970, 1971, 1972).

become a systematic component of the research design if the perpetual problem of "unrelated information" is to be avoided. It is necessary, therefore, that the matrix be expanded into a third dimension by addition of four levels of methodological analysis.

The "levels of analysis" notion has been around for some time. It was employed by Kroeber (1917) in connection with notions of the "super-organic." In attempts at handling massive and complex data coming from many sources, Bidney (1947), Hoebel (1949), White (1949), Sherif and Sherif (1969), and others have suggested and used variations of the concept. Buckley (1968) has found it convenient to order the content of his "systems" book by "level of analysis." The ordering of various science areas has been consistent, though the justification for the order was varied (see White 1949). The needs of the theorist may determine which levels are employed. For example, Yinger (1966) finds it convenient to separate social and cultural, and he has no need for the physical level of analysis. However, in general, the categories are ordered — physical, biological, psychological, and sociocultural — roughly the same order in which the sciences have progressed and developed historically.

It is probably unnecessary to resort to justifications of ordering in terms of history, complexity, or difficulty in retaining objectivity as the sciences approach man as an object of scientific study. It is easy, though, to document the greater ease and facility of translation of concepts within a "family" of related science areas (e.g. anthropology-sociology, physics-chemistry, anatomy-physiology, etc.). Translations across the borders of science families become more difficult (e.g. between physics and anthropology, or between anatomy and sociology). The conceptual tools developed in various science areas tend to form clusters within which translations are relatively easy and between which translations are relatively difficult. Transaction flow analysis as developed by Deutsch (1964) and Tascano (1964) should support this common observation.

If levels of analysis are added, each cell in the 10 by 8 by 4 matrix thus constructed represents some combination of specifiable behavioral and environmental variables under study at a prescribed level of analysis. The unity and integrity of the phenomena under examination is recognized and preserved, and the tasks of analysis and synthesis are facilitated.

The third dimension of the matrix may be more carefully defined as shown in Table 2.

A major advantage in employing "levels of analysis" notions is cross-checking findings for improved consensual validity (Sherif and Sherif

Table 2.   Third dimension of the Ecosystems Analysis Matrix

| Level of analysis | Object of study | Example disciplines |
| --- | --- | --- |
| Physical | Nonorganic world | Physics, chemistry, geology, etc. |
| Biological | Organisms and their part-systems | Botany, zoology, genetics, etc. |
| Psychological | Behavior of individual organisms | Psychology, psychiatry, ethology, etc. |
| Sociocultural | Men and their products | Anthropology, economics, sociology, linguistics, political science, etc. |

1969). For example, if a specialist working at the sociocultural level finds that the values of a group are changing, but another working at the psychological level finds that their individual attitudes are not changing, they just cannot both be right. Values (social norms) and attitudes

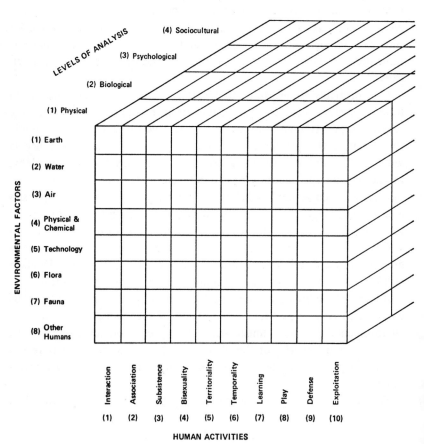

Figure 1.   The Ecosystems Analysis Matrix

are merely the collective and distributive aspects of a unitary phenomenon. Of course, translations between levels of analysis cannot always be made with comparable assurance.

The three-dimensional matrix provides a generalized, conceptual model that can be fitted to the analysis of any ecosystem. As used in the investigation of any particular ecosystem, cells will vary in importance and significance. For example, artificial environments in space (See Bresler 1966) would require greater emphasis at the physical and biological levels of analysis. Natural, terrestrial environments in which human culture and society loom large as determinants require emphasis on investigations at psychological and sociocultural levels. However, all cells will be meaningful in the analysis of any ecosystem involving humans-plus-environment.

The Ecosystems Analysis Matrix as depicted in Figure 1 consists of 320 cells. Each of the three dimensions of the matrix is labeled according to the following categories: human activities, environmental factors, and levels of analysis. Each of the components within the categories can be identified by a counting sequence. Thus, any one of the 320 cells can be identified by a set of three sequential numbers. The first number would indicate the human activity, (i.e. any number from 1 to 10); the second number in the sequence would identify the environmental factor, (i.e. any number from 1 to 8); and the third number would indicate the level of analysis, (i.e. any number from 1 to 4). For example, the upper, left, front cell would be 1-1-1 (i.e. interaction-earth-physical), and the cell at the diagonally opposite corner of the cube would be 10-8-4 (i.e. exploitation-other humans-sociocultural). With this counting sequence one can identify through the number's coordinates the topic of investigation, the level of analysis at which it is to be approached, the relevant fields of knowledge, and the disciplines and specialists to be involved. From these one can derive the necessary logistics for that part of the total operation, and the facilities and equipment required. It should be pointed out that this model differs from most systems models in that it models not just the system under investigation, but the system and the analysis of the system under different successional states.

Figure 2 depicts a vertical slice of the matrix taken at the human activity of subsistence (3) and the environmental factors of earth and water (1–2) at all four levels of analysis (i.e. 3–1; 2–1; 2.3.4). Each of the eight cells is numbered accordingly; a brief description of the possible variables for exploration included in each cell is also listed. For example, in cell 3–2–4, the social and religious sanctions of the use of water could be tied to individual differences of attitudes towards water (cell

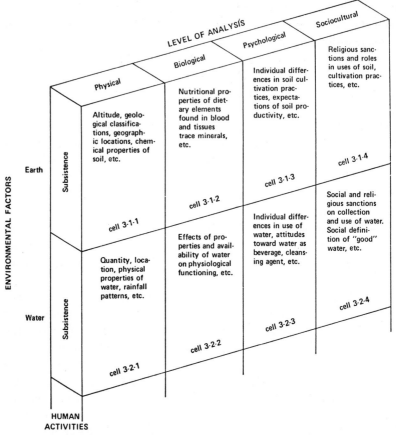

Figure 2.   Description of the content of a block of cells extracted from the Ecosystems Analysis Matrix

3–2–3), which also could be closely related to the water's availability (cell 3–2–2) and its physical properties (cell 3–2–1) as a function of its location. Thus, water as a source of subsistence could be more thoroughly understood if examined through the ecosystems approach.

Figure 3 is a more detailed examination of a particular configuration of cells within the matrix. Five contiguous cells have been extracted from the matrix and the various intercellular relationships are depicted. This cohort of the matrix is restricted to the sociocultural and psychological level of analysis rather than the physical and biological. In investigating human activities in natural or terrestrial environments, elements of human culture and society have proportionately more impact than, say, the actual physical environment itself, although its emphasis should not be totally discounted. If mental health of American

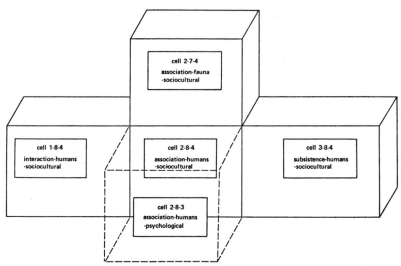

Figure 3. An example of a set of contiguous cells extracted from the Ecosystems Analysis Matrix

Indians is the concern, then it would be more logical to emphasize the sociocultural and psychological levels of analysis; the time it would take to explore the processes of mental health from physical and biological levels could well exceed the amount of information it would yield.

A distribution between the human activities of interaction and association should be made at this point (columns 1 and 2). As was previously indicated, the categories for human activities were adapted from Hall (1959). His model was developed to include the internal characteristics within cultures. To include the influence of and the relationships of ingroups (a cultural group) with outgroups, it was necessary to collapse Hall's categories of "association" and "interaction" into "association" alone. Thus, those cells whose coordinates are "association" (2) and "other humans" (8) contain data applicable to ingroup activities. Conversely, data concerned with intergroup relations is contained within the cells for "interaction" (1) and "other humans" (8).

Examples of the content of each of the contiguous cells within the cohort are discussed below.

*Cell 2–8–4 (the Center Cell in Figure 3):*
*Association (2)-Other Humans (8)-Sociocultural Level of Analysis (4)*

This is the primary cell for ingroup data (intrasocietal, intracultural).

All social structure and culture not related specifically to one of the other categories of Human Activities are included here. Some examples of structural factors would be society, government, caste, class, community, family, status, and roles. Normative cultural factors such as world-view, value systems (implicit and explicit) and communication (including vocal qualifiers and kinesics as well as language) would also be included here. Structure-to-value relations defining range of tolerable behavior would bring conceptions of conformity and deviation into the picture.

*Cell 2–7–4 (Top, Center Cell in Figure 3):*
*Association(2)-Fauna (7)-Sociocultural Level of Analysis (4)*

The content of this cell would include cultural definitions of proper breeding, care, and use of domesticated animals (relations and maintenace rather than subsistence or exploitation, for example). Social regulations of the nature of human-domesticated animal relations would be included (e.g. religion-related symbolism about animals). Cultural definitions of "domesticated" and "wild" animals would relate to the regulation of behavior (avoidance, approach, attack) toward species of animals defined as feral.

*Cell 3–8–4 (Cell on Right in Figure 3):*
*Subsistence (3)-Other Humans (8)-Sociocultural Level of Analysis (4)*

The content of this cell involves an aspect of intergroup relations – subsistence (economic) relations with nonmembers of the culture. Included would be sociocultural regulations of trading relations with outgroups and their members, particularly as foodstuffs are involved. Also, economic patterns of barter, exchange, money use, etc. as they relate to cooking utensils, food preparation, etc., and infusion of cultivation, gathering, and hunting practices from outgroups.

*Cell 1–8–4 (Cell on Left in Figure 3):*
*Interaction (1)-Other Humans (8)-Sociocultural Level of Analysis (4)*

Intergroup relations (intersocietal, intercultural) provide a focus for the content of this cell. In relatively closed, isolated ecosystems, this cell would require less emphasis than in the case of more open systems maintaining relations with a large number of outgroups. Included here would be the social distance scale, proscriptions, and prescriptions about relations with outgroups members (e.g. prejudice, discrimination, sexual relations, exogamy, etc.), cultural definitions of and expectations about characteristics and behavior of outgroupers, communication patterns between ingroup and outgroup, definitions of "negotiator" roles, etc.

*Cell 2–8–3 (Front Cell in Figure 3):*
*Association (2)-Other Humans (8)-Psychological Level of Analysis (3)*

Psychological aspects (e.g. attitudes, perception, judgment, etc.) of all the social and cultural content of cell 2-8-4 would be included here, for example, role perception and role behavior at the psychological level, permitting cross-checking of findings at different levels of analysis for improved validity. Also included would be individual differences with respect to perceptions and attitudes toward social structures and organizations, social norms and cultural values within the group.

The Ecosystems Analysis Matrix affords one the opportunity of examining the relationships between cells. The opportunity is especially valuable on the "levels of analysis" dimension, because a research team could cross-check their findings at various "levels" and thus improve the consensual validity of the data. More importantly, for example, one human activity could be examined simultaneously with one or more environmental factors at one or more levels of analysis. A pooling of the resulting data might reveal that the variables were more closely correlative than suspected, thus providing the research team with a greater insight into the phenomenon in question.

The possible relationships of the cells within the cohort in Figure 3 are discussed below.

*Relations between Cells 2–8–4 and 2–7–4:*
*Association (2)-Fauna and Other Humans (7.8)-Sociocultural Level (4)*

Included here would be social norms or cultural values (e.g. approval-disapproval) with respect to how other known peoples define and relate to "wild" and "domesticated" animals; shared attitudes about use of horses and vehicles by other groups as this relates to transportation habits of the ingroup; and group response to outgroup activities and practices with respect to protection from insects or insect-control programs.

*Relations between Cells 2–8–4 and 1–8–4:*
*Association and Interaction-(2.1)-Other Humans(8)-Sociocultural Level(4)*

Here would be included consequences of ingroup structure (or lack of) and social norms for the nature and flow of intergroup relations; perception of outgroup social organization and values in relation to those of the ingroup; and influence of ingroup communication patterns on the nature of intergroup relations.

*Relations between Cells 2–8–4 and 3–8–4:*
*Association and Subsistence-(2.3)-Other Humans (8)-Sociocultural Level (4)*

Included would be relations of ingroup social structures and cultural values to perceived outgroup economic practices, shared attitudes toward the money economy, packaged foodstuffs, and outgroup agricultural practices, hunting and gathering techniques, etc.

*Relations between Cells 2–8–4 and 2–8–3:*
*Association (2)-Other Humans (8)-Sociocultural and Psychological Levels (3.4)*

Included would be individual perceptions of and attitudes toward social structures, institutions, cultural values, and communication patterns of outgroups. Also included would be interpersonal relations with outgroup members (whether or not regulated by ingroup norms) and dispersion of individual attitudes inside and outside the range of tolerable behavior as defined by ingroup values with respect to outgroup associational-organizational factors.

It would appear that the cube exhaustively defines the content of any ecosystem as well as the process of any system under investigation. Yet there remains another dimension, one that attempts to handle the progress or change of any ecosystem. Quite conveniently, that dimension is time or "ecosystems succession." Time, in this instance, should not be confused with the human activity of temporality (column 6 in Figure 1), for that refers to a person's relationship with time in a normative and directive sense. Specifically, it refers to the manner in which time is used (or not used) by a person or a group (i.e. culture, society, etc.). For example, varying cultural groups have different criteria for identifying time (e.g. seasonal or climatic relationships, phases of the moon, migratory habits of fauna, variations in the developmental process of flora, solar variations, circadian rhythms, etc.), where each determines to a large extent when and where (and perhaps how) an activity will take place. Time as a dimension in the EAM (Ecosystems Analysis Matrix) refers to an interacting or transacting set of processes through and across some *a priori*-defined temporal spectrum. Odum (1969) refers to it as "ecological succession" and defines it as:

1) An orderly process of community development that is reasonably directional ...predictable; 2) it results from modification of the physical environment by the community; that is, succession is community-controlled even though the physical environment determines the pattern, the rate of change, and often sets limits as to how far development can go; [and] 3) it culminates in a stabilized ecosystem in which maximum biomass (or high information content) and symbiotic function between organisms are maintained per unit of available energy flow (Odum 1969:262).

Any ecosystem is constantly in a state of flux and thus could well be in a particular (and peculiar) stage of development at the time it is being investigated. Production, food chains, life cycles, etc. are all parts of successive development and hence are changing. Odum (1969) states "The degree of absolute change, the rate of change, and the time required to reach a steady state may vary not only with different climatic and physiographic situations but also with different ecosystem attributes in the same physical environment." Most of the social and behavioral research, past and present, has either ignored or neglected the effect that successive development has on variables. Even the use of the traditional pre-/post-methodological design leaves much to be desired despite its claims to the effect that it purportedly controls for certain maturational or developmental changes across time. The analysis of any ecosystem must, of necessity, consider and include the analysis of maturation or development. The diversity of change could shed much more additional light on the ecosystem and lead the investigators to a more conclusive understanding of the process.

To include the process of change and "ecosystems succession" it is necessary to depict the EAM in a temporal spectrum. Figure 4 represents this attempt.

To illustrate and further substantiate the need for the inclusion of "ecosystems succession" in the EAM two sets of contiguous cells or

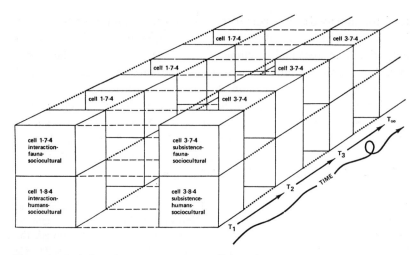

Figure 4.   Isolation of two connected intercellular cohorts showing possible systematic relationship as a function of investigation across a temporal spectrum

cohorts have been isolated (cells 1–7–4 and 1–8–4, or cohort 1, and cells 3–7–4 and 3–8–4, or cohort 2). Rather than attempt to illustrate the process with data pertaining to mental health, the basic notion of subsistence was used. To attempt to use mental health processes might have proven unmanageable at this point in the EAM's development. That problem can be looked at much later.

Many social systems rely heavily on the existence and availability of fauna for subsistence, so much so that at certain phylogenetic levels the dependency tends to be reciprocal and is based primarily on the law of supply and demand. For example, humans eat fish, the fish eat plankton and frogs feed on insects, the insects and plankton, in turn, feed on microorganisms and they feed on themselves. All of this depends heavily on the availability of the other, and each species or phylum seems to reproduce just enough so that the residue can be shared with the remainder left to continue the process. Intervention at any one level tends to offset the natural cycle of reciprocity to the extent that alternatives are sought; offsetting this apparent homeostatic process can and has, in many cases, led to the extinction of some species.

In an effort to insure the perpetuation of the human species, agriculture and the domestication of feral animals were developed. One would have to admit that the technology and ingenuity involved in both have more than insured the survival of humanity. Nevertheless, an increased awareness of the behavior of lower-order species and flora still reflects the notion of strong interdependency of one on the other. Cohort 1 (cells 1–7–4 and 1–8–4) at T1 (time one) attempts to illustrate this. For humans there exist cultural definitions and proscriptions about inter-group behavior extending from prescribed role expectations to inter-personal conflict that could resemble that of fauna. Investigating the two (i.e. humans and fauna) conjointly at a sociocultural level of analysis would bear this out, but more importantly it may reveal unique inter-group relationships that one may have with another. These relationships, however, are never static, and subsequent investigations at T2, T3, etc. would demonstrate how the relationships might covary across time. That covariation may turn out to be quite predictable and in retrospect the investigators may turn up data infinitely more valuable than that which has been garnered from "one-shot" studies.

Quite the same can be said for cohort 2 (cells 3–7–4 and 3–8–4). Subsistence as a human activity with other humans examined conjointly with fauna could reveal comparable behavioral patterns when studied at the sociocultural levels of analysis. Food gathering and hunting practices, bartering patterns, population densities and scarcities, and economic exchange may resemble each other for all species but may vary in one degree or another between and within each. But the seasons of the year as well as other possible contributing variables may well serve to change the patterns of interaction. If there is a drought, for example, the first to find water may not be the one who drinks first. Moreover, species may put aside outside natural conflicts at the only water hole in a barren area. And the seasons may well have a great deal to do with the amount of water that is available. Certainly the intergroup and ingroup relation-ships will vary as a function of water, for its amount will always vary. Thus, an investigation of both faunal and human activities must be examined in succession.

Combining the data generated by examining the two cohorts is the next step. Admittedly this appears to be an overwhelming task from an analytic perspective, but with the advent of increasing changes in computer technology the time needed to analyze the vast amount of data is greatly reduced. In this instance, investigators might produce data sets that could lend a much greater understanding of feeding the world's population and at the same time thwart any possible threat that could disrupt the systematic dependency of one species for another.

In short, the addition of the "ecosystem succession" component to the EAM may well be as essential as the inclusion of the notion of "level of analysis." "Ecosystems succession" is geared to analyzing trends preserving the particular level of integration of environmental factors and human activities. Its inclusion in the EAM is specifically to provide a check for, and an accounting of developmental stages. Odum (1969) suggests that such stages of change can be anticipated in community energetics, community structure, life history, nutrient cycling, selection pressures, and overall homeostasis. Not to include some of these considerations in any experimental design certainly would contribute invalidity to the decision-making process concerning the hypotheses as well as the generalizability of the results.

The EAM with its four components is thus complete, but let it quickly be said that its development is far from finished. The theories from which it was developed are incomplete in themselves as are the methodologies, experimental and statistical, that would be used to investigate any level of integration. The true test of the EAM rests with its implementation and use in the investigation of any component of an ecosystem, be it social, psychological, physiological, botanical, zoological, physical or historical, or any combination of these fields of study.

Finally, as we organize and interpret our massive data by means of this suggested or some other, better technique, what do we do? This is not merely an academic matter, an intellectual exercise; it is deadly serious. Disproportionate problems related to mental health among American Indian are apparently increasing in spite of our best efforts. How can that be, considering the appreciable expenditure of funds, energy, and genuine concern? Our efforts have been largely to control — to introduce negative feedback loops into the system through enforcement, treatment, and supporting research.

It must be that, somehow, the control system is being overpowered by some sort of positive feedback loops which amplify rather than control deviation. The implication of the theoretical model introduced here may well contribute to increasing, rather than decreasing the size of the very problems we are trying to deal with. We are well aware of this disturbing possibility.

## REFERENCES

ALEXANDER, T., R. ANDERSON
  1957   Children in a society under stress. *Behavioral Science* 2:46–55.
BERREMAN, G. D.
  1956   Drinking patterns of the Aleuts. *Quarterly Journal of Studies on Alcohol* 17:503–514.
BIDNEY, D.
  1947   On the concept of culture and some cultural fallacies. *American Anthropologist* 46:35–44.

BOYER, L. B., B. KLOPFER, R. M. BOYER, F. B. BRAWER, H. KAWAI
  1965  Effects of acculturation on the personality traits of the old people of
        the Mescalero and Chiricahua Apaches: Rorschach report. *Interna-
        tional Journal of Social Psychiatry* 23:264–270.

BRESLER, J. B.
  1966  *Human ecology: collected readings.* Reading, Massachusetts: Addison-
        Wesley.

BRILL, A. A.
  1913  Piblotoq or hysteria among Peary's Eskimos. *Journal of Nervous and
        Mental Disease* 40:514–520.

BRYDE, J. F.
  1966  "Indian education and mental health." Paper read at a meeting of the
        Association on American Indian Affairs, New York, N.Y., November
        14–15, 1966.

BUCKLEY, W.
  1968  *Modern systems research for the behavioral scientist: a sourcebook.*
        Chicago: Aldine.

CURLEY, R.
  1967  Drinking patterns of the Mescalero Apache. *Quarterly Journal of
        Studies on Alcohol* 28:116–131.

DEUTSCH, K. M.
  1964  "Transaction flows as indicators of political cohesion," in *The integra-
        tion of political communities.* Edited by P. E. Jacob and J. V. Toscano,
        75–97. Philadelphia: Lippincott.

DEVEREAUX, G.
  1948  The function of alcohol in Mohave society. *Quarterly Journal of
        Studies on Alcohol* 9:207–541.
  1956  "Normal and abnormal: the key problem of psychiatric anthropol-
        ogy," in *Some uses of anthropology: theoretical and applied.* Edited by
        J. B. Casagrande and T. Gladwin. Washington, D.C.: The Anthro-
        pological Society of Washington.

DEWEY, J., A. F. BENTLEY
  1949  *Knowing and the known.* Boston: Beacon Press.

DOBZHANSKY, T.
  1963  Evolutionary and population genetics. *Science* 142:1131–1135.

DOZIER, E. P.
  1966  Problem drinking among American Indians: the role of sociocultural
        deprivation. *Quarterly Journal of Studies on Alcohol* 27:72–87.

EGLER, F. E.
  1942  Vegetation as an object of study. *Philosophy of Science* 9(3):245–260.

ERIKSON, E. H.
  1939  Observations on Sioux education. *Journal of Psychology* 7:101–156.
  1963  *Childhood and society.* New York: W. W. Norton.

FERGUSON, F. N.
  1968  Navaho drinking: some tentative hypotheses. *Human Organization*
        27:159–167.

FRANK, P.
  1957  *Philosophy of science.* Englewood Cliffs: Prentice-Hall.

GEERTZ, C.
   1968    "The impact of the concept of culture on the concept of man," in *Man in adaptation: the cultural present.* Edited by Y. A. Cohen. Chicago: Aldine.
GOODENOUGH, W. H.
   1970    *Description and comparison in cultural anthropology.* Chicago: Aldine.
GRAVES, T.
   1967    Acculturation, access, and alcohol in a triethnic community. *American Anthropologist* 69:306–321.
GUSSOW, Z.
   1960    "Piblotoq (hysteria) among the Polar Eskimo: an ethnopsychiatric study," in *Psychoanalysis and the social sciences.* Edited by W. Muensterberger. New York: International Universities Press.
HALL, E. T.
   1959    *The silent language.* New York: Doubleday.
HAMER, J.
   1965    Acculturation stress and the functions of alcohol among the Potawatomi. *Quarterly Journal of Studies on Alcohol* 26:285–302.
HARE, A. P.
   1962    *Handbook of small group research.* New York: Free Press of Glencoe.
HARTMANN, H., E. KRIS, R. M. LOEWENSTEIN
   1951    "Some psychoanalytic comments on culture and personality," in *Psychoanalysis and culture.* Edited by G. B. Wilbur and W. Muensterberger, 3–31. New York: International Universities Press.
HERREID, C. F., J. R. HERREID
   1966    Differences in MMPI scores in native and nonnative Alaskans. *Journal of Social Psychology* 70:191–198.
HESSLER, R., P. NEW
   1972    Research as a process of exchange. *American Sociologist* 7:13–14.
HOEBEL, F. A.
   1949    *Man in the primitive world.* New York: McGraw-Hill.
HONIGMANN, J. J.
   1949    *Culture and ethos of Kaska society.* Yale University Publications in Anthropology 40. New Haven.
   1954    *Culture and personality.* New York: Harper and Row.
HONIGMANN, J. J., I. HONIGMANN
   1953    Some patterns of child rearing among the Great Whale River Eskimo. *Anthropological Papers of the University of Alaska* 2:31–47.
   1965    How Baffin Island Eskimo have learned to use alcohol. *Social Forces* 44:73–83.
HOOD, W. R.
   1968    "Scientific research and social responsibility." Paper presented at the Psychiatry and Behavioral Science Colloquium, The University of Oklahoma Health Sciences Center, Oklahoma City, Oklahoma, September.
   1969    "Impact of institutionalization on the aged." Unpublished manuscript. The University of Oklahoma Health Sciences Center.
   1970    "The Tarahumara Indians: an example of ecosystem analysis," in *Interdisciplinary approaches to understanding the American Indian.*

Chaired by J. Trimble. Symposium presented at the meeting of the Southwestern Psychological Association, St. Louis, April, 1970.

1971 "A bridge over troubled waters: ecology of Indian biosocial action," in *Research implications for native American social action*. Chaired by J. Trimble. Symposium presented at the meeting of the American Psychological Association, Washington, September, 1971.

1972 "Dirty words: genetic differences in response to alcohol," in *Taking the edge off of reality: alcohol consumption and the American Indian experience*. Chaired by J. Trimble. Symposium presented at the meeting of the American Psychological Association, Honolulu, September, 1972.

HORTON, D.
1943 The functions of alcohol in primitve societies: a cross-cultural study. *Quarterly Journal of Studies on Alcohol* 4:199–320.

HOYT, E. A.
1962 Young Indians: some problems and issues of mental hygiene. *Mental Hygiene* 46:41–47 (January).

HSU, F. L. K., *editor*
1972 *Psychological anthropology*. Cambridge, Massachusetts: Schenkman.

HURT, W. R., R. M. BROWN
1965 Social drinking patterns of the Yankton Sioux. *Human Organization* 24:222–230.

JEWELL, D. P.
1952 A case of a "psychotic" Navajo Indian male. *Human Organization* 11 (1):32–36.

KAPLAN, B.
1954 A study of Rorschach responses in four cultures. *Papers of the Peabody Museum of American Archaeology and Ethnology* 42:2.

KAPLAN, B.,*editor*
1961 *Studying personality cross-culturally*. New York: Harper and Row.

KARDINER, A.
1939 *The individual and his society*. New York: Columbia University Press.
1945 "The concept of basic personality structure as an operational tool in the social sciences," in *The science of man in the world crisis*. Edited by R. Linton, 107–122. New York: Columbia University Press.

KLUCKHOHN, C.
1954 "Culture and behavior," in *Handbook of social psychology*. Edited by G. Lindzey. Cambridge, Massachusetts: Addison-Wesley.

KROEBER, A. L.
1917 The superorganic. *American Anthropologist* 19:163–213.

KRUSH, T. P., J. W. BJORK, P. S. SINDALL, J. NELLE
1965 "Some thoughts on the formation of personality disorder: study of an Indian boarding school population." Paper read at the 121st annual meeting of the American Psychiatric Association, New York, New York, May 3–7, 1965.

KUNITZ, S. J., J. E. LEVY, M. EVERETT
1969 Alcoholic cirrhosis among the Navajo. *Quarterly Journal of Studies on Alcohol* 30:672–685.

KUTTNER, R. E., A. B. LORINEZ
  1967    Alcoholism and addiction in urbanized Sioux Indians. *Mental Hygiene*
          51:530–542.
LANDES, R.
  1938    The abnormal among the Ojibwa Indians. *Journal of Abnormal and
          Social Psychology* 33:14–33.
LEMERT, E. M.
  1958    The use of alcohol in three Salish Indian tribes. *Quarterly Journal of
          Studies on Alcohol* 19:90–107.
LEVY, D. M.
  1935    Sibling rivalry studies in children of primitive groups. *American
          Journal of Orthopsychiatry* 9:205–214.
LEVY, J. E.
  1965    Navajo suicide. *Human Organization* 24:308–318.
LEVY, J. E., S. J. KUNITZ
  1971    Indian reservations, anomie, and social pathologies. *Southwestern
          Journal of Anthropology* 27 (2):97–127 (Summer).
LEWIN, K.
  1935    *Dynamic theory of personality*. New York: McGraw-Hill.
LINCOLN, J. S.
  1935    *The dream in primitive cultures*. Baltimore: Williams and Wilkins.
LURIE, N. O.
  1971    The world's oldest on-going protest demonstration: North American
          Indian drinking patterns. *Pacific Historical Review* 40:311–332.
MAC GREGOR, G.
  1946    *Warriors without weapons*. Chicago: University of Chicago Press.
MALINOWSKI, B.
  1927    *Sex and repression in savage society*. London: Humanities Press.
MARTIN, H. W., S. S. SUTKER, R. L. LEON, W. M. HALES
  1968    Mental health of eastern Oklahoma Indians: an exploration. *Human
          Organization* 27 (4):308–315 (Winter).
MOHATT, G.
  1972    "The sacred water: the quest for personal power through drinking
          among the Teton Sioux," in *The drinking man: alcohol and human
          motivation*. Edited by David C. McClelland, W. S. Davis, R. Kalin,
          and E. Wanner, 261–275.
MURDOCK, G. P.
  1971    "Anthropology's mythology," in *Proceedings of the Royal Anthropol-
          ogical Institute of Great Britain and Ireland for 1971*. London: Royal
          Anthropological Institute of Great Britain and Ireland.
NADEL, S. F.
  1951    *Foundations of social anthropology*. Glencoe, Illinois: Free Press.
ODUM, E. P.
  1969    The strategy of ecosystem development. *Science* 164 (April 18):262–
          270.
OPLER, M. K.
  1956    *Culture, psychiatry, and human values*. Springfield, Illinois: Charles
          C. Thomas.

PHILLIPSON, J.
1966    *Ecological energetics.* New York: St. Martin's Press.
REISS, B. F.
1954    "Physiological psychology," in *Areas of psychology.* Edited by F. L. Marcuse. New York: Harper and Row.
RIPLEY, S. D., H. K. BUECHNER
1967    Ecosystem science as a point of synthesis. *Daedalus* 96 (4):1192–1199 (Fall).
ROHEIM, G.
1950    *Psychoanalysis and anthropology.* New York: International Universities Press.
SAINDON, J. E.
1933    Mental disorders among the James Bay Cree. *Primitive Man: Quarterly Bulletin of the Catholic Anthropological Conference* 6 (1): 1–12 (January).
SASAKI, T. T.
1960    "Sources of mental stress in Indian acculturation," in *Emotional problems of the Indian students in boarding schools and related public schools.* Workshop Proceeding edited by John C. Cobb.
SASLOW, H. L.
1972    "Alcoholism: the family and child personality development of the Native American," in *Taking the edge off of reality: alcohol consumption and the American Indian experience.* Chaired by J. Trimble. Symposium presented at the meeting of the American Psychological Association, Honolulu, September.
SASLOW, H. L., M. J. HARROVER
1968    Research on psychosocial adjustment of Indian youth. *American Journal of Psychiatry* 125:2 (August).
SCOTT, A. M.
1967    *The functioning of the international political system.* New York: Macmillan.
SELIGMAN, C. G.
1923    Type dreams: a request. *Folklore* 34:376–378.
1932    Anthropological perspective and psychological theory. *Journal of the Royal Anthropological Institute* 62:193–228.
SHERIF, M., C. SHERIF
1969    *Social psychology.* New York: Harper and Row.
SINGER, M.
1961    "A survey of culture and personality theory and research," in *Studying personality cross-culturally.* Edited by B. Kaplan, 9–90. New York: Harper and Row.
SZASZ, T.
1961    *The myth of mental illness: foundations of a theory of personal conduct.* New York: Hoeber-Harper.
TASCANO, J. V.
1964    "Transaction flow analysis in metropolitan areas," in *The integration of political communities.* Edited by P. E. Jacob and J. V. Tascano. Philadelphia: Lippincott.

THEODORSON, G. A.
   1961   *Studies in human ecology.* New York: Harper and Row.
TOFFELMIER, G., K. LUOMALA
   1936   Dreams and dream interpretation of the Diegueno Indians of Southern California. *Psychoanalytic Quarterly* 2:195–225.
WALLACE, A. F. C.
   1952   The modal personality structure of the Tuscarora Indians as revealed by the Rorschach Test. *Bulletin of the Bureau of American Ethnology* 169.
   1958   Dreams and wishes of the soul: a type of psycho-analytic theory among seventeenth-century Iroquois. *American Anthropologist* 60:234–248.
   1972   "Mental illness, biology, and culture," in *Psychological anthropology.* Edited by Francis L. K. Hsu. Cambridge, Massachusetts: Schenkman.
WEINBERG, S. K.
   1952   *Society and personality disorders.* New York: Prentice-Hall.
WESTERMEYER, J.
   1972   Options regarding alcoholic use among the Chippewa. *American Journal of Orthopsychiatry* 42:398–403.
WHITE, L. A.
   1949   *The science culture.* New York: Farrar-Strauss.
WHITTAKER, J. O.
   1963   Alcohol and the Standing Rock Sioux tribe (II): psychodynamic and cultural factors in drinking. *Quarterly Journal of Studies on Alcohol* 24:80–90.
WILBUR, G. B., W. MUENSTERBERGER
   1951   *Psychoanalysis and culture.* New York: International Universities Press.
WILSON, T. P.
   1970   Conceptions of interaction and forms of sociological explanation. *American Sociological Review* 35 (4):697–710.
WOODBURY, A. M.
   1954   *Principles of general ecology.* New York: Blakiston.
YINGER, J. M.
   1966   *Toward a field theory of behavior.* New York: McGraw-Hill.

# "Brainwashing" as Therapeutic Technique in Contemporary Canadian Indian Spirit Dancing: a Case of Theory Building

WOLFGANG G. JILEK

The winter spirit dances are the major ritual activity of Salish-speaking Indians of the Pacific Coast of North America. The Salish Indians regard winter as the appropriate time for ceremonies, when vitality is weakened, to be strengthened again by the annual return of the Spirit Powers. In the native view, spirit singing and dancing are means of restoring or preserving physical, mental, and social well-being. While much of traditional Salish Indian culture crumbled, the ceremonial was performed clandestinely by older people and survived in spite of previous efforts by government, church and school authorities to suppress this "pagan" ritual. In the Fraser Valley, spirit dancing was openly revived in 1967 and today has all the characteristics of a growing nativistic movement.

Indian ritualists consider native persons suffering from depression, anxiety, and somatic complaints which are unresponsive to Western treatment, as well as native persons with behavioral, alcohol, and drug problems, as candidates for spirit dance initiation. These persons often manifest an "anomic depression" syndrome of psychic, somatizing, and behavioral symptom formation in the context of cultural and social deprivation. The indigenous diagnosis of this condition as SPIRIT ILLNESS permits re-identification of an alienated person with his aboriginal culture via initiation into spirit dancing.

Data presented here are based on personal observation of Indian ceremonials and on information received during eight years of close contact with the native population as physician and mental health officer in the Fraser Valley of British Columbia, Canada.

## LITERATURE: THE BIOLOGY AND PSYCHOLOGY OF ALTERED STATES OF CONSCIOUSNESS.

Ludwig (1968) has explored and described altered states of consciousness in the context of trance and possession. Altered states of consciousness are characterized by the following symptomatology:

1.  Alterations in thinking, including predominance of archaic modes of thought, blurring of cause-effect distinction, and cognitive ambivalence.
2.  Disturbed time sense.
3.  Loss of control and inhibition.
4.  Change in emotional expression towards affective extremes.
5.  Body-image changes.
6.  Perceptual distortions.
7.  Change in meaning; attachment of increased or specific significance to subjective experience or external cues, leading to thrilling feelings of insight, and revelation of "truth" which then carries an unshakable conviction.
8.  Sense of the ineffable; the essence of the personal experience is felt to be not directly communicable, and this is often explained by varying degrees of amnesia.
9.  Feelings of rejuvenation, of renewed hope or of rebirth.
10. Hypersuggestibility.

Ludwig's altered states of consciousness correspond to what Bleuler (1961) has defined as *Bewusstseinsverschiebung* [shifting of consciousness], a state of mind attributable to either cerebro-organic or, more frequently, to psychogenic processes. In Western culture, altered states of consciousness of a psychogenic type are mainly observed in (1) hypnosis, (2) religious revelation, and (3) "hysterical" dissociation. The term TRANCE STATE is in usage for all these phenomena, while POSSESSION STATE has been reserved for non-Western cultures and for cases not approved of by Christian authorities — an arbitrary convention indicative of Eurocentric bias. The differences between these states are cultural, not psychological or neurophysiological. Schlesinger (1962) has accumulated evidence for a neuropsychological clarification of these hitherto vaguely defined experiences. His conclusions are briefly summarized here:

The term trance designates a "state of double consciousness, i.e. the constricted state of awareness of the personal self which co-exists with the dreamlike state of consciousness of the para-personal self." The neuropsychological basis of any trance or possession state is the dissociation of the self, which loses its experiential unity and is converted into a secondary "dual system of relational experience," namely, the personal self and the para-personal self. A mild degree of dissociation of the central experiential agency involves the dominant or conscious sphere of mentation only; a more profound dissociation, the dominant and the subsidiary or unconscious sphere; and a maximal degree of dissociation would also effect cleavage of the mnemonic sphere, i.e. the memory functions.

There is no evidence of cerebro-organic changes as manifested in electro-encephalography in either hypnotic or so-called hysterical trance states (Lindsley 1960; Kugler 1966; Hill [1963] cited by Prince 1968). Some authors have found an inhibition of alpha-blocking under hypnosis (Loomis, et al. 1936; Titeca and Kluyskens 1962). Electroencephalogram (EEG) data of this kind which point to specific alterations of attention and consciousness were also obtained during Zen exercises in Japan (Kasamatsu and Shimazono 1957; Kasamatsu and Hirai 1966).

The capacity for attaining altered states of consciousness is a universal property of the human central nervous system, as evidenced by the ubiquitous occurrence of trance phenomena through time and space. However, the prevalence of these phenomena appears to be a function of sociocultural variables. Under the impact of rationalistic-positivistic ideologies, the normal faculty of manifesting psychogenic dissociation appears to have diminished among members of the Western urban middle class who nowadays would not be expected to readily enter hysterical twilight reactions, demoniac possessions, or religious frenzy, while these states are by no means rare in more tradition-oriented pockets of Western culture (see Jilek and Jilek-Aall 1970).

Experimental studies of hypnotic trance have demonstrated beyond any doubt (1) that the subject's motivation is essential for the induction of a hypnotic reaction; (2) that the hypnotist is of importance only as a culturally approved sanctioning figure in whose influence the subject firmly believes, and as a focus for the projection of omnipotence fantasies; and (3) that the hypnotic state serves the subject's wish-fulfillment and the achievement of consciously or unconsciously desired goals (Schilder 1953; Barber 1958; Van der Walde 1965, 1968). Above all, hypnotic trance is a "product of situational and cultural demands" (Van der Walde 1968). This is equally true of nonexperimental trance states. We may say that in trance the subject makes use of his capacity to enter a dissociative state in order to enact most efficiently a goal-directed role which his culture in certain situations permits or demands him to do.

While the induction of psychogenic dissociation unquestionably depends on the subject's motivation, it may be facilitated by the employment of techniques which result in changes of brain function with demonstrable electroencephalographic indicators. Such "somato-psychological factors"

(Ludwig 1968) producing altered states of consciousness are hypoxyventi-
lation and hyperventilation which both can be carried on until loss of
consciousness ensues, and which are associated with stage-specific EEG
changes (Davis, et al. 1938); further, hypoglycemia and dehydration due
to fasting; sleep deprivation; and exposure to extreme temperatures. The
role of rhythmic sensory stimulation in the production of altered states of
consciousness deserves our special attention. While PHOTIC DRIVING, i.e.
the effects of stroboscopic photostimulation on electrical brain activity,
perception and consciousness, has been the main concern of neurophysiological research in this field ever since the pioneering work of Adrian
and Matthews (1934), an analogous significance of acoustic stimulation
has long been surmised by observers of rituals and ceremonies in which
rhythmic sounds appeared to have a direct effect on the central nervous
system. This was clearly expressed by Huxley (1961:369):

No man, however highly civilised, can listen for very long to African drumming,
or Indian chanting, or Welsh hymn-singing, and retain intact his critical and
self-conscious personality... if exposed long enough to the tom-toms and the
singing, every one of our philosophers would end by capering and howling with
the savages.

In their now classical treatise on rhythmic sensory stimulation, Walter
and Grey Walter recorded the well-known physiological and psychological effects of photic flicker stimulation. With regard to acoustic stimulation, they concluded that

...rhythmic stimulation of the organ of hearing as a whole can be accomplished
only by using a sound stimulus containing components of supra-liminal intensity over the whole gamut of audible frequencies — in effect a steep fronted
sound such as that produced by an UNTUNED PERCUSSION INSTRUMENT or an
explosion (1949:82; emphasis added).

This lead was not to be followed for some time. Instead of using rhythmic
percussion, other researchers experimented with intermittent pure-tone
sound stimulation, for example, Gastaut, et al. (1949) who elicited clinical
responses in two patients suffering from photogenic epilepsy, and Goldman (1952) who could show "acoustic driving" in the EEG of two normal
subjects. More recently, Kugler (1966) was able to elicit spikes in the EEG
of patients suffering from temporal lobe epilepsy when using loud noises
at a repetition rate of two to six per second. It was not until Neher's (1961,
1962) investigations that the neurophysiological effects of rhythmic drumming were demonstrated in controlled experiments. The significance of
Neher's findings for the anthropological and psychological study of ritual

trance and possession states can hardly be overestimated. Neher (1961) exposed clinically and electroencephalographically normal subjects to a low-frequency, high-amplitude stimulus obtained from a snare drum without snares — an instrument quite similar to the Salish Indian deerskin drums employed in winter ceremonials. AUDITORY DRIVING responses were demonstrated in the EEG of all subjects at the fundamental of each stimulus frequency (three, four, six, and eight beats per second), also at second harmonics and second subharmonics of some stimulus frequencies.

Subjective responses were similar to those obtained with photic driving by Walter and Grey Walter (1949), and included "fear, astonishment, amusement, back pulsing, muscle tightening, stiffness in chest, tone in back-ground, humming, rattling, visual and auditory imagery." Due to the presence of theta rhythms (four to seven cycles per second) in the temporal auditory region of the cerebral cortex, sound stimulation by drumming in this frequency range appears to be most effective and would, therefore, be expected to predominate in ceremonies associated with trance behavior. As cited by Neher (1962) the response is heightened by accompanying rhythms reinforcing the main rhythm, and by concomitant rhythmic stimulation in other sensory modes, such as tactual and kinesthetic; susceptibility to rhythmic stimulation is increased by stress in general, hyperventilation, hypoglycemia and adrenaline secretion resulting from exertion and fatigue. At the same time, strong sensory stimulation inhibits the transmission of pain signals to the conscious areas of the brain.

In the light of his findings, Neher (1962) reviewed some ethnographic reports on ceremonies involving rhythmic drumming from Siberia, Africa, Haiti, and Indonesia. A comparison of these data appeared to suggest that "unusual behaviour observed in drum ceremonies is mainly the result of rhythmic drumming which affects the central nervous system." However, such a conclusion awaits final confirmation by electroencephalographic examination of subjects while participating in appropriate ceremonies. Prince (1968) discusses the possibility that auditory driving is a "commonly used portal of entry into the dissociative state." His practical suggestions for the study of possession states by telemetering the EEG of fully mobile "native" participants in ceremonies have not yet been taken up by field researchers.

Sargant (1959) explains the induction of states of religious enthusiasm and spirit possession, as well as the so-called brainwashing and related therapeutic techniques, in terms of Pavlovian theory as TRANSMARGINAL inhibition. He marshals evidence from historical and contemporary reports on methods of religious and ideological conversion and indoctrination and shows that the basic processes involved are analogous in all significant aspects, paralleling those Pavlov deduced from his experimental observations in dogs. Given the fact that human cerebral organization varies within very narrow limits, we should not be surprised to find the most heterogeneous ideologies introduced successfully by very similar techniques, as Sargant asserted.

Ludwig (1968) presents a classification of factors in the production of altered states of consciousness under the following headings:

1. Reduction of exteroceptive stimulation and/or motor activity.
2. Increase of exteroceptive stimulation and motor hyperactivity, emotional arousal leading to exertion and mental fatigue.
3. Focused and selective hyperalertness.
4. Decreased alertness, relaxation of critical faculties.
5. Somato-psychological factors such as hyperventilation, hypoxemia, hypoglycemia, sleep deprivation.

From the foregoing we conclude that TRANCE and POSSESSION are altered states of consciousness involving the universally human mechanism of mental dissociation without cerebro-organic lesion. Their introduction is largely dependent on the subject's motivation and on the situational and sociocultural context but may be facilitated by certain conditions and techniques, some of which effect temporary changes of brain function.

It may be appropriate here to raise the question of the functional relevance of altered states of consciousness for the individual and for the collective. This question has recently been answered by Wittkower (1970) in a discussion of his observations on trance and possession states in non-Western societies:

Trance and possession states have undoubtedly an adaptive function culturally as well as individually. Their individual psychological effects consist of drive release, ego support, problem solution, relief from superego pressures and atonement.... There can be no doubt in anybody's mind that trance and possession states in the countries in which they play part of religious rituals have an important distress relieving, integrative, adaptive function. As far as mental illness is concerned, they may be of prophylactic value. An increase in mental illness may have to be expected when as a result of culture change they have ceased to exist.

## DATA: OBSERVATIONS ON THE THERAPEUTIC PROCESS OF CONTEMPORARY SALISH SPIRIT DANCING.

The death-and-rebirth myth is the central theme of the collective suggestions surrounding the spirit-dance initiation. In the view of contemporary

Salish Indian ritualists, the gift to obtain power, and to heal through power, was universal to all Indians in the distant past as part of their "Indian ways," but has been lost by most of them today as a result of their emulation of the white man who, by definition, lacks this "Indian power." The genuine shamanic healing power was a divine compensation for the technological assets of white civilization. In contemporary Salish theory, as taught by the ritualists, it is the spirit power, *sya'wən*, which acts through the initiator on the initiates, and it is this spirit power, not the initiator, which cures the novice, burying his ailments and conflicts together with his old personality and at the same time giving him rebirth into a new life. As the shaman's or medicine man's healing craft has to be sanctioned by supernatural powers (see Jilek 1971), so the initiator here is a healer by the power of *sya'wən* — just as in Christian tradition the physician is a healer only by the power of God.[1] As such an instrument of *sya'wən* the initiating ritualist is empowered to "club to death" the initiate's faulty and diseased old self, to let him awaken with a new potential for total change, and to guide him on the path of Indian tradition through the teachings of his elders. The "newborn" initiate is not only called "baby" and "helpless," he also is treated as such: bathed, later fed and dressed, constantly attended and guarded by "babysitters." Regression to a state of complete infantile dependency is at first imposed on the initiate who, in the quasi-uterine shelter of the dark longhouse cubicle, hatches his power, prepared to grow with it into a more rewarding and healthier existence. Henceforth, he will count his spiritual age from the day his initiation started.

The techniques employed today in spirit-dance initiation in the Fraser Valley are patterned after traditional models provided by the littoral Salish tribes, whose ritualists were instrumental in reviving spirit dancing in the region. In the whole process of initiation, three major therapeutic approaches can be discerned: (1) depatterning through shock treatment, followed by (2) physical training, with (3) indoctrination.

The candidate is kept in the longhouse, secluded in a dark cubicle or "smokehouse tent" for a period of usually ten days, which in a few privileged cases may be reduced to four days but which may also be prolonged

---

[1]    The traditional Christian theory of the physician's healing power has found a classical expression in the worlds of Paracelsus (1922–1933:172) in 1537: *"on got wird nichts . darumb so muss der arzt seine principia im selben auch nemen und on in ist er nichts als ein pseudomedicus und ein errant eins fliegenden geists"* [nothing will be achieved without God... therefore the physician must take the essential elements of his art from God, and without Him he is nothing but a fake doctor and the errant of a flighty mind].

for several weeks, or even the whole season. The length of the seclusion, which after four days of passive endurance is interrupted by frequent strenuous exercises, varies with candidates and ritualists. It seems to depend on the novice's motivation and his — unconscious or conscious — cooperation in "finding his song and dance," which is the professed purpose of the initiation process. The principal therapeutic functions of this process — personality depatterning and reorientation — are not unknown to the ritualists. In the words of a senior participant:

It is an Indian treatment, it is a kind of BRAINWASHING, four to ten days of torture. Through this torture they soften up, their brain gets soft. During that time you're the weakest and YOUR BRAIN IS BACK TO NIL,[2] anything you're taught during those ten days is going to stick with you, you'll never forget it.

Personality depatterning starts with an initial shock treatment known as the "clubbing," "grabbing," or "doctoring up" of the candidates, aiming at rapid induction of an altered state of consciousness, often via temporary loss of consciousness. In the cases we witnessed this was the result of a repeated and prolonged treatment which included (1) sudden bodily seizure of the allegedly unsuspecting candidate; (2) immobilization of his limbs by physical restraint; (3) blindfolding, (4) hitting, biting, and tickling of exposed body parts (abdomen, sides, foot soles). At the same time the candidate was subjected to (5) kinetic stimulation — uplifted and dropped, hurriedly carried around the longhouse; whirled about and swayed — and (6) to intensive acoustic stimulation — loud drumming and rattling in rapid rhythms, singing and howling close to his ears. This "grabbing" procedure is repeated at least four times, each time the eight "workers" complete four circles around the longhouse hall with their candidate, whose moaning cries become progressively weaker until he appears lifeless, pale, and rigid when finally bedded in the cubicle.

Through the four days of the depatterning phase, the initiate is blindfolded, he has to lie still, is forbidden to talk or to move even in sleep or when sweating under his heavy covers on the fringes of which sit the "babysitters" or "watchmen." He is starved and his fluid intake is restricted; at the same time he is "teased" and "tested" with tasty salmon bits held close to his mouth. Every day he is again exposed to the initial shock of the "grabbing" procedure in order to make him "die" again. The novice's reentry into the desired altered state of consciousness is facilitated by the ceremonial workers' frequent "singing and drumming to him." These maneuvers aim at bringing forth the novice's "song." They are

---

[2]   Compare with John Locke's (1632–1714) *tabula rasa* concept.

supplemented by more subtle methods such as placing two eager candidates together with one recalcitrant fellow or by instilling anxiety and guilt feelings.[3] While lying in his "tent," the initiate perceives his song, dance movements and face painting in a state between sleep-dream and wakefulness.[4]

The strict regime of "sacrifices" and "torture" is continued until the initiate "gets his song straight" — usually within four days — to be duly invested then with the traditional "uniform, hat and stick" in sign of his "rebirth in *syə'wən.*" The guardian spirit itself — today referred to by the young dancers as the "Indian" or the "Power Animal" — appears in a dream to the novice in the longhouse cubicle, or in a visionary experience under conditions of physical exertion in the context of the training which follows the initiate's investiture.

The phase of physical training is associated with intense indoctrination, and is supposed to "make the newborn baby strong." It lasts for at least one week and consists of (1) daily "runs" around the longhouse hall or outside, often barefoot in snow; (2) daily swimming — the new dancers have to jump into ice-cold waters and then rub their bodies with cedar boughs; (3) frequent rounds of dancing in the longhouse, to the fast rhythms of many drums, which drive the novice to exhaustion. Released from their incubation, the initiates feel their newly acquired power when the song bursts forth from them and the leaping steps of their first dance carry them through the longhouse, spurred on by the rhythms of deerhide drums and the chanting and clapping of the crowd. In view of Neher's (1961) findings on the neurophysiological effects of rhythmic drumming, this type of sensory stimulation has to be considered as a major factor operating in the induction of altered states of consciousness during Indian spirit-dance initiation.

Physical analysis of records of drumming[5] revealed that rhythmic drumming encompasses a frequency range from 0.8 to 5.0, with a mean frequency of 2.95 cycles per second [cps]. One-third of the recorded frequencies are above 3.0 cps, i.e. within, or close to the frequency of the theta waves of the human electroencephalogram. Frequencies in this range are entirely predominant in drumming during initiation procedures.

[3]   Cf. Sargant (1959:130): "Brainwashers use a technique of conversion which does not depend only on the heightening of group suggestibility, but also on the fomenting in an individual of anxiety, of a sense of real or imaginary guilt... strong and prolonged enough to bring about the desired collapse."
[4]   Reminiscent of the therapeutic dream-revelations to patients during incubation in the Aesculapian Temples of Healing of ancient Greece.
[5]   For this physical analysis we are indebted to Dr. Helmut Ormestad of the Fysisk Institutt Blindern of the University of Oslo.

As a stimulus frequency in the theta range of the EEG (4 to 7 cps) is expected to be most effective in the production of trance states, Neher assumed drumming rhythms close to such frequencies to be preponderant in ceremonies associated with trance behavior. The analysis of our data confirms this hypothesis, as far as contemporary Indian spirit dancing is concerned. It need not be emphasized that rhythmic acoustic stimulation in this ceremonial is far more intensive than in Neher's experiments: not one, but up to fifty drums may be employed. Indeed, the effects of rhythmic drumming, more than other factors, may contribute to the "contagiousness" of a spirit power which often seizes uninitiated persons present at ceremonials.

Modern spirit dancers refer to the initiation as a salutary learning experience: "It teaches you physical, emotional, and mental well-being." While much of this learning is effected through nonverbal conditioning processes, theoretical indoctrination also plays an important role. It includes the direct teaching of the rules and sanctions of spirit power, the indirect reinforcement of collective suggestion by recounting of traditional lore, presenting examples of the works of spirit, or "spiritual" power. Furthermore, it also includes what may be called culture propaganda, the propagation of an OPPOSITION IDEOLOGY (Schwimmer 1970), instrumental in helping the young Indian achieve a positive cultural identification.

When teaching the new dancers, the ritualists speak with ancestral spiritual authority, they teach the *syə'wən* rules — traditional prescriptions and proscriptions — and instill in the initiate a sense of personal responsibility toward his elders and his people. Of practical therapeutic importance is the prohibition of alcohol drinking, and also of smoking and "dope" taking.

The initiation process ends with the disrobing ceremony. The therapeutic implication of this ceremony is that it documents the candidate's successful cure from spirit illness through a duly performed initiation treatment. Together with his uniform, the initiate sheds the last vestiges of his old personality as the snake sloughs off its old skin. The new dancer is presented to the public as yet another testifier to the healing and regenerating power of *syə'wən*.

Not only for those who have become active spirit dancers through initiation, and therefore continue to dance on frequent occasions each subsequent winter season, but also for their relatives and for many other Indian families who are involved in the ceremonial, the winter time now brings every year an immersion in SEASONAL SPIRIT-DANCE THERAPY, a complex therapeutic enterprise which in scope and duration is unparallelled in non-Indian society. Seen from the mental health worker's perspective, it combines occupational and activity therapy, group psychotherapy, cathartic abreaction, psychodrama, direct suggestive ego-support and physical exercise.

Specific shamanistic curing rites are observed during the dances, also for non-initiated patients requiring immediate therapeutic attention. The main area of native Indian therapy is that of conditions in which psycho-reactive and psychophysiologic mechanisms are prominent. In our experience (Jilek and Todd 1974), the therapeutic effectiveness of indigenous treatment methods compares favorably with current Western therapies as far as such Indian patients are concerned, and with Western correctional management of Indian behavior disorders associated with alcohol or drug abuse.

## CONCLUSION

I have reviewed elsewhere the presentation and interpretation in anthropological literature of the Salish Guardian Spirit Complex, of which spirit dancing forms an integral part (see Jilek 1972). In the current article, I offer my observations on this sociocultural phenomenon in the light of physiologic and psychologic theories. In doing so, I hope to provide an example for the linkage of biopsychic and sociocultural events, and to do justice to Bohannan's (1963) anthropological view of man as a sentient and social mammal living by culture, the study of which calls for the concerted application of physical and social sciences.

By the example of Salish spirit dancing it can be demonstrated that traditional therapeutic principles, developed in a very specific, non-Western cultural and historical context, confirm the transcultural validity of certain theoretical propositions of modern physiology and psychology regarding altered states of consciousness, which in turn are illuminated by this particular cultural paradigm.

In order to arrive at a holistic theory of human societies, sociocultural data will have to be linked up with those of other sciences of man. Lévi-Strauss (1962:174) reminds us that *"l'ethnologie est d'abord une psychologie,"* to which we may add that psychology itself is first of all physiology.

## REFERENCES

ADRIAN, E. D., B. H. C. MATTHEWS
  1934   The Berger rhythm; potential changes from the occipital lobes in man. *Brain* 57: 355–385.

BARBER, T. X.
1958   The concept of "hypnosis." *Journal of Psychology* 45:115–131.

BLEULER, M.
1961   "Bewusstseinsstörungen in der Psychiatrie," in *Bewusstseinsstörungen*. Edited by H. Staub and H. Thölen, 199–213. Stuttgart: Thieme.

BOHANNAN, P.
1963   *Social anthropology*. New York: Holt, Rinehart and Winston.

DAVIS, P. A., H. DAVIS, J. W. THOMPSON
1938   Progressive changes in the human electroencephalogram under low oxygen tension. *American Journal of Physiology* 123:51–52.

GASTAUT, H., J. ROGER, J. CORRIOL, Y. GASTAUT
1949   L'épilepsie induite par la stimulation auditive intermittente rhythmée ou épilepsie "psophogénique." *E.E.G. and Clinical Neurophysiology* 1: 121.

GOLDMAN, D.
1952   The effect of rhythmic auditory stimulation on the human electroencephalogram. *E.E.G. and Clinical Neurophysiology* 4:370.

HUXLEY, A
1961   *The devils of Loudon*. London: Chatto and Windus.

JILEK, W. G.
1971   From crazy witch doctor to auxiliary psychotherapist — the changing image of the medicine man. *Psychiatria Clinica* 4:200–220.
1972   "Psychohygienic and therapeutic aspects of the Salish Guardian Spirit Ceremonial." Unpublished master's thesis, University of British Columbia, Vancouver.

JILEK, W. G., L. M. JILEK-AALL
1970   Transient psychoses in Africans. *Psychiatria Clinica* 3:337–364.

JILEK, W. G., N. TODD
1974   Witchdoctors succeed where doctors fail — the role of indigenous psychotherapy in a Canadian Indian population today. *Canadian Psychiatric Association Journal* 19:351–356.

KASAMATSU, A., T. HIRAI
1966   An electroencephalographic study on the Zen meditation (*Zazen*). *Folia Psychiatrica et Neurologica Japonica* 20:315–336.

KASAMATSU, A., Y. SHIMAZONO
1957   Clinical concept and neurophysiological basis of the disturbance of consciousness. *Folia Psychiatrica et Neurologica Japonica* 11:969–999.

KUGLER, J.
1966   *Elektroencephalographie in Klinik und Praxis*. Stuttgart: Thieme.

LINDSLEY, D. B.
1960   "Attention, consciousness, sleep and wakefulness," in *Handbook of physiology, section 1: neurophysiology*. Edited by J. Field and H. W. Magoun, volume three, 1553–1593. Washington D.C.: American Physiological Society.

LÉVI-STRAUSS, C
1962   *La pensée sauvage*. Paris: Plon.

LOOMIS, A. L., E. N. HARVEY, G. HOBART
1936   Electrical potentials of the human brain. *Journal of Experimental Psychology* 19:249–279.

LUDWIG, A. M.
1968   "Altered states of consciousness," in *Trance and possession states.* Edited by R. Prince, 69–95. Montreal: R. M. Bucke Memorial Society.

NEHER, A.
1961   Auditory driving observed with scalp electrodes in normal subjects. *Electroencephalography and Clinical Neurophysiology* 13:449–451.
1962   A physiological explanation of unusual behaviour in ceremonies involving drums. *Human Biology* 34:151–160.

PARACELSUS (THEOPHRASTUS VON HOHENHEIM)
1922–1933   *Sämtliche Werke,* volume eleven: *Labyrinthus medicorum errantium.* Edited by K. Sudhoff. Munich: Alber. (Originally published in 1537.)

PRINCE, R.
1968   "Can the E.E.G. be used in the study of possession states?" in *Trance and possession states.* Edited by R. Prince, 121–137. Montreal: R. M. Bucke Memorial Society.

SARGANT, W
1959   *Battle for the mind.* London: Pan Books.

SCHILDER, P .
1953   *Medical psychology.* New York: International University Press.

SCHLESINGER, B.
1962   *Higher cerebral functions and their clinical disorders — the organic basis of psychology and psychiatry.* New York and London: Grune and Stratton.

SCHWIMMER, E. G.
1970   "Symbolic competition." Paper presented at a Symposium on Canadian Indian Social Organization, Winnipeg, May, 1970.

TITECA, J., A. KLUYSKENS
1962   Etude électroencéphalographique des altérations du champ visuel induites par hypnose. *Bulletin Académie Royale de Médecine Belgique* 7:413–441.

VAN DER WALDE, P. H.
1965   Interpretation of hypnosis in terms of ego psychology. *Archives of General Psychiatry* 12:438–447.
1968   "Trance states and ego psychology," in *Trance and possession states.* Edited by R. Prince, 57–68. Montreal: R. M. Bucke Memorial Society.

WALTER, V. J., W. GREY WALTER
1949   The central effects of rhythmic sensory stimulation. *E.E.G. and Clinical Neurophysiology* 1:57–86.

WITTKOWER, E. D.
1970   Trance and possession states. *The International Journal of Social Psychiatry* 16:153–160.

# SECTION SIX

*Methods and Models*

# Introduction

"Anthropology and mental health" has provided an active intersection for the transfer of methodologies among social scientists and clinicians. Moreover, it has been a field in which concepts and models developed and tested within one discipline are tested with methods employed by another discipline. The field continues to serve these important functions actively.

Correlating selected behaviors across cultures has been a methodological hallmark of anthropologists. Especially in the mental health field, however, other social and behavioral scientists have used the cross-cultural method widely over the last thirty years. Schaefer's paper describes the modifications and sophistication which have occurred in this method during the last several years. In order to distinguish it from more in-depth comparisons between a few cultures and from studies in which investigator and subjects differ in ethnicity, a new term has evolved for such surveys: the holocultural method. As you can note from Schaefer's paper and a careful reading of the paper by Rosenblatt, et al., one does not merely think up interesting associations for the computer to match. Indeed, such an approach would produce a considerable number of spuriously positive correlations merely by coincidence alone. Rather, careful controls, thorough knowledge of the topic at hand, and creative tests for possible sources of bias have made this strategy a finely honed instrument for one schooled in its usage (and an impossible quagmire for the uninitiated).

Billig, Burton-Bradley, and Doermann have resurrected a method for the study of mental disorder which had been largely abandoned in recent years. They use the art of psychiatric patients in New Guinea (with some comparison to American patients), but again with an increased sophistication which lends itself to expanded theory testing. Beginning with the study of ordinary New Guinea art forms, they deduce rules which govern the form, content, style, color, and so forth. Proceeding then to the art of psychotic patients, they demonstrate how these rules gradually fragmented in the psychotic process. Finally, comparing New Guinea and American patients, they show how form (a cross-cultural constant) disintegrates regardless of ethnic group. Their method provides a means for handling emic-etic problems in mental disorder, since the content must be evaluated within the framework of the individual's own ethnic group (an emic process) whereas the form can then be compared across cultures (an etic process).

The vector model for measuring value change, as developed by Hartog also promises to aid in dealing with emic-etic problems. Questionnaires for evaluating value change would have to be developed separately within each culture group (though presumably one could employ some "etic" guidelines based on assumptions about what values are apt to be important to people). Once such vectors are determined, they might then be related to specific kinds of social problems (e.g. divorce, homicide, theft). While Hartog has not proceeded as far as Billig, et al. in testing his model, his "emic" vectors could potentially be compared among various ethnic groups to see whether general principles could be educed.

In his pithy review on animal models of psychopathology, McKinney also returns to our purview a model which has been largely abandoned in recent years, However, recent neurochemical and chronobiological discoveries in affective disorders (stimulated by the pharmacological studies of antidepressant medication) have recaptured the interests of physiologists and biochemists in mental disorder. Refined behavioral psychology has also sharpened the research tools available to investigators. Armed with careful criteria for animal models of psychopathology, this cross-species research may add to our understanding of disordered behavior without the anthropomorphizing (by proponents) and counter-anthropomorphizing (by critics) which have impeded similar efforts in the past.

The paper by Cowan and Meyers applies systems theory to a recent therapeutic modality and suggest an analysis of treatment goals and patient motivation in a drug treatment unit. Their model rings true for anyone involved in the treatment of chemical dependency, though operationalizing their "goals" and especially their "motivations" in a quantifiable way would be no easy task. That is not to say that the model should not receive serious attention. Until such studies can be carried out in a valid and replicable manner, government agencies will continue to spend public funds for alcohol and drug programs without knowing the efficacy of their expenditures.

# A Review of Methods in Holocultural Studies in Mental Health/Illness

JAMES M. SCHAEFER

One of the most humane fields of inquiry that anthropologists have dealt with over the years is that of human health and illness. Questions in this area ask whether or not certain cultures or life-styles encourage certain mental illnesses, exacerbate rates of anxiety, or engender and maintain pathologic institutions. There are questions about whether some societies are easier to live in than others. There are related questions, too (indeed there are major ideological contentions), about how our American culture compares with Russian, Chinese, Tanzanian, Czechoslovakian, Chilean, and other cultures with respect to mental health or illness. There is also the classic question about the relative influence of biological and cultural factors in these matters of health and illness.

Useful theoretical reviews on mental health/illness and comprehensive bibliographies are included in the works of Kavolis (1969), Plog and Edgerton (1969), Naroll (1970a), and Hsu (1972).

Anthropological research in the past century has opened up a new way of thinking about these many distinctively human problems. Our ever-broadening perspective on mental health and illness owes much to ethnographic field studies of diverse cultural groups around the world. For many years the primary contribution of field studies has been the richly detailed observations about the way of life in a local group, or within local groups, in a delimited cultural region. Ethnographic reports have long been the repository of theoretical linkages about a variety of behaviors, including aspects of individual and group well-being. The

I would like to thank the Department of Anthropology of the University of Montana for secretarial support. In addition, the University of Montana Foundation provided support for this work under Grant Number 841–O/L.

theories we can derive from such studies, however, are tenuous at best and often cannot account adequately for similar behavior elsewhere. Generalizations from case studies are risky.

This problem of generalizing broadly about human behavior is what comparative anthropologists attempted to deal with many years ago (Morgan 1871; Tylor 1889; Rivers 1911:490–499). These early efforts were fraught with difficulties (Boas 1896, 1940; Lowie 1948: Chapter 3). The problems in testing theoretical propositions by the comparative method were overcome, in part, by the influence of Radcliffe-Brown (1952:113–114), Nadel (1951:222–255), and Eggan (1953:743–763). These scholars fostered the controlled comparison style of research. In controlled comparison studies theoretical traits (sociocultural variables) are studied in situations where the variables vary, or where they don't vary. Other factors are "controlled," depending on the scope of the study (see Redfield 1941 and Spicer 1954 for contrastive styles). In the field of mental health and illness Nadel's study of witchcraft in four African societies (1952:18–29) is a classic. The most thoroughgoing critique of the strengths and weaknesses of the controlled comparison study style is by Clignet (1970:597–619).

Another research method is that of the cross-cultural survey. It is a century-old comparative style of research in anthropology that recently has shed some of its shortcomings and has emerged as a formidable theory-testing tool. Cross-cultural surveys test broad, general hypotheses on a global scale by simultaneously comparing predicted and nonpredicted trait-type frequencies in random probability samples of whole societies. The greatest strength of the cross-cultural or holocultural method is that one can test rival hypotheses in a relatively short period of time. Its greatest weakness is that the globally supported theoretical linkages are often too broadly conceived, too generally argued, and too simplistic for ready application in a specific cultural scene or to individual problems. A more general category for globally based sample survey studies is hologeistic research (Naroll 1970a: 1227).

The term hologeistic was introduced into the anthropological literature by Kobben (1952:133; see Moore 1961:170). Hologeistic refers to Greek *holos* [whole], and *ge* [earth], studies. Hologeistic thus becomes a generic term for cross-cultural surveys, cross-polity surveys, cross-historical surveys and cross-archaeological surveys. The form *holo-* has been adopted by a growing number of researchers as a prefix replacing "cross" in each of the above-mentioned styles of study. These usages and the rejuvenation of the method have been stimulated largely by Raoul Naroll. During the last decade it is through his works, as well as others (see below), that we have come, through the hologeistic method, to a better understanding of the major problems, as well as many of the possible solutions to these problems.

Naroll (1970a:1230–1231) has suggested that three "generations" of hologeistic study may be distinguished by methodological accomplishment. The first generation encompasses the years 1889–1934, starting with E. B. Tylor and ending with J. Unwin. The first-generation hologeists "sampled" by taking data from all available "societies." They often include data on the same society under a different name (Hobhouse, et al. 1915; see Naroll 1970a).

The second generation encompasses the years 1935 to the mid-1960's. Second-generation hologeists have tended to follow the methodological suggestions of George P. Murdock (1949) and John W. M. Whiting (Whiting and Child 1953). Hologeistic studies during this period used specific sampling techniques and mathematical statistics to test associations and significance levels; and they worked out elaborate concept definitions and taxonomies. They typically ignored unit definition and control, Galton's problem, data quality controls, null hypotheses (mud-sticking problems), adequate documentation, and many other desirable control procedures and tests.

As to the future, Naroll has given a succinct challenge to hologeistic researchers:

In third-generation studies as I envision them, samples are to be probability samples from a universe comprising substantially all adequately described tribes. Societal units are to be pinpointed in time and space on particular communities, and the societal unit is to be measured for ethnic distinctiveness. Formal reliability tests are to check for random factual error and formal data quality control tests are to check for systematic error. All concepts, classifications, and coding rules are to be explicit and highly reliable. Formal tests of clustering or neighboring resemblances are to establish that correlations are functional (semidiffusional) rather than mere artifacts of migration or borrowing (hyperdiffusional). Formal significance tests are to consider not only the significance levels of individual associations but also those of the entire group. Separate regional correlations are to show that the association concerned is worldwide, not merely found in only one or two regions. Deviant case analyses are to seek to explain exceptions systematically. Finally, and most important, formal causal analysis of correlational matrices is to establish the direction of causality at least among all variables considered in the study; these are to include all those considered relevant by any professional social scientist (Naroll 1970a: 1230–1231).

Setting forth expectations is one thing; proceeding with practical details is altogether another. Progress is being made in each of the problem areas that Naroll has suggested we concern ourselves with. Briefly, let me direct the reader's attention to the most recent study guides.

Otterbein (1969) sets forth a thumbnail sketch of how a cross-cultural survey may be carried out. Schaefer (1973, 1974), in a theoretical study on drunkenness provides an example of how a holocultural survey is performed, and includes most of the suggested third-generation control techniques. Sipes (1972) reviews how hologeistic studies may be rated. We have learned a great deal from introspective criticism as well as the criticisms leveled by Kobben (1952, 1967), Schapera (1953), and Lewis (1956).

From all these works it seems clear that we need to be concerned with the following problems in holocultural method: sampling (what were the sample size, sample universe, sampling methods?), units of study (what was being counted in order to compute tests of association and significance?) Galton's problem (was diffusion a plausible factor in explaining theoretical findings?), statistics (what statistical tests were used?), data quality controls (how do we get trustworthy data from untrustworthy sources like ethnographic monographs?), coding reliability, validity, and documentation (how can the critic be assured that the data used for evidence is reliable?), categorization (how do indicators used relate to theories or how were theories operationalized?), and deviant cases (why were there exceptions?).

Here is a summary of topics and studies bearing on problems raised:
1.  Sampling (Naroll 1967, 1970d, 1970e; Chaney and Ruiz Revilla 1969; Murdock and White 1969).
2.  Societal unit definition (Naroll 1964a, 1964b, 1970b, 1971b; Helm 1968; Murdock and White 1969).
3.  Data accuracy coding and bias (Naroll 1962, 1970g; Rosenthal 1966; Webb, et al. 1966; Janda 1970; O'Leary 1970; Rummel 1970; Vansina 1970.
4.  Conceptualization, categories and taxonomy (Ford 1967; Moore 1969; Tatje 1970; Ember 1970; Goodenough 1970; LeBar 1970; Naroll 1970b).
5.  Galton's problem-cultural diffusion (Murdock and White 1969; Schaefer 1969; Schaefer [ed.] 1974; Naroll 1970f; Driver and Chaney 1970; Driver 1970).
6.  Causal analysis of correlations (Blalock 1960, 1964; Boudon 1967, 1970; Kobben 1970a, 1970b; Rozelle and Campbell 1969; Tanter 1970).
7.  Regional variation and scope (Sawyer and LeVine 1966; Driver and Schuessler 1967; Chaney and Ruiz Revilla 1969; Erickson 1972).
8.  Deviant case analysis (Kobben 1967; Rosenblatt 1967).

9. Statistical significance (Winch and Campbell 1969; Naroll 1971a).
10. Group probability (Tatje, Naroll, and Textor 1970; Textor 1967; White 1970).

Our vision has been sharpened by the problems raised and the solutions proposed in hologeistic research during the past decade; however, we must bear in mind the fact that our predecessors, whose studies I review below, were not always aware of the methodological revolution going on around them.

In his recent general review of holocultural studies, Naroll (1970a) included over seventy studies whose theoretical emphasis was in the area of mental health/illness. I will briefly review these in summary fashion (see Table 1) in an effort to indicate how these studies stand with respect to holocultural studies on other theoretical topics. I include in my selection any study that dealt with such topics as suicide, culture stress, drunkenness, moral order, mother-infant separation, sexual behavior, abortion, dreams, friendship, socialization practices, disassociational states, warfare, ordeals, permissiveness, sorcery, and love magic. In general, I include studies which fall primarily under the purview of the National Institute of Mental Health. In fact, many of the studies selected were funded by NIMH.

In Naroll's evaluation (1970a:1231–1238) of holocultural surveys he was primarily interested in ascertaining the general validity of the theories tested. His evaluation thus inquired into the degree to which a specific researcher lowered the plausibility of rivaling hypotheses. As I have already suggested, there are many possible rival explanations and sources for error in holocultural surveys. Naroll, therefore, made note of researchers in his review who had formally tested rival hypotheses and who used otherwise rigorous procedures in an effort to reduce error in the study (noted as * in Table 1). Where a researcher failed to test a rival hypothesis or otherwise use some procedure to control for a problem area, Naroll made note of it ($^\circ$ in Table 1). Finally where a researcher appeared to use a procedure erroneously or otherwise failed to demonstrate his procedures convincingly, Naroll raised a question about the whole study (noted as a question mark in Table 1). See Naroll (1970a: 1231–1238) for a full presentation; also Schaefer (1973).

It is clear from Table 1 that the vast majority of holocultural studies on mental health/illness stand out as important theoretical contributions. This is apparent from the large number of studies (52 of 73) that stand up to the test of the null hypothesis. The null hypothesis is concerned with the issue of whether or not the number of correlations cited as supportive evidence for theoretical propositions could plausibly be an artifact of

Table 1.  Summary of evaluations of holocultural studies on mental health/illness

| Sampling bias | n | N |
|---|---|---|
| * | 8 | 28 |
| o | 57 | 97 |
| ? | 8 | 28 |
|  | 73 | 153 |

| Galton's problem | n | N |
|---|---|---|
| * | 11 | 27 |
| o | 45 | 82 |
| ? | 17 | 33 |
|  | 73 | 142 |

| Unit definition | n | N |
|---|---|---|
| * | 3 | 9 |
| o | 69 | 135 |
| ? | 1 | 4 |
|  | 73 | 148 |

| Theoretical indicators | n | N |
|---|---|---|
| * | 36 | 86** |
| o | 29 | 53 |
| ? | 8 | 9** |
|  | 73 | 148 |

| Taxonomic validity | n | N |
|---|---|---|
| * | 38 | 84** |
| o | 32 | 57 |
| ? | 3 | 7 |
|  | 73 | 148 |

| Data documentation | n | N |
|---|---|---|
| * | 8 | 18 |
| o | 57 | 116 |
| ? | 8 | 14** |
|  | 73 | 148 |

| Reliability tests | n | N |
|---|---|---|
| * | 34 | 49** |
| o | 33 | 87 |
| ? | 6 | 12 |
|  | 73 | 148 |

| Coding bias | n | N |
|---|---|---|
| * | 2 | 4 |
| o | 67 | 138 |
| ? | 4 | 4** |
|  | 73 | 146 |

| Ethnographer bias | n | N |
|---|---|---|
| * | 4 | 8 |
| o | 63 | 132 |
| ? | 6 | 7** |
|  | 73 | 147 |

| Informant bias | n | N |
|---|---|---|
| * | 2 | 4 |
| o | 71 | 143 |
| ? | 0 | 0 |
|  | 73 | 147 |

| Causation test | n | N |
|---|---|---|
| * | 9 | 12** |
| o | 51 | 85 |
| ? | 13 | 21** |
|  | 73 | 118 |

| Multiple strategy | n | N |
|---|---|---|
| * | 24 | 40** |
| o | 49 | 104 |
| ? | 0 | 2 |
|  | 73 | 146 |

| Null hypothesis | n | N |
|---|---|---|
| * | 52 | 92** |
| o | 9 | 19 |
| ? | 12 | 29 |
|  | 73 | 140 |

Key:  n   mental health/illness subsample
N   total sample in Naroll (1970a)
*   supportive evidence present
o   no support or nonsupport
?   questionable support
**  noteworthy for this grouping

chance by virtue of the large number of correlations calculated in such a study. In the case of the mental health/illness studies and, by and large, the whole of the holocultural studies reviewed by Naroll (1970a), the number of correlations cited far outnumber the chance expectations for the number of correlations calculated.

Other noteworthy trends in the holocultural studies reviewed that have a bearing on the theoretical contentions of these studies include a better-than-average rate of carefully constructed theoretical taxonomies and indicators, as well as frequent reportage of intercoder reliability tests for theoretical variables. A small number ( < 10 percent) of the mental health/illness studies had questionable theoretical indicators; however, in comparison with all other holocultural studies reviewed here and in Naroll (1970a), nearly all the questionable studies (8 out of 9) were studies in the area of mental health/illness.

General shortcomings of all the studies in mental health and illness were the failure to define sample societies precisely (unit definition); failure to control for the possibility that cultural diffusion could explain correlation patterns (Galton's problem); failure to control for representativeness in the sample (sample bias); failure to present documentation of codings and source references (data documentation); and failure to deal with the problem of systematic bias among coders, ethnographers, and informants. Noteworthy among the problems of questionable evidence were the handful of mental health/illness studies that failed to report codings and documentation and test for coding and ethnographer bias. The mental health/illness studies with such problems stand out among the holocultural studies reviewed by Naroll (1970a).

The most problematic methodological issue in holocultural studies on mental health/illness is causal analysis. A large number of these studies had questionable evidence regarding the plausibility of a particular theoretician's tendency to argue a theory in the way he did. In other words, the assertion that variable A preceded variable B on the basis of mere correlations was found to be unwarranted in many cases. In fact, the reverse (i.e. B causing A) was not disproven beyond a reasonable doubt. I think it equally important to point out that even though holocultural studies in mental health/illness fared badly in terms of causal analysis (*vis-à-vis* all other holocultural studies reviewed by Naroll), of those studies with outstanding merit ( < 10 percent) among all holocultural studies, a very large percentage were in the area of mental health/illness (9 out of 12). That causal analysis is a problem in studies on mental health/illness is not terribly surprising, because it is the leading methodological problem in hologeistic research. Attempts to overcome this problem are taking two forms: first, there are the correlation matrix experimenters (cited above under causal analysis) and second, there are those who are attempting to obtain time-sequenced data so that cross-lagged correlations may be used to help causal analysis (see Rozelle and Campbell 1969). It is conceivable that an exciting theoretical breakthrough may come when historical documents, ethnohistorical documents, and archaeological documents are systematically organized in time sequence. This is true in the area of mental health/illness, as it will be for other anthropological areas of interest.

In summary, we have learned a great deal so far from holocultural studies in mental health/illness. At least we have a growing number of studies that have made theoretical linkages on a wide variety of topics within the general subject area. No general theory has yet emerged which economically ties together in a parsimonious manner the diverse aspects of the human condition. However, we are at an advanced stage of theory testing, and we may hope that the next few years will provide us with some theoretical syntheses toward which we all have been working. It is hoped, too, that the hologeistic comparativist's problem as well as their advantages in theory testing will become better understood by the field-oriented theory testers. The interplay of these noncomparativists with the comparativists is a paramount concern if the rise of anthropological theory is to continue.

## REFERENCES

BLALOCK, HUBERT M., JR.
   1960   Correlational analysis and causal inferences. *American Anthropologist* 62:624–653.
   1964   *Causal inferences in nonexperimental research*. Chapel Hill: University of North Carolina Press.
BOAS, FRANZ
   1896   "The limitations of the comparative method of anthropology," in *Race, language and culture*. Edited by F. Boas. New York: Macmillan.
   1940   *Race, language and culture*. New York: Macmillan.
BOUDON, RAYMOND
   1967   *L'Analyse mathématique des faits sociaux*. Paris: Plon.
   1970   "A method of linear causal analysis-dependence analysis," in *A handbook of method in cultural anthropology*, Edited by R. Naroll and R. Cohen, 99–108. Garden City, N. Y.: Natural History Press.
CHANEY, RICHARD P., ROGELIO RUIZ REVILLA
   1969   Sampling methods and interpretation of correlation: a comparative analysis of seven cross-cultural samples. *American Anthropologist* 71:597–633.

CLIGNET, R.
1970 "A critical evaluation of concomitant variation studies," in *A handbook of method in cultural anthropology*. Edited by R. Naroll and R. Cohen. Garden City, N. Y.: Natural History Press.

DRIVER, HAROLD E.
1970 "Statistical studies of continuous geographic distributions," in *A handbook of method in cultural anthropology*. Edited by R. Naroll and R. Cohen, 620–639. Garden City, N. Y.: Natural History Press.

DRIVER, HAROLD E., RICHARD P. CHANEY
1970 "Cross-cultural sampling and Galton's problem," in *A handbook of method in cultural anthropology*. Edited by R. Naroll and R. Cohen, 990–1003. Garden City, N. Y.: Natural History Press.

DRIVER, HAROLD E., KARL F. SCHUESSLER
1967 Correlational analysis of Murdock's 1957 ethnographic sample. *American Anthropologist* 69:332–352.

EGGAN, FRED
1953 Social anthropology and the method of controlled comparison. *American Anthropologist* 56 (5): 743–763.
1961 "Social anthropology and the method of controlled comparison," in *Readings in cross-cultural methodology*. Edited by F. W. Moore. New Haven: Human Relations Area Files Press.

EMBER, MELVIN
1970 "Taxonomy in comparative studies," in *A handbook of method in cultural anthropology*. Edited by R. Naroll and R. Cohen, 697–706. Garden City, N. Y.: Natural History Press.

ERICKSON, EDWIN E.
1972 Other cultural dimensions: selective rations of Sawyer and LeVine. Factor analysis of the World Ethnographic Sample. *Behavior Science Notes* 7 (2): 95–156.

FORD, CLELLAN S.
1967 *Cross-cultural approaches: readings in comparative research*. New Haven: Human Relations Area File Press.

GOODENOUGH, WARD H.
1970 *Description and comparison in cultural anthropology*. Chicago: Aldine.

HELM, JUNE, *editor*
1968 *Essays on the problem of tribe*. Proceedings of the 1967 Annual Spring Meeting of the American Ethnological Society. Seattle: University of Washington Press.

HOBHOUSE, L. T., G. C. WHEELER, M. GINSBURG
1915 *The material culture and social institutions of simpler peoples*. London: Chapman and Hall.

HSU, FRANCIS L. K., *editor*
1972 *Psychological anthropology*. New York: Schenkman.

JANDA, KENNETH
1970 "Data quality control and library research on political parties." in *A handbook of method in cultural anthropology*. Edited by R. Naroll and R. Cohen. Garden City, N. Y.: Natural History Press.

KAVOLIS, V., *editor*
1969 *The comparative approach to social problems*. Boston: Little, Brown.

KOBBEN, A.
1952 New ways of presenting an old idea: the statistical method in social anthropology. *Journal of the Royal Anthropological Institute of Great Britain and Ireland* 82:129–146.
1967 Why exceptions? The logic of cross-cultural comparison. *Current Anthropology* 8:3–34.
1970a "Cause and intention," in *A handbook of method in cultural anthropology*. Edited by R. Naroll and R. Cohen. Garden City, N. Y.: Natural History Press.
1970b "Comparativists and noncomparativists," in *A handbook of method in cultural anthropology*. Edited by R. Naroll and R. Cohen. Garden City, N. Y.: Natural History Press.

LE BAR, FRANK M.
1970 "Coding ethnographic materials," in *A handbook of method in cultural anthropology*. Edited by R. Naroll and R. Cohen, 707–720. Garden City, N. Y.: Natural History Press.

LEWIS, O.
1956 "Comparisons in cultural anthropology," in *Readings in cross-cultural methodology*. Edited by F. Moore. New Haven: Human Relations Area File Press.

LOWIE, ROBERT H.
1948 *Social organization*. New York: Holt, Rinehart and Winston.

MOORE, FRANK W., *editor*
1961 *Readings in cross-cultural methodology*. New Haven: Human Relations Area File Press.
1969 Codes and coding. *Behavior Science Notes* 4:247–66.

MORGAN, L. H.
1871 *Systems of consanguinity and affinity of the human family*. Washington: Smithsonian Institution.

MURDOCK, G. P.
1949 *Social structure*. New York: Macmillan.

MURDOCK, G. P., DOUGLAS R. WHITE
1969 Standard cross-cultural sample. *Ethnology* 8:329–369.

NADEL, S. F.
1951 *The foundations of social anthropology*. Glencoe, Ill.: Free Press.
1952 Witchcraft in four African societies: an essay in comparison. *American Anthropologist* 54. (Also in Ford 1967:207–220.)

NAROLL, R.
1961 Two solutions to Galton's problem. *Philosophy of Science* 28:16–39.
1962 *Data quality control*. New York: Free Press.
1964a A fifth solution to Galton's problem. *American Anthropologist* 66: 853–867.
1964b On ethnic unit classification. *Current Anthropology* 5:283–312.
1967 The proposed HRAF probability sample. *Behavior Science Notes* 2:70–80.
1968 "Some thoughts on comparative method in cultural anthropology," in *Methodology in social research*. Edited by H. M. Blalock and A. Blalock. New York: McGraw-Hill.

1970a What have we learned from cross-cultural surveys. *American Anthropologist* 72:1227–1288.

1970b "The culture-bearing unit in cross-cultural surveys," in *A handbook of method in cultural anthropology*. Edited by R. Naroll and R. Cohen, 721–765. Garden City, N.Y.: Natural History Press.

1970c "The logic of generalization, Part I: Epistemology," in *A handbook of method in cultural anthropology*. Edited by R. Naroll and R. Cohen. Garden City, N.Y.: Natural History Press.

1970d Chaney and Ruiz Revilla: a comment. *American Anthropologist* 72: 1450–1453.

1970e "Cross-cultural sampling," in *A handbook of method in cultural anthropology*. Edited by R. Naroll and R. Cohen, 889–926. Garden City, N.Y.: Natural History Press.

1970f "Galton's problem," in *A handbook of method in cultural anthropology*. Edited by R. Naroll and R. Cohen, 974–989. Garden City, N.Y.: Natural History Press.

1970g "Data quality control in cross-cultural surveys," in *A handbook of method in cultural anthropology*. Edited by R. Naroll and R. Cohen, 927–945. Garden City, N.Y.: Natural History Press.

1970h Stratified sampling and Galton's problem (a comment on "Evaluation of a stratified versus an unstratified universe of cultures in comparative research" by Lenora Greenbaum). *Behavior Science Notes* 4:282–283.

1971a Review: of the significance test controversy, a reader. *American Anthropologist* 73:1437–1439.

1971b The double language boundary. *Behavior Science Notes* 6:95–102.

NAROLL, R., R. COHEN, *editors*
1970 *A handbook of method in cultural anthropology*. Garden City, N.Y.: Natural History Press.

NAROLL, R., R. D'ANDRADE
1963 Two further solutions to Galton's problem. *American Anthropologist* 65:1063–1067.

NAROLL, R., F. NAROLL
1963 On bias of exotic data. *Man, Journal of the Royal Anthropological Institute* 25.

O'LEARY, TIMOTHY J.
1970 "Ethnographic bibliographies," in *A handbook of method in cultural anthropology*. Edited by R. Naroll and R. Cohen, 128–146. Garden City, N.Y.: Natural History Press.

OTTERBEIN, KEITH F.
1969 Basic steps in conducting a cross-cultural study. *Behavior Science Notes* 4:221–36.

PLOG, STANLEY C., ROBERT F. EDGERTON, *editors*
1969 *Changing perspectives in mental illness*. New York: Holt, Rinehart and Winston.

RADCLIFFE-BROWN, A. R.
1952 "The sociological theory of totemism," in *Structure and function in primitive society*. Edited by A. R. Radcliffe-Brown. Glencoe, Ill.: Free Press.

REDFIELD, ROBERT
1941 *Folk culture of Yucatan.* Chicago: University of Chicago Press.
RIVERS, W. H. R.
1911 *The ethnological analyses of culture.* Report of the British Association for the Advancement of Science 81.
ROSENTHAL, ROBERT
1966 *Experimenter effects in behavioral research.* New York: Appleton-Century-Crofts.
ROZELLE R. M., DONALD T. CAMPBELL
1969 More plausible rival hypotheses in the cross-lagged panel correlation. *Psychological Bulletin* 72:74–80.
RUMMEL, RUDOLPH J.
1970 "Dimensions of error in cross-national data," in *A handbook of method in cultural anthropology.* Edited by R. Naroll and R. Cohen 946–961. Garden City, N.Y.: Natural History Press.
SAWYER, JACK, ROBERT A. LE VINE
1966 Cultural dimensions: a factor analysis of the World Ethnographic Sample. *American Anthropologist* 63:708–713.
SCHAEFER, JAMES M.
1969 Linked pair alignments for the HRAF quality control sample universe. *Behavior Science Notes* 4:299–320.
1973 "A hologeistic study of family structure and sentiment, supernatural beliefs and drunkenness." Doctoral dissertation microfilm at Buffalo: SUNY and Ann Arbor: University Microfilms. (Dissertation Abstracts Index Vol. 34, No. 6: 73–29, 131.)
1974 *Studies in cultural diffusion: Galton's problem.* New Haven: Human Relations Area File Press.
1976 "Drunkenness: a holocultural treatise," in *Cross-cultural appoaches to the study of alcohol: an interdisciplinary perspective.* Edited by M. W. Everett, J.O. Waddell, and D. B. Heath 469–529. World Anthropology. The Hague: Mouton.
SCHAPERA, I.
1953 Some comments on comparative method in social anthropology. *American Anthropologist* 55:353–361.
SIPES, R. G.
1972 Rating hologeistic method. *Behavior Science Notes* 7:157–198.
SPICER, EDWARD H.
1954 *Potam: A Yaqui village in Sonora.* American Anthropological Association Memoir 77.
TANTER, RAYMOND
1970 Toward a theory of political development," in *A handbook of method in cultural anthropology.* Edited by R. Naroll and R. Cohen, 111–127. Garden City, N.Y.: Natural History Press.
TATJE, TERRANCE
1970 "Problems of concept definition for comparative studies," in *A handbook of method in cultural anthropology.* Edited by R. Naroll and R. Cohen. Garden City, N.Y.: Natural History Press.
TATJE, TERRANCE A., R. NAROLL, R. B. TEXTOR
1970 "The methodological finds of the cross-cultural summary, in *A hand-*

*book of method in cultural anthropology.* Edited by R. Naroll and R. Cohen. Garden City, N. Y.: Natural History Press.

TEXTOR, ROBERT B.
1967   *A cross-cultural summary.* New Haven: Human Relations Area File Press.

TYLOR, E. B.
1889   On a method of investigating the development of institutions: applied to laws of marriage and descent. *Journal of the Royal Anthropological Institute* 18:245–269.

VANSINA, JAN
1970   "Cultures through time," in *A handbook of method in cultural anthropology.* Edited by R. Naroll and R. Cohen. Garden City, N.Y.: Natural History Press.

WEBB, EUGENE J., DONALD T. CAMPBELL, RICHARD D. SCHWARTZ, LEE SECHREST
1966   *Unobtrusive measures: non-reactive research in the social sciences.* Chicago: Rand, McNally.

WHITE, DOUGLAS R.
1970   "Societal research archives system: retrieval, quality control and analysis of comparative data," in *A handbook of method in cultural anthropology.* Edited by R. Naroll and R. Cohen. Garden City, N.Y.: Natural History Press.

WHITING, J. W. M., I. CHILD
1953   *Child training and personality, a cross-cultural study.* New Haven: Yale University Press.

WINCH, R. F., D. T. CAMPBELL
1969   Proof? No. Evidence? Yes. The significance of tests of significance. *The American Sociologist* 4: 140–143.

## FURTHER REFERENCES

ALLEN, MARTIN G.
1962   The development of universal criteria for the measurement of the health of a society. *Journal of Social Psychology* 57:363–382.
1963   The study and evaluation of societies in cross-cultural research. *International Mental Health Research Newsletter* 5:1, 4–5.
1967   Childhood experience and adult personality: a cross-cultural study using the concept of ego strength. *Journal of Social Psychology* 71:53–68.

APPLE, DORRIAN
1956   The social structure of grandparenthood. *American Anthropologist* 58:53–68.

ASUNI, T.
1962   Suicide in western Nigeria. *The British Medical Journal*, October 22. (Reprinted in *International Journal of Psychiatry* 1:52–61, 1965.)

AYRES, BARBARA
1967   "Pregnancy magic: a study of food taboos and sex avoidances, '

in *Cross-cultural approaches: readings in comparative research*. Edited by Clellan S. Ford, 111–125. New Haven: Human Relations Area File Press.

BACON, MARGARET K., HERBERT BARRY, III, IRVIN L. CHILD

1965   A cross-cultural study of drinking. *Quarterly Journal of Studies on Alcohol*, supplement 3.

BACON, MARGARET K., IRVIN L. CHILD, HERBERT BARRY, III

1963   A cross-cultural study of correlates of crime. *Journal of Abnormal and Social Psychology* 66:241–300.

BARRY, HERBERT, III

1952   "Influence of socialization on the graphic arts: a cross-cultural study." Unpublished honors thesis, Harvard College, Department of Social Relations, Cambridge, Mass.

1957   Relationships between child training and the pictorial arts. *Journal of Abnormal and Social Psychology* 54:380–383.

BARRY, HERBERT, III, MARGARET K. BACON, IRVIN L. CHILD

1957   A cross-cultural survey of some sex differences in socialization. *Journal of Abnormal and Social Psychology* 55:327–332.

BARRY, HERBERT, III, IRVIN L. CHILD, MARGARET K. BACON

1959   Relation of child training to subsistence economy. *American Anthropologist* 61:51–53.

BOURGUIGNON, ERIKA

1968   *A cross-cultural study of disassociational states*. Columbus: Ohio State University Research Foundation.

BROWN, JUDITH

1963   A cross-cultural study of female initiation rites. *American Anthropologist* 65:837–853.

BURTON, ROGER V., JOHN W. M. WHITING

1961   The absent father and cross-sex identity. *Merill-Palmer Quarterly of Behavior and Development* 7:85–95.

CHILD, IRVIN L., THOMAS STORM, JOSEPH VEROFF

1958   "Achievement themes in folk tales related to socialization practice," in *Motives, fantasy, action, and society: a method of assessment and study*. Edited by John W. Atkinson. Princeton: Van Nostrand.

COHEN, YEHUDI A.

1961a   "Food and its vicissitudes: a cross-cultural study of sharing and non-sharing," in *Social structure and personality: a casebook*. Edited by Yehudi A. Cohen, 312–350. New York: Holt, Rinehart and Winston.

1961b   "Patterns of friendship," in *Social structure and personality: a casebook*. Edited by Yehudi A. Cohen, 351–383. New York: Holt, Rinehart and Winston.

1964a   The establishment of identity in a social nexus: the special case of initiation ceremonies and their relation to value and legal systems. *American Anthropologist* 66:529–552.

1964b   *The transition from childhood to adolescence: cross-cultural studies of initiation ceremonies, legal systems, and incest taboos*. Chicago: Aldine.

1969   Ends and means in political control: state organization and the punishment of adultery, incest, and the violation of celibacy. *American Anthropologist* 71:658–687.

COLBY, KENNETH MARK
  1963    Sex differences in dreams of primitive tribes. *American Anthropologist*
          65:1116–1122.
COPPINGER, ROBERT M., PAUL C. ROSENBLATT
  1968    Romantic love and subsistence dependence of spouses. *Southwestern
          Journal of Anthropology* 24:310–319.
D'ANDRADE, ROY G.
  1961    "Anthropological studies of dreams," in *Psychological anthropology:
          approaches to culture and personality*. Edited by Francis L. K. Hsu,
          296–332. Homewood, Ill: Dorsey.
DEVEREUX GEORGE
  1955    *A study of abortion in primitive societies*. New York: Julian Press.
FIELD, PETER B.
  1962    "A new cross-cultural study of drunkenness," in *Society, culture,
          and drinking patterns*. Edited by D. J. Pittman and C. R. Snyder,
          48–74. New York: Wiley.
FORD, CLELLAN S., FRANK A. BEACH
  1951    *Patterns of sexual behavior*. New York: Harper.
GOULDNER, ALVAIN W., RICHARD A. PETERSON
  1962    *Notes on technology and the moral order*. Indianapolis: Bobbs-
          Merrill.
GUNDERS, SHULAMITH MARCUS, JOHN W. M. WHITING
  1968    Mother-infant separation and physical growth. *Ethnology* 7:196–206.
HARRINGTON, CHARLES
  1968    Sexual differentiation in socialization and some male genital mutila-
          tions. *American Anthropologist* 70:951–956.
HORTON, DONALD
  1943    The functions of alcohol in primitive societies: a cross-cultural study.
          *Quarterly Journal of Studies on Alcohol* 4:199–320.
KALIN, RUDOLF, WILLIAM N. DAVIS, DAVID C. MC CLELLAND
  1966    "The relationship between use of alcohol and thematic content of
          folktales in primitive societies," in *The general inquirer: a computer
          approach to content analysis*. Edited by Philip J. Stone, et al., 569–588.
          Cambridge, Mass.: MIT Press.
KRAUSS, HERBERT H.
  1966    "A cross-cultural study of suicide." Doctoral dissertation, Depart-
          ment of Psychology, Northwestern University.
KRAUSS, HERBERT H., BEATRICE J. KRAUSS
  1968    Cross-cultural study of the thwarting-disorientation theory of suicide.
          *Journal of Abnormal Psychology* 73:353–357.
LAMBERT, WILLIAM W., LEIGH MINTURN TRIANDIS, MARGARET WOLF
  1959    Some correlates of beliefs in the malevolence and benevolence of
          supernatural beings: a cross-cultural study. *Journal of Abnormal and
          Social Psychology* 58:162–169.
LANDAUER, THOMAS K., JOHN W. M. WHITING
  1964    Infantile stimulation and adult stature of human males. *American
          Anthropologist* 66:1007–1028.
LESTER, DAVID
  1966    Antecedents of the fear of the dead. *Psychological Reports* 19:741–742.

1967a The relation between discipline experiences and the expression of aggression. *American Anthropologist* 69:734–737.

1967b Suicide, homicide and the effects of socialization. *Journal of Personality and Social Psychology* 5:466–468.

LE VINE, ROBERT A.

1960   The role of the family in authority systems: a cross-cultural application of stimulus-generalization theory. *Behavioral Science* 5:291–296.

1962   Witchcraft and co-wife proximity in southwestern Kenya. *Ethnology* 1:39–45.

MC CLELLAND, DAVID C., WILLIAM DAVIS, ERIC WANNER, RUDOLF KALIN

1966   A cross-cultural study of folk-tale content and drinking. *Sociometry* 29:308–333.

MINTURN, LEIGH, MARTIN GROSSE, SANTOAH HAIDER

1969   Cultural patterning of sexual beliefs and behavior. *Ethnology* 8: 301–318.

MURDOCK, GEORGE PETER

1964   "Cultural correlates of the regulation of premarital sex behavior," in *Process and pattern in culture: essays in honor of Julian H. Steward.* Edited by Robert A. Manners, 399–410 Chicago: Aldine.

NAG, MONI

1962   *Factors affecting human fertility in nonindustrial societies: a cross-cultural study.* New Haven: Yale University Publicationsin Anthropology 66.

NAROLL, RAOUL

1959   A tentative index of culture stress. *International Journal of Social Psychiatry* 5:107–116.

1969   "Cultural determinants and the concept of the sick society," in *Changing perspectives in mental illness.* Edited by Robert B. Edgerton and Stanley C. Plog. New York: Holt, Rinehart and Winston.

OSMOND, MARIE W.

1965   Toward monogamy: a cross-cultural study of correlates of a type of marriage. *Social Forces* 44:8–16.

OTTERBEIN, KEITH F.

1968b Internal war: a cross-cultural study. *American Anthropologist* 70: 277–289.

OTTERBEIN, KEITH F., CHARLOTTE SWANSON OTTERBEIN

1965   An eye for an eye, a tooth for a tooth: across-cultural study of feuding. *American Anthropologist* 67:1470–1482.

PALMER, STUART

1965   Murder and suicide in forty nonliterate societies. *Journal of Criminal Law, Criminology, and Police Science* 56:320–324.

PROTHRO, E. TERRY

1960   Patterns of permissiveness among preliterate peoples. *Journal of Abnormal and Social Psychology* 51:151–154.

ROBERTS, JOHN M.

1965   Oaths, autonomic ordeals, and power. *American Anthropologist* 67 (6, 2):186–212.

ROBERTS, JOHN M., BRIAN SUTTON-SMITH

1962   Child training and game involvement. *Ethnology* 1:166–185.

1966 Cross-cultural correlates of games of chance. *Behavior Science Notes* 1:131–144.

ROBERTS, JOHN M., BRIAN SUTTON-SMITH, ADAM KENDON
1963 Strategy in games and folk tales. *Journal of Social Psychology* 61: 185–199.

ROSENBLATT, PAUL C.
1966 A cross-cultural study of child rearing and romantic love. *Journal of Personality and Social Psychology* 4:336–338.
1967 Marital residence and the functions of romantic love. *Ethnology* 6:471–479.

ROSENBLATT, PAUL C., STEPHEN S. FUGITA, KENNETH V. MC DOWELL
1969 Wealth transfer and restrictions on sexual relations during betrothal. *Ethnology* 8:319–328.

SHANKMANN, PAUL
1969 *Le rôti et le bouilli*: Lévi-Strauss's theory of cannibalism. *American Anthropologist* 71:54–69.

SHIRLEY, ROBERT W., A. KIMBALL ROMNEY
1962 Love magic and socialization anxiety: a cross-cultural study. *American Anthropologist* 64:1028–1031.

SLATER, PHILIP E.
n.d. "Culture, sexuality and narcissism: a cross-cultural study." Mimeographed manuscript, Brandeis University.

SLATER, PHILIP E., DORI A. SLATER
1965 Maternal ambivalence and narcissism: a cross-cultural study. *Merrill-Palmer Quarterly of Behavior and Development* 11:241–259.

STEINMETZ, RUDOLPH S.
1896 Endokannibalismus. *Mittheilungen der Anthropologischen Gesellschaft in Wien* 54:211–231. (Reprinted: Rudolf S. Steinmetz, *Gesammelte kleinere Schriften zur Ethnologie und Soziologie*, two volumes. Volume one, 132–271. Groningen: Noordhoff.

STEPHENS, WILLIAM N.
1961 A cross-cultural study of menstrual taboos. *Genetics Psychology Monographs* 64:385–416.
1962 *The Oedipus complex: cross-cultural evidence*. With a chapter on kin avoidances written in collaboration with Roy G. D'Andrade. New York: Free Press.
1963 *The family in cross-cultural perspective*. New York: Holt, Rinehart and Winston.
1969 "A cross-cultural study of modesty and obscenity." Mimeographed manuscript, Dalhousie University, Halifax.

SWEETSER, DORRIAN APPLE
1966 On the incompatability of duty and affection: a note on the role of the mother's brother. *American Anthropologist* 68:1009–1013.

TRIANDIS, HARRY C., LEIGH MINTURN, WILLIAM W. LAMBERT
1961 Sources of frustration and targets of aggression. *Journal of Abnormal and Social Psychology* 61:640–648.

UNWIN, JOSEPH D.
1934 *Sex and culture*. London: Oxford University Press.

WHITING, BEATRICE BLYTH
  1950   *Paiute sorcery*. Viking Fund Publications in Anthropology 15.
WHITING, JOHN W. M.
  1959   Sorcery, sin and the superego: a cross-cultural study of some mecha-
         nisms of social control. Nebraska Symposium on Motivation. (Re-
         printed in *Cross-cultural approaches: readings in comparative research*.
         Edited by Clelland S. Ford, 147–168. New Haven: Human Relations
         Area File Press.)
WHITING, JOHN W. M., IRVIN L. CHILD
  1953   *Child training and personality: a cross-cultural study*. New Haven:
         Yale University Press.
WHITING, JOHN W. M., RICHARD KLUCKHOHN, ALBERT S. ANTHONY
  1958   "The function of male initiation ceremonies at puberty," in *Readings
         in social psychology* (third edition). Edited by Eleanor E. Maccoby,
         Theodore M. Newcomb, and Eugene L. Hartley, 359–370. New York:
         Holt, Rinehart and Winston.
WRIGHT, GEORGE O.
  1954   Projection and displacement: a cross-cultural study of folk-tale
         aggression. *Journal of Abnormal and Social Psychology* 49:523–528.
YOUNG, FRANK
  1965   *Initiation ceremonies: a cross-cultural study of status dramatization*.
         Indianapolis: Bobbs-Merrill.
YOUNG, FRANK, ALBERT A. BACDAYAN
  1965   Menstrual taboos and social rigidity. *Ethnology* 4:225–240.

# Schizophrenic Graphic Expression and Tribal Art in New Guinea

OTTO BILLIG, B. G. BURTON-BRADLEY, and
ELLEN DOERMANN

The present study examines and compares Western schizophrenic graphic expression and that of indigenous patients from New Guinea and Papua. Graphics function not only as a vehicle of individual expression, but also as a medium through which cultural elements are expressed (Billig 1966, 1970, 1971). These elements are evaluated in terms of regional cultural influences.

The term GRAPHIC EXPRESSION should be distinguished from ART. Art appears to have a societally oriented function, while psychotic expression originates as an individual's attempt to communicate his inner feelings, having become less capable of expressing such feelings verbally. Creativity, essential in the shaping of art forms, links the existing concepts in the unconscious into cohesive entities. The psychotic has lost the ability to reconstruct the fragmented images into cohesive patterns; consequently such images lack both cohesiveness and societal significance (Arnheim 1969).

Verbal language is a more intricate system than visual language (Arnheim 1969). Verbal communication depends upon an adequate interaction between the individual and his environment, a condition that is highly limited in the schizophrenic, who has lost the necessary sequential and "linear" order of thinking that is a prerequisite for verbal communication (Arnheim 1969). Being subjectively aware of this limitation, schizophrenic patients, in their attempt to find a substitute, often begin to draw spontaneously during the course of their illness (Billig 1970). Graphic expressions facilitate the expression of simultaneous concepts. However, as the individual becomes more reintegrated, linear thinking and therefore verbal language are reestablished. Consequently, as patients improve, they may no longer feel the need to express themselves through graphics.

Psychiatric diagnosis in transcultural settings tends to be complex and "cannot be based on the content of delusions alone, but has to be based on the structure of the disorder" (Wynne 1963). The content of the delusions as well as the content of the graphics executed by psychotics seems to be influenced by cultural factors as long as the patient remains relatively well integrated. Accordingly, meaning and content must be considered within the appropriate cultural context. At the beginning of the psychosis, delusions are strongly culture-bound. Control by spirit-beings and magic concepts may be part of a paranoid delusion or part of a cultural belief. However, it assumes significance on a pathological level if the patient's behavior is considered culturally deviant and therefore rejected by the adequately adjusted members of his own community (Ackerknect 1943).

## METHOD

In order to assess the universality of such "core features," graphics produced by Western patients were compared with those of other cultures. Previous cross-cultural studies concerning schizophrenic expression related the spatial structure observed in drawings to clinical manifestations of psychotic disintegration in both Western and non-Western cultures. These patients' productions included material from North America, Western Europe, Kenya, Hong Kong, Japan, and Lebanon (Billig 1966).

New Guinea was selected for our study because it remains in a state of cultural transition. Various regions exhibit different levels of enculturation: tribal traditions and customs still play a significant role in the more isolated areas. The relative isolation of the social groups results primarily from a lack of adequate transportation and existing language difficulties; the 2,000,000 inhabitants of the island speak 700 different languages and dialects. The vast variety of local languages in New Guinea and Papua generates considerable communication difficulty, even among neighboring tribes. The language barrier complicates the psychiatric interview; relatively few patients speak the common neo-Melanesian. Often more than one interpreter is required in cases where the patient comes from one of the more remote areas. The schizophrenic's neologisms and condensations are often difficult to understand, even in the patient's own language. The difficulties are greatly enhanced when translation into a completely different language becomes necessary. Pathological thought processes tend to remain in a state of flux, resulting in an unstable linkage of concepts and therefore a tendency to revise or deny statements that have been made previously. Graphic expression is a more stable form of communication and may facilitate the understanding of patients in various cultures.[1]

## DATA

We collected more than 500 graphics, from which a small number were selected. Because outpatient facilities are extremely limited, all of our patients were hospitalized. We selected patients of different ages and from different regions in order to determine if the duration and intensity of cultural change affected the content and structure of the drawings. The cultural change in various regions of New Guinea depends on when "European" contacts were made. The first "penetrations" during the nineteenth century attempted to change the cultural patterns forcefully, while a more tolerant attitude toward the existing life-styles prevailed in recent contacts in the Highlands (Berndt 1962).

Art has always played a significant role in the cultural life of New Guinea. A large portion of that art was intended to create strong emotional feelings (Beier and Kiki 1970). Many of our patients who are now middle-aged grew up prior to "European penetration" (Berndt 1962). In such cases, traditional cultural influences played an essential part in their personality development, and tribal art primarily fulfilled important societal needs. It protected the individual and society from the threatening unknown by the magic of imagery. It required a strict adherence to established traditional design patterns (Biebuyck 1969). Only the well-integrated personality is able to establish the inner cohesiveness and stable concepts necessary to meet the strict societal demands. The artist and the group share essentially the same set of values (Gebrands 1969); common interests and concerns are linked into overall goal-directed systems (Billig 1966). While the imagery of the tribal artist is socially determined in accord with standards set by the group, psychotic imagery remains solipsistic in nature.

In order to determine the degree of psychotic disintegration, it may be necessary to consider the nonpsychotic traditional art as a basis from which the disintegration of the graphics took place. Traditional art is fundamentally cult art; it forms an essential part of any ceremony performed by the whole group. Decorative art exists; "its motifs and usages

---

[1]    The term TRIBAL is used here to indicate the traditional unit of the nonliterate society. We are aware that most groups in New Guinea are not tribes; they are clans, lineages, moieties, and similar forms of organization.

are derived from cult art" (Forge 1970). Traditional paintings tend to be two-dimensional; "there is no attempt of any sort to establish any visual correspondence with either nature or three-dimensional art" (Forge 1970). Bright colors and overly elaborated patterns are not acceptable (Beier and Kiki 1970; Mead 1963). The forms and styles in traditional art are limited and their production is considered a "sacred" activity (Forge 1970). The traditional colors are "low-toned" earth colors and include four basic hues: red ocher, yellow ocher, white, and black. On some occasions non-traditional colors, such as blue or green, are substituted for one of these four basic colors. Such substitutions have no significant meaning and do not suggest any particular distinction.

Other frequently observed characteristics in tribal art include multiple polychrome lines that are used generally as borders surrounding an object. Not more than three colors are observed in any single work (Newton 1961). The art is abstract and two dimensional, with emphasis placed upon simplicity and tightness of design; the use of bilateral symmetry is common. The entire work forms a cohesive entity and spatial integrity is maintained.

*Case Material*

CASE A

The first patient came from Ihu in the Gulf of Papua. He had always been seclusive, not participating in the customary clan activities that took place in the men's houses. He exhibited a marked personality change following the death of his wife. While fishing with two other women, she was supposedly attacked and killed by a crocodile. Her husband attributed the sudden death to sorcery, an accusation not unusual in the area. He offered a large reward for the person who would identify the crocodile and the presumed sorcerer. A woman accused a particular man in the village of being the sorcerer. When the patient attacked and attempted to kill him, the patient was hospitalized. Even before attacking the "sorcerer," he had lost interest in activities and had neglected his farm. He had broken into the villagers' huts and threatened them with an ax. Such behavior led to his being considered *long-long* [mentally ill] by the villagers.

During hospitalization the patient appeared incoherent, confused, and he hallucinated. He reported that his wife's spirit had appeared to him, admonishing him "not to think about her." If he would not follow her warnings, he would become *long-long*. In order to protect himself against the spirit of his wife, he had produced a large number of imitations of Hohao ancestral plaques, which had been traditionally used in that region.

Hohaos were large boards that "came into their own during time of crisis" (Beier and Kiki 1970); they were considered a powerful symbolic force in

Plate 1.   Hohao ancestral plaque; Gulf of Papua (courtesy of the Field Museum of Natural History, Chicago, Illinois)

Plate 2a.  Schizophrenic distortion and perseveration (Hohao ancestral plaque)

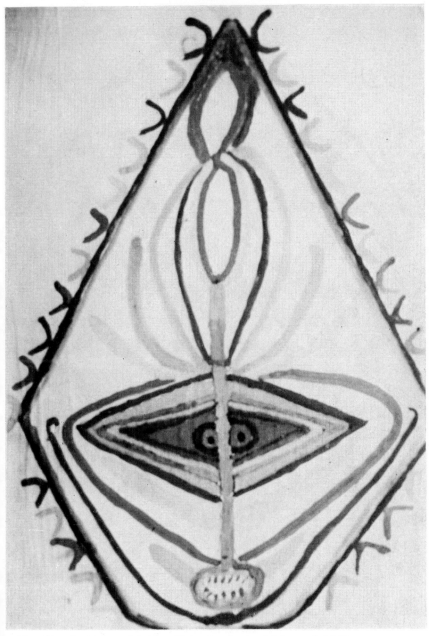

Plate 2b.   Reduction of design with increased geometricism and rigidity

Plate 2c.   Further disintegration of the basic design

Plate 2d.   Increased reduction and two-dimensionality

Plate 2e.   Reduction to baseline with vertical projection; elongation and perseveration of curlicues

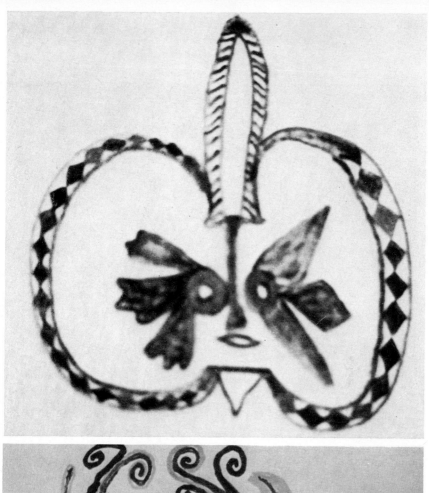

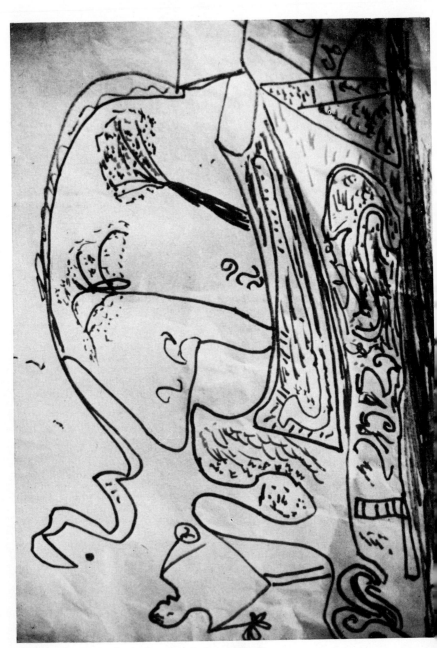

Plate 3a. Lack of cohesion; "vertical projection"

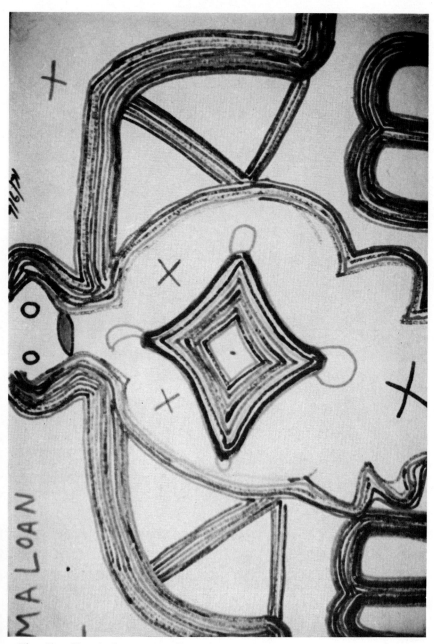

Plate 3b.   "Inarticulate structures"

Plate 3c.  Rigid geometric repetition of design

Plate 3d. Compulsively controlled, rigid geometry

Plate 4.   Vertical projection (North America)

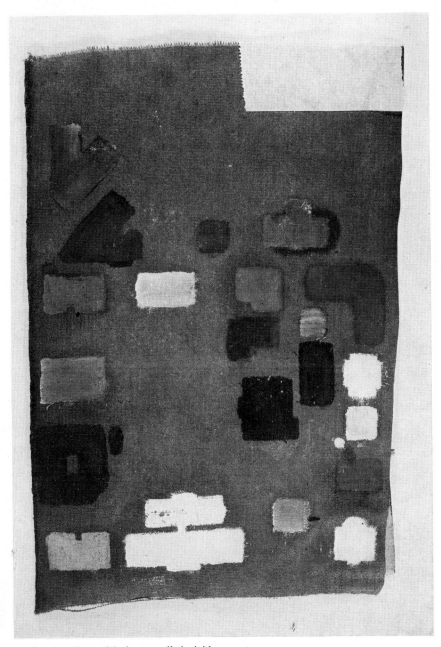

Plate 5.   Compulsively controlled, rigid geometry

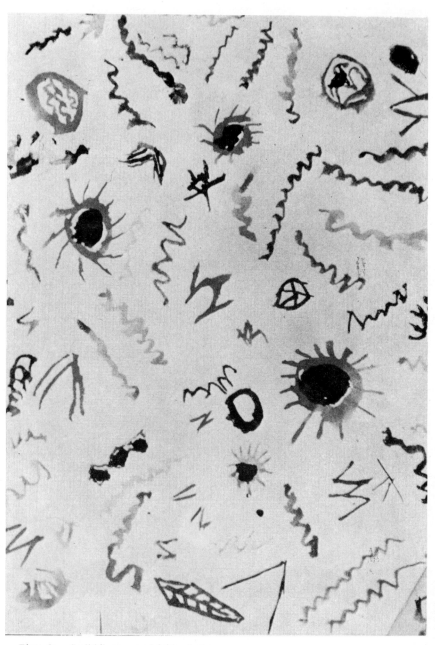

Plate 6a.    Scribblings, mandalalike designs

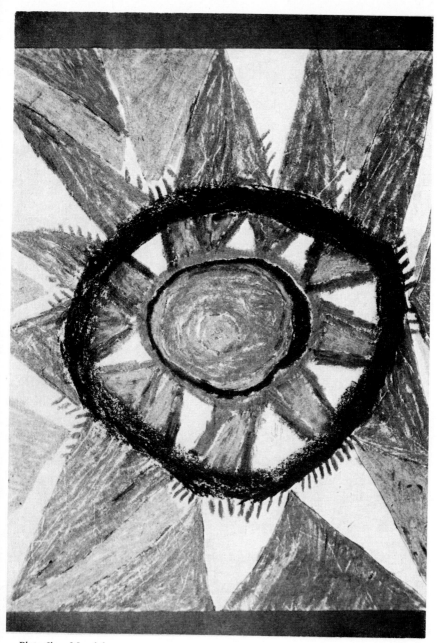

Plate 6b.   Mandala

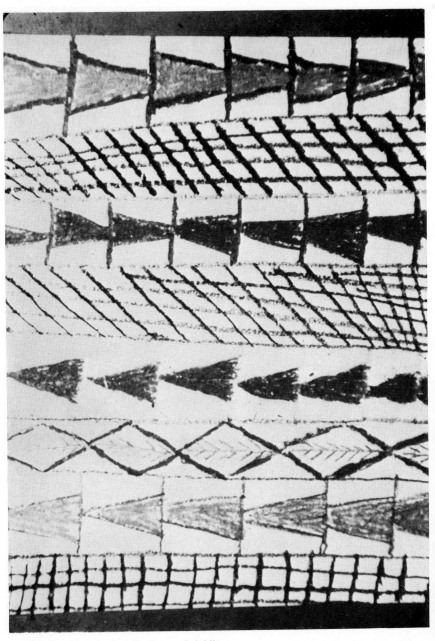

Plate 6c.    Increased stylization and rigidity

Plate 6d.  Elongation

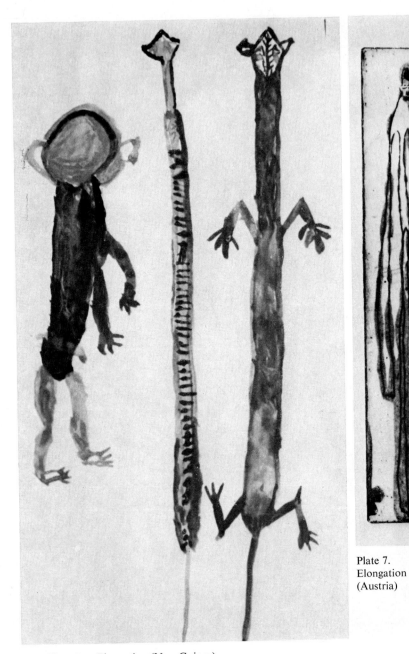

Plate 7.
Elongation
(Austria)

Plate 6e.   Elongation (New Guinea)

protecting the clan (Newton 1961). The many plaques produced by this patient suggest his need of such a protective device. While the traditional plaques had served the needs of the community, the patient's productions had become interwoven in the structure of his delusional system.

The stages of regression exhibited by the patient are illustrated by a series of graphics (see Table 1). Plate 2a shows an attempt to preserve most of the features found in traditional Hohao designs, yet some of the characteristics are becoming rather distorted. The headdress, which in traditional tribal art is cohesive and symmetrical (see Plate 1), has become markedly distorted. The teeth and oral cavity are absent. The traditionally small body is lacking in this drawing. Aside from the dissolving bilateral symmetry, the borders of the plaque are increased from the usual three layers to six layers. Such perseverations produced "too much color or design" and were regarded as unacceptable (Beier and Kiki 1970; Mead 1963). The patient uses bright colors in all his paintings, in contrast to the traditional muted colors.

As further regression takes place, the entire design becomes more rigid and geometric (see Plate 2b); the organic shapes are replaced by more linear, flattened ones. Basic features are structurally altered and reduced.

Table 1. Regressive levels of disintegration

| *Clinical condition* | *Spatial structure* (after Arnheim 1969) |
| --- | --- |
| Beginning withdrawal of object relationships | Emptying space; shadowy figures; elongation and distortions |
| Disintegration of the boundaries existing between the self and the environment | Perseveration<br>Spatial relations destroyed |
| Inadequate balance between external reality and the self | Impoverished and condensed design<br>Mixing of planes<br>"X-ray pictures" (transparencies)<br>Vertical projection |
| More advanced disintegration | *Horror vacui*<br>Fragmentation of concepts |
| Appearance of universal concepts | Inarticulated structures |
| Severe repression of relations to external reality | Baseline with vertical direction<br>Geometric designs<br>Abstract mandala-like designs |
| Feelings of undifferentiated oneness between the self and external reality | Multidirectional space; "scribblings" |

The chevrons surrounding the eyes are now mere triangular encasements. Multiple colored lines repeat these triangular structures. Geometricism and rigidity appear as an attempt to establish order in the threatening personality disintegration.

The dissolution of the basic design progresses further (see Plate 2c). The conventional boundaries with zigzag designs disappear and the plaque becomes partially open; the previous rigid attempt to form a cohesive, intact entity can no longer be maintained and the borders partially dissolve. The borders above the eyes, which are surrounded by modified chevrons, disintegrate. This change may reflect the disintegration of the personality and its increasing lack of separation from the surrounding space. The structures appearing in the lower portion of the mask are perseverated and distorted, while the colors remain untraditionally bright.

Further condensation is shown in the next graphic (see Plate 2d). The entire design has become impoverished, flattened, and more compact. The original oval-shaped face is rounded, with small diamonds forming the border. Eyes are painted as circles flanked by chevrons. The vertical line that originally represented the nose remains, having a small triangle on its base. The headdress has become elongated, although the symmetry is maintained. The outstanding feature of this watercolor is its relative emptiness.

Plate 2e was executed by the patient during a period of severe psychotic disintegration. It has lost the facial features of the original design. Only the vertical lines observed in previous watercolors remain. A horizontal line has been added to the vertical line, thereby forming a cross. Several layers of bright colors that have been surrounded by the traditional curlicues are perseverated and elongated. A continuous boundary is lacking and the entire structure has lost its cohesiveness and spatial integrity. The basic design has disintegrated. An adequate control of the concept formation can no longer be maintained and realistic relations of objects to one another no longer exist. Object relationships, which were used not only to separate but also to identify concepts, become weakened (Burnham and Burnham 1969).

CASE B

The people of Buka, a small island in the Solomon group, have been in contact with "Europeans" for more than 100 years. At intervals, reactions against Western colonization have emerged in the form of cargo cults (Burton-Bradley 1972). Patient B led one such movement, and at one time he had been a successful and comparatively wealthy man. The government had appointed him as the headman of his village. Some years later, a gradual personality change began. He developed increasing anxieties and irritability; he became querulous, which led to fights with the local police for which he was jailed for a short time. Following his arrest, he lost interest in his affairs and neglected his businesses; though the villagers formerly respected him highly, they now considered him strange. He joined the Hahalis Welfare Society, a group dedicated to forcing social and political changes. Private property was abolished within the group and an economic and sexual commune was established (Burton-Bradley 1972).

The patient began preaching to his people about the emergence of a new millennium of everlasting wealth; ancestors would return with a cargo filled with building materials, food, and other goods. Such cargo cults have sprung up periodically for more than a century and express the conflict arising from the impact of Western culture on tribal tradition (Burton-Bradley 1969a, 1969b, 1972). In order to induce his ancestors to bring the cargo, he sacrificially killed his sister's daughter's son by cutting the boy's throat. During the preliminary hearing, he appeared indifferent and paid little attention to the proceedings. When at the end of the hearings he attempted suicide by cutting his throat, he was hospitalized (Burton-Bradley 1972). The patient considered himself to have superior powers, believing that he had become God as a result of his sacrificial act; he considered it to be his right to sacrifice others or himself. This patient had developed a slowly progressive paranoid system that was rather well organized and interwoven with traditional beliefs. He had no insight into his delusions, which remained fixed. The more discerning members of his own group recognized them as being psychotic (Ackerknect 1943).

The patient's disintegration is reflected in the first crayon drawing (see Plate 3a). Its organization is loose, lacking cohesiveness. He had become unable to maintain an adequate sequence of thoughts; conceptual links had become inteerrupted. The patient was overwhelmed by the simultaneous presence of concepts (Billig 1966). He attempted a partial restitution, which is reflected in his drawing as "vertical continuance" (Arnheim 1969). The objects lack an adequate sequence, being placed on three "baselines," one over the other. Vertical projection (see Table 1) was previously reported in schizophrenic paintings of other non-Western and Western cultures (see Plate 4).

Plate 3b shows comparatively unstructured elements, or "inarticulate structures" (Billig 1966, 1970, 1971; Ehrenzweig 1969). A rudimentary figure is painted with ten to twelve layers of bright colors, a marked perseveration of the traditional use of three layers (Mead 1963). The arms and legs in the drawing are highly stylized, giving the entire figure the appearance of being frozen in this highly regressed form. The face is almost empty, consisting of two holes representing the eyes and mouth. Similar "inarticulate" structures were described in the paintings of Western patients (Billig 1971).

The patient's increasing concern with structure and organization is shown in Plate 3c.

This graphic was executed in an extremely rigid fashion. Organic forms (smooth, rounded, flowing shapes) have given way to rigid geometric forms. The house has been constructed solely from the juxtaposition and addition of various triangles and rectangles. A symmetrical composition is attempted by arranging similar parts at equal distances from the baseline. The entire work is completely flat (compare with Plate 4). The graphic was drawn after the patient had undergone treatment for more than two years. He still expressed the same clinical delusional system, but his anxieties were markedly reduced.

The last drawing (Plate 3d) suggests an attempt at restitution on the part of the patient (Burnham and Burnham 1969). The previous flooding of simultaneous concepts becomes compulsively controlled by the production of rigid geometrical designs (compare with Plate 5). The patient's delusions were interwoven with culture-bound material; his actions were controlled by traditional beliefs. His personality disintegration is reflected to a far greater extent in his graphics. Their structure demonstrates changes similar to those in patients of other cultures (Billig 1966, 1971).

CASE C

The patient is a fifty-three-year-old male from the Chimbu district in the Highlands who reportedly had committed several murders. He became noticeably psychotic following the death of his wife, at which time he performed necrophilic relations with her. His behavior was considered to be completely unacceptable in his own group and subsequently led to his hospitalization. He appeared confused when hospitalized; he hallucinated, hearing the voice of his dead wife. His thought processes were circumstantial and vague. However, he did not appear highly disintegrated and he improved under treatment.

In contrast to the previous patient's productions, the content of the drawings produced by Patient C is more culture-bound. The first watercolor demonstrates a lack of cohesiveness (see Plate 6a). Scribblings executed in various bright colors are interspersed with small mandalalike objects in red and yellow. The mandala, which is surrounded by yellow chevrons, consists of a simple red disk devoid of the inner structuralizations that appear later. The considerable perseveration of design, rigidity, and elaborations differentiate this watercolor from the traditional patterns (Abramson and Holst 1973).

As the patient's clinical condition improved, the scribblings disappeared and the small forms were replaced by more cohesive and uniform shapes. The patient then produced a number of designs that were similar to traditional patterns (see Plate 6b). However, he elaborated these patterns considerably, and furthermore he filled in the entire available space with geometric figures. The disintegrated personality, having lost adequate contacts with reality, defends itself against the threat of surrounding emptiness (Billig 1966) by "obliterating space" (Read 1961) and filling it with abstract designs (*horror vacui*). The patient used bright colors, particularly, red, green, and blue, in contrast to the usual muted tones.

Increased rigidity and stylization are evident in Plate 6c. The basic units are geometrically proportioned, executed in traditional design. However, perseveration and the considerable repetition of the individual components deviate from the traditional patterns. A drawing in red and blue crayon shows a markedly elongated animal (see Plate 6d).

Articulated anthropomorphic structures are lacking and are replaced by more stylized, geometric components. Such figures are found, although infrequently, in bark paintings of the Highlands (Abramson and Holst 1973). The arms are bent at the elbows in a culturally characteristic position. The entire figure appears overly rigid and stiff. Two areas of perseverated cross-hatching place the central figure within a restricted space. Organic articulation has been replaced with more abstract and flattened designs.

The elongations, a characteristic previously observed in Western paintings (see Table 1), are considerably overemphasized in the three figures painted by the patient (see Plate 6e). The left, humanlike figure is "shadowy"; it appears stiff, in twisted perspective (*perspective tordue* [Giedion 1962]). The middle figure represents an unspecified animal with horizontal stippling, while the right figure appears to be a lizard with a human face, a theme not uncommonly observed in New Guinea art. Such elongation of the body with a disproportionally small head is a recurrent design observed in schizophrenic paintings, regardless of cultural background (see Plate 7).

The graphics of these three patients suggest that characteristic structural changes correspond to various levels of psychotic disintegration. The stages may be differentiated from one another as demonstrated in Table 1. Regressive structural features such as elongation, perseveration, excessive ornamentation, and "baseline" emerge.

## DISCUSSION

Two aspects of the graphics produced by patients from New Guinea were investigated: structure and content. Structural characteristics correspond more directly to personality disintegration and reflect the concepts of reality, while content is related to individual cultural factors. However, as regression advances in any cultural setting, fewer elements of that culture remain and more universal elements emerge. Acutely regressed patients produce structures similar to those of Western patients of corresponding levels of personality disintegration. Simple inarticulated shapes, two-dimensionality, and mere scribblings are observed. These characteristics appear regardless of any artistic experience, dexterity, or cultural level (Billig 1966). The structural changes seem to be controlled by the level of personality organization: more advanced regression leads to earlier levels of spatial organization (Billig 1971) and to decreasing cultural influences (see Table 1).

The content of the graphics shows a great interdependency with cultural elements. In cases where considerable enculturation has taken place, graphics are produced in Western style. However, traditional patterns appear wherever European culture has made only a superficial impact. Specifically, Patient B came from a societal group that has been subjected to Western influences for more than 100 years. The patient himself had experienced intimate European contacts. As he became psychotic, he relinquished his adopted European life-style and joined the Hahalis Welfare Society. He expressed his ambivalence and conflicts concerning Western influences by desiring the material advantages of the white man but attempting to attain these goals by cultural practices of the past such as human sacrifices. In spite of a partial regression, which led to traditional behavior, it was actually the Western influences that were instrumental in creating his "wish to break with the past" (Burton-Bradley 1972). The patient demonstrated clinically a preoccupation with the culture-bound concepts of the cargo cult, while most of his drawings express culture-free universal concepts as well as a Western graphic style.

Patient C lived in the comparative cultural isolation of the Highlands. As long as he appeared severely disintegrated, his drawings contained no significant cultural concepts; such patterns of psychotic disintegration have been observed in patients regardless of cultural background. As this patient's personality reintegrated, regional cultural concepts became more prominent in his graphics.


## SUMMARY AND CONCLUSIONS

In considering cross-cultural studies pertaining to psychotic disintegration, one must consider the obvious conclusion that a psychosis develops within its specific cultural setting (characteristics of tribal art and psychotic expressions are compared in Table 2). Cultural patterns seemingly influence the content of the indigenous graphics in a manner similar to that

Table 2. Cultural and personality functions in tribal art and psychotic expressions

|  | *Tribal art* | *Psychotic expressions or "art"* |
|---|---|---|
| Structure of personality | Integrated | Disintegrated |
| Boundaries between the self and the environment | Intact | Dissolved |
| Concept formation | Stable, often rigid, cohesive well delineated | Unstable linkage, vague, overlapping, fragmented |
| Defense mechanisms | Goal-directed, adapted to cultural group images; magical thinking; rigidity; omnipotence | Lacking goal ideas; unconscious mechanisms overwhelm the poorly integrated personality; magical thinking; omnipotence |
| Symbolism | Culturally determined; societal values | Solipsistic |
| Relation to external reality | Societal organization may disregard individual needs; stylistic characteristics often developed because of societal needs | Individual may sacrifice external reality |
| Summary | Shared, common reality within which the individual functions | Common reality is reduced |

of the language patterns (Lévi-Strauss 1963). The art style of a specific region appears as a form of expression related to cultural and social influences: "It must be characterized by a typical combination of elements which identifies the objects from one area" (Myers 1967). In addition, individual stylistic differences within the cultural group remain significant in "tribal" society, as they do in Western art (Gebrands 1969), despite rigid societal rules (Mead 1963).

In New Guinea, as in other preliterate societies, the artist and psychotic alike express themselves by means of "visual language." Art as "a visual mode of communication comes into existence as soon as human society comes into existence and can be found wherever society exists" (Read 1961). According to Read, art exists prior to verbal language. Verbal language, being a more complex system, depends upon the interaction between the individual and his environment, whereas graphic productions depend far less on such interaction. The inability to preserve and maintain "linear sequential thinking" (Arnheim 1969) renders graphic productions more successful as vehicles of expression concerning the psychotic's concepts of reality (Billig 1966).

In cases where the regional style is unfamiliar, psychotic painting may appear as foreign to the layman as that produced by nonpsychotics, as exemplified by Case A. The pathological effect upon the structure, its alteration, and the significance of content requires a familiarity with the culture from which the work originates. The personality disintegration modifies the content of the cultural patterns in accord with the level of disintegration. As regression advances, cultural influences recede and universal culture-free patterns develop. Disintegration leads to a "return to an archaic psychic organization" (Wynne 1963). As demonstrated in the regressive patterns of Cases A and C, culture-bound concepts, such as Hohao plaques, disintegrated to abstractions, while anthropomorphic figures regressed to a form of scribbling.

While the content is more culture-bound, spatial structural changes seem to be universal (Billig 1970, 1971). Giedion (1962), an art historian, states that "man's attitude toward space is the psychic reflection of his visual world. The all embracing quality of any art is how man experiences space: space conception."

Psychotic disintegration leads to a regression to the latent "universals" that were formerly repressed. As these early spatial structures reappear, they are related to the level of disintegration. Concepts become controlled by emotionally charged material rather than by existing reality factors. The psychotic lacks the ability to connect concepts in a stable linkage; they exist in a state of flux, remaining vague and overlapping, and exhibit inadequate cohesiveness. The resulting concepts lead to the formation of a new ideation based on apparent similarities and lacking an adequate goal system (Billig 1971). As the personality undergoes greater disintegration, the individual becomes less able to interrelate the multiple determinants necessary to maintain an adequate level of mental functioning (Hallowell 1965); therefore a regression to "psychobiological universals" is observed. Subtle structural changes may be overlooked at first and may be hidden by cultural elements. As regression progresses, however, the structural characteristics emerge more clearly and can be observed in all stages of disintegration.

In summary, the data collected from New Guinea and Papua appear to support theories of universal factors of behavior: "Every man has numerous latent functions which lead under certain conditions, compulsorily and essentially, to the same course" (Wynne 1963). Psychotic reintegration proceeds "from a state of relative globality and lack of differentiation to a state of increased differentiation, articulation and hierarchic integration." Enculturation exerts a profound influence upon the individual and his society; however, in cases of pronounced personality disintegration, cultural influences become less significant and more universal elements appear.

## REFERENCES

ABRAMSON, J. A., R. HOLST
1973   Hewa sacred painting and style in New Guinea Art. *Records of the Papua New Guinea Museum and Art Gallery* 3. Port Moresby.
ACKERKNECT, E. H.
1943   Psychopathology: primitive medicine and primitive culture. *Bulletin of the Institute of the History of Medicine* 14. Johns Hopkins University.
ARNHEIM, R.
1969   *Visual thinking*. Los Angeles: University of California Press.
BEIER, ULLI, ALBERT MAORI KIKI
1970   *Hohao*. Melbourne: Nelson.
BERNDT, R. M.
1962   *Excess and restraint*. Chicago: University of Chicago Press.
BIEBUYCK, D., editor
1969   *Tradition and creativity in tribal art*. Berkeley: University of California Press.
BILLIG, OTTO
1966   Cross-cultural factors in schizophrenic art. *Proceedings of the Fourth World Congress of Psychiatry*, Madrid, 1966. Excerpta Medica International Congress Series 150:600–612.
1970   Structures of schizophrenic forms of expression. *Psychiatric Quarterly* 44:187–222.
1971   Is schizophrenic expression art? *Journal of Nervous and Mental Disorders* 153:149–164.
BURNHAM, D. L., A. L. BURNHAM
1969   *Schizophrenia and the need-fear dilemma*, 282–305. New York: International Universities Press.
BURTON-BRADLEY, B. G.
1969a  Papua and New Guinea, transcultural psychiatry I. *Australia and New Zealand Journal of Psychiatry* 3:124–129.
1969b  Papua and New Guinea, transcultural psychiatry II. *Australia and New Zealand Journal of Psychiatry* 3:130–136.
1972   Human sacrifice for cargo. *Medical Journal of Australia* 2:668–670.
DE VOS, G.
1965   "Transcultural diagnosis of mental health," in *Transcultural psychiatry*. Edited by A. V. S. De Reuck and Ruth Porter, 328–353. Boston: Little, Brown.
EHRENZWEIG, A.
1969   *The hidden order of art*. Berkeley: University of California Press.

FORGE, A.
  1970    "Learning to see in New Guinea," in *Socialization*. Edited by P. Mayer. Association of Social Anthropologists Monograph 8. London: Tavistock.
GEBRANDS, A
  1969    "The concept of non-Western art," In *Tradition and creativity in tribal art*. Edited by D. Biebuyck, 58–70. Berkeley: University of California Press.
GIEDION, S.
  1962    *The eternal present: the beginning of art*. New York: Random House.
HALLOWELL, A. E.
  1965    "Hominid evolution, cultural adaptation, and mental dysfunctioning," in *Transcultural psychiatry*. Edited by A. V. S. De Reuck and Ruth Porter, 26–53. Boston: Little, Brown.
LÉVI-STRAUSS, C.
  1963    *Structural anthropology*. New York: Basic Books.
MEAD, M.
  1963    "The bark paintings of the Mountain Arapesh of New Guinea," in *Technique and personality in primitive art*. By M. Mead, J. B. Bird, and H. Himmelheber. New York: Museum of Primitive Art.
MYERS, B. S.
  1967    *Art and civilization*. New York: McGraw-Hill.
NEWTON, D.
  1961    *Art styles of the Papuan Gulf*. New York: Museum of Primitive Art.
READ, H.
  1961    "Art in aboriginal society," in *The artist in tribal society*. Edited by M. W. Smith, 14–32, 126. New York: Free Press.
RUESCH, J.
  1955    Non-verbal language and therapy. *Psychiatry* 18:323–330.
RYAN, J.
  1971    *The hot land: focus on New Guinea*. Melbourne: Macmillan.
WILLIAMS, F. E.
  1969    *Drama of Orokolo*. London: Clarendon Press.
WYNNE, L. C.
  1963    The transcultural study of schizophrenics and their families. *Transcultural Research* 15:10–13.

# The Vectors of Changing Values: A Model for Predicting Change in Mental Deviance Rates in Developing Countries

JOSEPH HARTOG

## INTRODUCTION

The possibility, formulated by Florence Kluckhohn, (Kluckhohn and Strodtbeck 1961) of systematically assessing a culture's value orientations gives us the opportunity to build some hypotheses. One group of hypotheses might relate different rates of mental deviance to different configurations of values (value orientations) across cultures. However, such cross-cultural comparisons present many pitfalls of comparability, definitions, linguistics, and epidemiology (Hartog 1972, 1973). I wish to offer a model for longitudinal study of one culture at a time to predict for developing countries (a) changes in rates and kinds of mental deviance from certain characteristics and interrelationships of present values, and (b) future value stances.

This proposal emerged from preliminary baseline work I performed in Malaysia in 1966–1968 as part of a broad study of mental health among Malays. I prepared a value survey (Hartog n.d.) in which respondents were asked to indicate the value choice that "traditional," "in between," and "modern" Malays would make for each of forty-three items. The items were of various levels of logical abstraction, ranging from Kluckhohn's five cosmic areas (man's relation to man, nature, being, time, and innate

The research for this paper was done under the auspices of the G. W. Hooper Foundation and the Department of International Health of the University of California, San Francisco, and the Faculty of Medicine (Department of Psychological Medicine), University of Malaya. Work was supported by the University of California International Center for Medical Research through research grant A1 10051 from the National Institutes of Health, United States Public Health Service.

good or evil) to everyday prosaic concerns about interpersonal relations and choices, sexuality, and aesthetics. This rather crude instrument, with many technical flaws, was offered to approximately 100 English-speaking Malays, experienced United States Peace Corps volunteers, and non-Malay experts on Malay life and culture. It has not been revised, and except for a comparison of "supportiveness toward women" among Malays, Chinese, and Iban for Karl Schmidt,[1] the results have not been tabulated or analyzed. The model presented here evolved from this survey. The specific instrument is of secondary concern for the moment.

If the model works in one culture, it should be adaptable to other cultures with due regard for cultural linguistics, and definitional differences, because the main hurdle is circumvented by using an INTERNAL comparison rather than a cross-cultural one. For instance, to quantify change it does not matter so much what is universally defined as mental deviance so long as internal measurable consistency is maintained. Similarly, it does not matter so much if "man is basically evil" means different things in different cultures so long as the same meaning is attributed to it within the single culture throughout the period of initial and follow-up studies.

Furthermore, the problem of determining whether a respondent's assessment of Malay values is valid creates a whole, possibly needless, technology of assessment materials and techniques, from interviews and questionnaires to essay-type hypothetical problems and situation formats. I contend that given an internally consistent research model, any of the techniques will be adequate because in a longitudinal study, distorted responses — to please, deceive, or defeat the researcher, or because of imperfect communication — will nevertheless have predictive use. For instance, in psychotherapy the patient's free associations, memories, dreams, expectations, apprehensions, etc., need not be "real" or factual in order to be predictive, prognostic, or of dynamic significance.

"Values" and "value orientations," used interchangeably here, mean those opinions and attitudes that influence how people actually behave and feel, or what they believe they should be or do.

"Mental deviance," as used here, encompasses mental illness, social illness (violent and nonviolent crime and delinquency), suicide, drug and alcohol addiction, and sexual and marital disorders, as perceived and defined by the community and outsiders. This large and fine net should reduce the probability of a speciously low overall rate of mental deviance resulting, for example, from too great a dependence on hospital data. A society with a low rate of hospitalizable mental illness may have a high

---

[1]   Formerly of Kuching, Sarawak, and now of Nouméa, New Caledonia.

rate of alcoholism or homicide, just as adolescents who do not show clinical depression may become delinquent instead. The model does not imply an etiology of mental deviance except insofar as value conflict is one of several environmental factors in addition to the hereditary, congenital, nutritional, intrapsychic, and interpersonal ones. It does strongly imply, however, that susceptible individuals, the "weak links," will be pushed toward culturally selected forms of deviance.

HYPOTHESIS 1: *Value orientations will change over time toward those now judged "modern."* This is essentially the self-fulfilling prophecy on a communal scale. If Malay peasants in a traditional village believe, correctly or not, that modern Malays are less religious, the hypothesis predicts a change toward secularism. Similarly, if the same respondents believe that more modern Malays engage in premarital sexual relations, the hypothesis translates that into a prediction.

HYPOTHESIS 2: *The vectors of changing values can graphically and quantitatively predict the direction and specific forms of future mental deviance.* Not only are there hierarchies of importance and different degrees of adherence to different values, but actions may not even follow stated or felt values. In the survey, respondents were asked to indicate, as much as possible, the values observed and acted upon. At least as an indicator, if the hypothesis concerning the self-fulfilling prophecy has any merit, the deviant members of a society will act out the stated values literally.

As used here, "vector" refers to a graphic summation of the direction and quantity of movement of a cluster of related values from a point of origin toward "traditional" and "modern" poles. Because vectors are directional, value changes that are opposed, conflicting, or contradictory within a cluster will reduce the total length of the vector. It is in the setting of excessive value conflict and short vectors that mental deviance will grow. Each cluster represents values subsumed under, and including, a value of higher abstraction, such as one of Kluckhohn's five.

The idea of the vectors is that the interaction of related values, particularly conflict and strain, will be more predictive than mere change in isolated values. I believe that individuals and cultures can withstand, without mental and social harm, massive value changes if the sweep of these changes is relatively consistent, noncontradictory, and congruous in such a way as to minimize conflict among the core values. Although at this stage one must defer any categorical definition of core values or any estimate of how much value conflict or strain is critical, the model itself should empirically throw light on these issues.

The model requires assumptions about how to cluster the values and about which forms of deviance will follow from conflict within certain clusters.

*Example*:   One can assign an arbitrary weight to an item dealing with some supraordinate value — e.g. the universe and everything within it is measurable, limited, and explainable (closed system), OR the universe... is immeasurable, limitless, and unexplainable (open system), OR a mixture of the two — and equal or lower weights to items dealing with other related values of a similar or lower order of abstraction within the same cluster (open versus closed system). Some items that could belong to the cluster in this example (and possibly to other clusters) are:

A.   Man's behavior and decisions are determined by forces not under his control — either outside him or within him (determinism) — OR man has free will in his choices and behavior.[2]

B.   There is a right way to live and do things, OR one lives and does things according to the method that seems to work.

C.   In relations with other people, one should generally try to take control, OR one should generally try to follow the lead of others and submit to the wishes of others ,OR neither of these two.

D.   One must live life for itself (being, spontaneity), OR one must live life to improve oneself (being-in-becoming, growth, maturity, knowledge), OR one must live life by doing and changing the world (doing).

E.   Man must control and tame nature, OR be in harmony with nature, OR submit to nature.

F.   Man must control and tame those forces outside of nature (godly, supernatural, metaphysical), OR be in harmony with those forces, OR submit to those forces.

G.   Which is more valued by the Malays of each category:
   1. Reason or faith
   2. Intellect or emotions
   3. Science or inspiration
   4. Logic or imagination
   5. Facts or mysteries
   6. Heredity or environment

H.   Is man accountable and responsible:
   1. For his fellow man

_____

[2]   In the value survey, respondents were asked to ascribe to each column of "traditional," "in-between," and "modern" Malays a preferred or acted upon value, indicated by a code letter, numeral, or abbreviation.

2. To God

3. Regarding his own health

a. Physical

b. Mental

I.    How concerned are the Malays of each category with neatness and cleanliness?

After each item is assigned a numerical weight and a directional (+ or —) character, the completed surveys are tabulated (Figures 1 and 2). We then represent the vectors in two dimensions for simplicity (other methods are available [Keats 1962; Stephenson 1968; Schnaiberg 1970]).

Total consistent value change to modern will appear as an arrow vector proportional in length to the total of value weights in the directions of the modern pole; total consistent unmodified traditional values will be represented by an arrow vector in the direction of the traditional pole; and

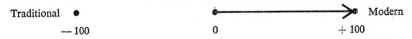

Traditional    ●                                                  ➤● Modern

   — 100                     0                    + 100

Totally "modern" value choices

Traditional    ◄————————————————●              ● Modern

   — 100                     0                    + 100

Totally "traditional" value choices

Traditional    ●                    (●)                    ● Modern

   — 100                     0                    + 100

Totally balanced (conflicted) "modern" and "traditional" value choices

Figure 1.   Hypothetical vectors for clusters of totally "modern," "traditional," and conflicted values

maximum conflict or strain will appear as a zero-length resultant vector indicating equal totals of traditional and modern value choices within one cluster (see Figure 1).

If, in the cluster of values cited earlier (open versus closed system), some items were rated as changing little or not at all, some were rated as changing toward modern, and others were rated as changing toward traditional, the vector for the cluster would show little movement, hence much conflict. Suppose item B (orthodoxy versus pragmatism) is perceived by most respondents as changing to greater pragmatism among modern Malays, while on the other hand, the respondents see Malays of all categories as agreeing on a traditional view of items C (follow the leader) and G1 (reason or faith). A summation of similar contradiction would contribute to a small, high-conflict vector.

The next task, also involving assumptions, is the prediction of which area of mental deviance will increase in the future in view of the low vector and high conflict represented in the above cluster. I would venture another hypothesis.

HYPOTHESIS 3: *The form of mental deviance predicted to increase in response to value conflict reflects the main human issue inherent in the value cluster involved.* For instance, in the hypothetical example cited above, the predominant issue is control and helplessness in the world. If increasing conflict is predicted, then it should manifest itself in forms of deviance, expressed by vulnerable individuals, aimed at homeostatically restoring psychological control or reflecting a loss of psychological control. Anxiety should be a prominent symptom and projection a common psychological mechanism of defense. Hence the forms of deviance to increase should be mostly paranoid forms of psychoses, anxiety neuroses, psychosomatic disorders, and antisocial behaviors, all commonly seen in people who feel powerless and helpless.

Another cluster of values — for example, concerning man's relationship to man, whether the orientation is vertical (authoritarian), horizontal (equalitarian), or individualistic; and whether the area of concern is law, violence, good and evil, sex, familial and extrafamilial allegiances, reciprocal relations, honesty, etc. — will predict deviance in the areas of crime, delinquency, marriage, and sex.

The usefulness and the complexity of the model can expand to accommodate each different cluster of values by assigning a different angle to each cluster's vector. This would allow for a visual, perhaps even three-dimensional, representation, a value-change profile or "valueprint" for each culture (see Figure 2).

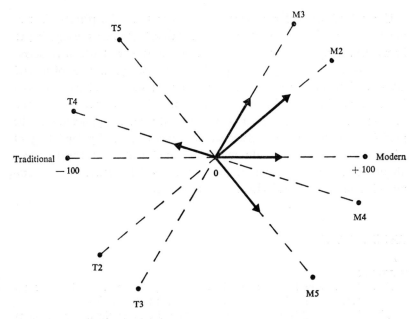

Figure 2.  Hypothetical vectors for five clusters of changing values

## CONCLUSION

I have presented preliminary thoughts on a model for predicting value change and changes in mental deviance rates in developing countries. I have argued that a longitudinal study within a culture will provide internal consistency and a dynamic picture not available with a cross-cultural approach. The clash of conflicting changes within a value cluster probably influences mental deviance more than does mere value change by itself. Change in values does not "cause" mental deviance in and of itself but rather shapes the expression of symptoms that susceptible individuals will show. I have described a simplified graphic representation and analysis of value change using a crude survey of "traditional" and "modern" values of Malays.

The hypotheses to be tested by the model are: (1) Value orientations will change over time toward those that are now judged "modern." This is a version of the self-fulfilling prophecy hypothesis. (2) The vectors of changing values can graphically and quantitatively predict the direction and specific forms of future mental deviance. (3) The form of mental deviance predicted to increase in response to value conflict reflects the main human issue inherent in the value cluster involved.

Unresolved research problems include perfection of a primary instrument for obtaining value ratings for more than forty items, weighting of items, and determination of the point on the vector at which sufficient conflict is indicated to predict any significant change in rates of mental deviance. Technical problems, such as sampling for value survey respondents, determining useful mental and social deviance parameters, and accurate data collection, must be worked out prior to application of the model (see References and Selected References on the Epidemiology of Mental Disorders). Also, although the author makes informed guesses about which forms of deviance follow from which clashing values, empirical confirmation awaits the test of the model.

## REFERENCES

HARTOG, J.
   1972   Institutions for the mentally and socially deviant in Malaysia: some ethnic comparisons. *Asian Journal of Medicine* 8:170–177.
   1973   Ninety-six Malay psychiatric patients: characteristics and preliminary epidemiology. *International Journal of Social Psychiatry* 19:49–59.
   n.d.   "Value survey." Unpublished manuscript.
KEATS, J. A.
   1962   Attitudes towards idealized types in Australia and Malaya. *Journal of Social Psychology* 57:353–362.
KLUCKHOHN, F. R., F. L. STRODTBECK
   1961   *Variations in value orientations*. Evanston: Row, Peterson.
SCHNAIBERG, A.
   1970   Measuring modernism: theoretical and empirical explorations. *American Journal of Sociology* 76:399–425.
STEPHENSON, J. B.
   1968   Is everyone going modern? a critique and a suggestion for measuring modernism. *American Journal of Sociology* 74:265–275.

# Animal Modeling of Psychopathology: Current Status of the Field

WILLIAM T. McKINNEY, Jr.

During the last ten years the field of experimental psychopathology in nonhuman primates has undergone considerable development. It is now possible through utilization of certain social and biological induction methods to produce syndromes of abnormal behavior which can be objectively documented and evaluated. If behavioral and biochemical studies whose findings may subsequently be applied to human beings are to be performed, ideally one should use a species as close to man as possible. From this viewpoint, the great apes might be the logical choice. However, due to the scarcity and the difficulties and expense of working with large primates in a laboratory, much of the work to be referred to here has utilized rhesus monkeys and other species of monkeys as subjects. Also the life span of monkeys is considerably compressed in comparison to man or the apes, thus facilitating longitudinal studies.

The interest of most clinicians in the experimental simulation of abnormal behavior states in nonhumans has ranged from excessive anthropomorphism to indifference to hostility to confusion. The skepticism with which much animal behavioral work has been received lies partly in the history of the field and partly in the attitude of some clinicians who refuse to accept animal work as relevant to human disorders. This latter school of thought has been actively represented by Kubie (1939) who states "Thus, the imitation in animals of the emotional states which attend neuroses in man is not the experimental production of the essence of neuroses itself." Kubie's contention is that behavior is only the "sign language" of an underlying symbolic disorder which is the real core of psychopathology. He feels that animals do not have symbolic capacities and therefore, it is not possible to produce a "true" neurotic or psychotic state in nonhumans. This position is predicated on an assumption about human psychopathology that many would disagree with, namely, that behavior is important only as an indicator of something more important which is the "real" disorder.

Others would insist that observations of behavior are the only way to define disorders reliably. Also, the assumption that higher order primates do not have symbolic capacities is open to serious question. However, Kubie in his criticisms did focus on an important issue in the field of animal modeling of human psychopathology. Various terms have been applied far too loosely to the abnormal behavioral states created in different species. Labels such as "experimental neuroses," "phobia," "anxiety," "behavioral disorder," "chronic emotional disorder," "experimental neurasthenia," and "depression" have been utilized often without adequate behavioral descriptions. The laxity in labeling has often alienated clinicians who fail to see the similarities between conditions used to produce abnormal behavior in many animal studies and those that are thought to predispose to human psychopathology.

Many criticisms of the field of experimental psychopathology are justified. However, there is no intrinsic reason why specific forms of human psychopathology cannot be examined at an animal level. It has been pointed out by Seligman and Grores (1970) and by McKinney and Bunney (1969) that the difficulty in moving from a dramatic analogue to animal models has been due in large part to the lack of ground rules or criteria which might validate the model. These will be reviewed below.

It should be mentioned that this discussion is concerned only with experimental laboratory investigations and does not deal with the broader range of important field studies that are available. However, field studies and laboratory studies of primates should be viewed as complimentary rather than competitive with each having inherent advantages and disadvantages.

In addition to a discussion of the criteria involved in producing animal models for human psychopathology, we will refer to the major social induction techniques which are being used in animals. These include (1) social isolation, (2) experimental helplessness, and (3) attachment behavior and separation studies. Recent approaches to biochemical studies in primate models will also be outlined.

## CRITERIA FOR ANIMAL MODELS

The basic controversy that has developed from previous work in this field as well as from recent data is whether a laboratory phenomenon in animals can model a form or forms of psychopathology in man. The theoretical considerations regarding this general issue have been discussed by Senay (1966), McKinney and Bunney (1969), Harlow and McKinney (1971), Seligman and Maier (1967), and Mitchell (1970). The above authors stated their criteria in different terms but the content of what each has said is very similar. Much of the work which has been done earlier in this field suffered from the lack of prior criteria by which the syndromes produced could be evaluated and there was too loose a use of clinical terms.

Forms of human psychopathology are not entities that can be studied on an animal level unless appropriate criteria have been previously established. The following criteria have been proposed by several workers as being useful in evaluating nonhuman experimental psychopathology research:

1. The behavioral manifestations of the syndrome being modeled should be similar to those seen in the human condition.
2. The behavioral changes should be able to be objectively detected by independent observers in different laboratories.
3. The behavioral state induced should be persistent and generalizable.
4. Etiological inducing conditions used in animals should be similar to those in human psychopathology.
5. Treatment modalities effective in reversing the human disorder should be effective in the animal model.
6. There must be sufficient reference control data available.

While these criteria suggest needed research in the creation of models it should also be remembered that the condition being modeled is often itself poorly defined from behavioral standpoints. While this point can be used as a rebuttal to critics who demand more preciseness from "models" research than is currently available, it also delineates one of the potential values of animal model research, that is, to aid in more clearly defining human syndromes from a behavioral standpoint.

In essence, what is being attempted in the creation of experimental models in primates is the production of a syndrome or syndromes which meets the criteria outlined above. The value of the model system in animals is that it lends itself to more direct manipulation of social and biological variables than is possible in human beings from ethical and/or practical standpoints. This is not to contend that monkeys are humans or vice versa. Obviously there are differences, but the similarities far outweigh most differences especially with regard to social development and affectional systems.

## SOCIAL ISOLATION[1]

The technique of social isolation involves rearing animals from birth either in total social isolation chambers where they have no social contact with other monkeys or in bare wire cages where their only contact is visual and auditory. Social isolation is only one of many different rearing conditions that are possible in a controlled laboratory setting. Each of the other rearing conditions, of course, has its influence on the rapidity and/or nature of the development of social behaviors, but, in general, all except social isolation can be used to rear socially normal rhesus monkeys in a laboratory. Social isolation early in life on the other hand produces severe and persistent syndromes of abnormal behavior involving the destruction or severe disruption of the major affectional systems. The dramatic effects of social isolation rearing conditions are well stated in previous publications in the scientific literature. The mechanisms by which such an early rearing condition has such drastic effects are far from clear and some current research is being directed along these lines. Also, what the social isolation syndrome might represent in terms of human models is not clear at this point. Probably it is modeling something on the psychotic spectrum, although the exact labeling of the syndrome in human terms would be premature. Words such as infantile autism, psychoses, schizophrenia, and depression have all been used often without sufficient clarification as to the choice of the particular label.

There have been two types of recent rehabilitation studies. One involved a social technique (Suomi, Harlow, and McKinney 1972; Harlow and Suomi 1971) by which six-month total isolates were paired with younger three month old "therapist" monkeys and allowed to have a scheduled social interaction. Over a period of time such experience was effective in reversing the abnormal behavior shown by the social isolates and rendering them socially normal animals. The long term follow-up on these subjects so far indicates that they maintain their mprovement and are eventually able to socialize with equal aged peers.

---

[1]   See Turner, Davenport, and Rogers 1969; Menzel, Davenport, and Rogers 1963a, 1963b; Mason 1963; Cross and Harlow 1965; Suomi, Harlow, and Kimball 1971; Harlow and Harlow 1969; Sackett 1968; Harlow 1964; Harlow, Rowland, and Griffin 1964; Mason and Sponholz 1963; Mitchell and Clark 1968; Harlow, Joslyn, Senko, and Dopp 1966; Harlow, Harlow, Dodsworth, and Arling 1966; Seay, Alexander, and Harlow 1964; Miller, Mirsky, Carl, and Sakata 1969; Griffin and Harlow 1966; Mirsky 1968; Clark n.d.; Pratt 1969; Heath 1972.

There has also been recent pilot work indicating that partial socially isolated monkeys responded to chlorpromazine treatment in terms of a decrease in the frequency of most of their abnormal behaviors although they do not become as socialized as the socially treated monkeys (McKinney, Young, Suomi, and Davis 1973).

## LEARNED HELPLESSNESS

Seligman (see Seligman and Grores 1970; Seligman and Maier 1967; Seligman, Maier, and Geer 1968) uses the term "learned helplessness" to describe the interference with adaptive responding produced by inescapable shock. Most of their work has been conducted with dogs but they note that a similar phenomenon can be observed in rats, cats, dogs, fish, mice and men. In the paradigm used to produce learned helplessness subjects were first given a series of sixty-four unsignaled inescapable shocks. The shocks occurred randomly in time. Twenty-four hours later the subjects were given ten trials of signaled escaped avoidance training. During this phase if the subjects jumped a barrier when the conditioned stimulus was presented, they avoided shock. Failure to jump led to a shock which continued until the subject jumped the barrier. Learned helplessness is an operational concept used to describe subjects that have had experience with uncontrollable shock and failed to initiate responses to escape the shock or were much slower to make responses than naïve dogs.

Also, if the subject did happen to make a response which turned off shock it had more trouble than a naïve subject learning that responding was effective. In other words, after an initial experience in which responding could not control reinforcers, that is, uncontrollable shock, the animal ceased to respond even when responding could now control reinforcers.

Such a model for learned helplessness has been suggested as a type of animal model for certain aspects of human depression by those who would see at least reactive depression, especially the passivity components, as having its roots in loss of control over reinforcers, for example, gratification and alleviation of suffering. In this model experimental helplessness is cured by letting the animal make repeated responses that turn off the shock. This has been likened to one of the important features in the treatment of depressed patients which involves changing the patient's perception of himself as hopeless to one in which he believes that he has control over his environment.

## SEPARATION STUDIES[2]

Separation experiences, that is, object losses, are thought to precede development of severe depression as well as other forms of psychopathology in human beings. The theories that postulate the importance of separation are largely based on retrospective studies which start with a population of clinically depressed people who have undergone separation. There is little understanding of the mechanisms underlying the apparent close connection between separation and depression, though the terms separation and object loss have themselves become well accepted phrases among clinicians. They have been used to describe many diverse states, ranging from an infant's response to separation from its mother to an adult's loss of self-esteem when certain defense mechnisms are no longer effective. Unfortunately, separation is becoming a greatly overused term in the sense that its usage has far outstripped our basic understanding of its meaning. Separation is certainly more than just an event and needs to be defined in terms of many parameters. If this is not done there exists the risk that the term will continue to be used so broadly and loosely as to become meaningless. It is in the area of clarifying the mechanisms underlying separation that primate models have perhaps been most useful thus far.

Rhesus monkeys develop strong affectional systems and form close social bonds, factors which have facilitated the study of separation and depression in primate models. Separation of a rhesus infant from its mother has produced a laboratory syndrome behaviorally analogous to the anaclitic depression syndrome as described by Spitz and Bowlby in human infants. Recently separation studies in primate models have been extended to peer separation studies during the first year of life as well as during the third year of life. Parameters such as the length of the attachment bond prior to separation, the duration of separation, the conditions of housing during separation, and the nature of the reunion response have all been studied in animal models. Recent data would suggest that either maternal separation or peer separation during the first year of life produces a biphasic protest and despair reaction whereas peer separation occurring during the third year of life produces only a

---

[2]   See Seithi 1964; Paykel 1969; Robertson and Bowlby 1952; Spitz 1945; Seay, Hansen, and Harlow 1962; Seay and Harlow 1965; Jensen and Tvemen 1962; Kaufman and Rosenblum 1967; Rosenblum and Kaufman 1968; Hinde and Spencer-Booth 1971; Hinde, Spencer-Booth, and Bruce 1966; Suomi, Domek, and Harlow 1970; McKinney, Suomi, and Harlow 1972; Young, Suomi, Harlow, and McKinney 1973; Young, McKinney, et al. 1973.

uniphasic protest type reaction. Recent biological data indicate that maternal separation during the fifth month of life is accompanied by marked activation of the peripheral sympathetic system and by increases in the central serotonergic system.

## AN APPROACH TO BIOCHEMICAL STUDIES IN PRIMATE MODELS

One of the reasons for creating primate models for behavioral disorders is to be able to do direct biochemical studies. It is hoped to study rhesus monkeys with induced syndromes of psychopathology by directly examining the relationship between brain neurotransmitters and the abnormal behaviors exhibited. This area of research has been recently developed and is currently an active one. One technique involves experimental alteration of the brain amine levels by drugs and a study of the consequent social effects of this manipulation. A second approach involves socially inducing psychopathology and studying the biological consequences of social induction techniques, for example, separation and social isolation. A third approach involves attempts to reverse socially induced syndromes of psychopathology by biological means. In this regard a study using chlorpromazine in partial isolates has been referred to previously. Such types of rehabilitative studies have the potential for helping to clarify what the syndrome being produced represents as well as offering a system for better preclinical evaluation of certain drugs.

## PERSPECTIVES

Experimental psychopathology in nonhuman primates is at the same time a new and an old field. To start with, it has suffered from a too loose use of clinical terms without adequate behavioral descriptions and the exclusive use of conditioning techniques. As a result, clinicians have been uninterested in this field. This lack of interest is, of course, overdetermined but hopefully is changing somewhat in recent years as the field itself matures and clinicians become increasingly aware of the potential relevance of many fields of inquiry.

The major areas of interest in animal models for clinicians includes the development of attachment behaviors, the effects of social isolation, separation studies, the possible experimental simulation of learned helplessness and various biological approaches which are being developed.

It is in these areas that work has been and is being conducted which has potential clinical usefulness. Investigators may be close to developing viable animal models for depression that may facilitate a more comprehensive understanding of this particular syndrome and enable studies to be done which are currently impossible to perform utilizing human beings. The rest of medicine has long used nonhuman primates to advance knowledge about their fields and there is no particular reason why psychiatrists should not do the same.

## REFERENCES

CLARK, D. L.
   n.d.   "Immediate and delayed effects of early, intermediate, and late social isolation in the rhesus monkey." Unpublished doctoral dissertation, University of Wisconsin.
CROSS, HENRY A., HARRY F. HARLOW
   1965   Prolonged and progressive effects of partial isolation on the behavior of Macaque monkeys. *Journal of Experimental Research in Personality* 1(1):39–49.
GRIFFIN. GARY A., HARRY F. HARLOW
   1966   Effects of three months of total social deprivation on social adjustment and learning in the rhesus monkey. *Child Development* 37(3): 533–547.
HARLOW, HARRY F.
   1964   "Early social deprivation and later behavior in the monkey," in *Unfinished tasks in the behavioral sciences*. Edited by A. Abrams, H. H. Garner, and J. E. P. Tomal, 154–173. Baltimore: Williams and Wilkins.
HARLOW, HARRY F., MARGARET K. HARLOW.
   1969   "Effects of various mother-infant relationships on rhesus monkey behaviors," in *Determinants of infant behaviors*, volume four. Edited by B. Foss, 15–36. London: Methuen.
HARLOW, HARRY F., MARGARET K. HARLOW, R. D. DODSWORTH, G. L. ARLING
   1966   "Maternal behavior of rhesus monkeys deprived of mothering and peer associations in infancy," in *Proceedings of the American Philosophical Society* 110:58–66.
HARLOW, HARRY F., W. D. JOSLYN, M. SENKO, A. DOPP
   1966   Behavioral aspects of reproduction in primates. *Journal of Animal Science* 25:45–67.
HARLOW, HARRY F., WILLIAM T. MC KINNEY.
   1971   Non-human primates and psychoses. *Journal of Autism and Childhood Schizophrenia* 1:368.
HARLOW, HARRY F., GUY L. ROWLAND, GARY A. GRIFFIN
   1964   "The effect of total social deprivation on the development of monkey behavior," in *Psychiatric Research Report* 19. Edited by P. Solomon and B. C. Glueck, 116–135. American Psychiatric Association.

HARLOW, HARRY F., STEPHEN J. SUOMI
1971   Social recovery by isolation-reared monkeys. *Proceedings of the National Academy of Sciences* 68:1534–1538.

HEATH, ROBERT G.
1972   Electroencephalographic studies in isolation-raised monkeys with behavioral impairment. *Diseases of the Nervous System* 33:157–163.

HINDE, R. A., Y. SPENCER-BOOTH
1971   Effects of brief separation from mother on rhesus monkeys. *Science* 173:111–119.

HINDE, R. A., Y. SPENCER-BOOTH, M. BRUCE
1966   Effects of 6-day maternal deprivation on rhesus monkey infants. *Nature* 210:1021–1023.

JENSEN, G. D., C. W. TVEMEN
1962   Mother-infant relationship in the monkey, Macaca Nemestrina: the effect of brief separation and mother-infant specificity. *Journal of Comparative and Physiological Psychology* 55:131–136.

KAUFMAN, I. C., L. A. ROSENBLUM
1967   Depression in infant monkeys separated from their mothers. *Science* 155:1030–1031.

KUBIE, LAWRENCE S.
1939   The experimental induction of neurotic reactions in man. *Yale Journal of Biology and Medicine* 11:541–545.

MASON, W. A.
1963   "The effects of environmental restriction on the social development of rhesus Monkeys," in *Primate social behavior*. Southwick, 161–173. Princeton: Van Nostrand.
1968   "Early social deprivation in the non-human primates: implications for human behavior," in *Environmental influences*. Edited by D. C. Glass, 70–100. New York: Russel Sage foundation.

MASON, W. A., SPONHOLZ, R. R.
1963   Behavior of rhesus monkeys raised in isolation. *Journal of Psychiatric Research* 1:298–306.

MC KINNEY, WILLIAM T., WILLIAM F. BUNNEY
1969   Animal model of depression: review of evidence. *Archives of General Psychiatry* 21:240.

MC KINNEY, WILLIAM T., LAURENS YOUNG, STEPHEN J. SUOMI, JOHN M. DAVIS
1973   Chlorpromazine treatment of disturbed monkeys. *Archives of General Psychiatry* 29:490–495.

MC KINNEY, W. T., S. J. SUOMI, HARRY F. HARLOW
1971   Depression in primates. *American Journal of Psychiatry* 127:1313–1320.
1972   Repetitive peer separations of juvenile age rhesus monkeys. *Archives of General Psychiatry* 200–203.

MENZEL, EMIL W., RICHARD K. DAVENPORT, CHARLES M. ROGERS
1963a  The effects of environmental restriction upon the chimpanzee's responsiveness to objects. *Journal of Comparative and Physiological Psychology* 56(1):78–85.
1963b  Effects of environmental restriction upon the chimpanzee's responsiveness to novel situations. *Journal of Comparative and Physiological Psychology* 56(2):329–334.

MILLER, ROBERT E., I. ARTHUR MIRSKY, WILLIAM F. CARL, TOSHIE SAKATA
   1969   Hyperphagia and polydipsia in socially isolated rhesus monkeys. *Science* 165:1027–1028.

MIRSKY, I. ARTHUR
   1968   "Communication of affects in monkeys," in *Environmental influences*. Edited by David L. Glass, 129–137. New York: Rockefeller University Press and Russell Sage Foundation.

MITCHELL, G. D.
   1970   "Abnormal behavior in primates," in *Primate behavior*. Edited by L. Rosenblum. New York: Academic Press.

MITCHELL, G. D., D. L. CLARK
   1968   Long term effects of social isolation in non-socially adapted rhesus monkeys. *Journal of Genetic Psychology* 113:117–128.

PAYKEL, E. S.
   1969   Life events and depression. *Archives of General Psychiatry* 21:753–760.

PRATT, C. L.
   1969   "The developmental consequences of variations in early social stimulation." Unpublished doctoral dissertation, University of Wisconsin.

ROBERTSON, J., J. BOWLBY
   1952   Responses of young children to separation from their mothers. *Courier du Centre International de l'Enfant* 2:131–142.

ROSENBLUM, L. A., I. C. KAUFMAN
   1968   Variations in infant development and response to maternal loss in monkeys. *American Journal of Orthopsychiatry* 83:418–426.

SACKETT, GENE P.
   1968   "The persistence of abnormal behaviour in monkeys following isolation rearing," in *CIBA Foundation symposium on the role of learning in psychotherapy*. Edited by R. Porter, 3–25. London: J. and A. Churchill.

SEAY, W., BRUCE K. ALEXANDER, HARRY F. HARLOW
   1964   Maternal behavior of socially deprived rhesus monkeys. *Journal of Abnormal and Social Psychology* 69 (4):345–354.

SEAY, W., E. HANSEN, HARRY F. HARLOW
   1962   Mother-infant separation in monkeys. *Journal of Child Psychology and Psychiatry* 3:123–132.

SEAY, W., HARRY F. HARLOW
   1965   Maternal separation in the rhesus monkey. *Journal of Nervous and Mental Disease* 140(6):434–441.

SEITHI, B. B.
   1964   Relationship of separation to depression. *Archives of General Psychiatry* 10:486–496.

SELIGMAN, M. E. P., D. GRORES
   1970   Non-transient learned helplessness. *Psychonomic Science* 19:191–192.

SELIGMAN, M. E. P., S. F. MAIER
   1967   Failure to escape traumatic shock. *Journal of Experimental Psychology* 74:1–9.

SELIGMAN, M. E. P., S. F. MAIER, J. GEER
   1968   The alleviation of learned helplessness in the dog. *Journal of Abnormal and Social Psychology* 73:256–262.

SENAY, EDWARD C.
1966    Toward an animal model of depression: a study of separation behavior in dogs. *Journal of Psychiatric Research* 4:65–71.

SPITZ, RENE A.
1945    "Hospitalism," in *The psychoanalytic study of the child*, two volumes. New York: International University Press.

SUOMI, S. J., C. J. DOMEK, HARRY F. HARLOW
1970    Effects of repetitive infant-infant separation of young monkeys. *Journal of Abnormal Psychology* 76:161–172.

SUOMI, STEPHEN J., HARRY F. HARLOW, DAVID S. KIMBALL
1971    Behavioral effects of prolonged partial social isolation in the rhesus monkey. *Psychological Reports* 29:1171–1177.

SUOMI, STEPHEN J., HARRY F. HARLOW, WILLIAM T. MC KINNEY
1972    Monkey psychiatrists. *American Journal of Psychiatry* 128(8):927–932.

TURNER, CORBETT, RICHARD K. DAVENPORT, CHARLES M. ROGERS
1969    The effect of early deprivation on the social behavior of adolescent chimpanzees. *American Journal of Psychiatry* 125:85–90.

YOUNG, LAURENS, W. T. MC KINNEY, J. K. LEWIS, G. R. BREESE, R. D. SMITHER,
R. A. MUELLER, J. L. HOWARD, A. J. PRANGE, M. A. LIPTON
1973    Induction of adrenal catecholamine synthesizing enzymes following mother-infant separation. *Nature* 246:94–96.

YOUNG, L. D., S. J. SUOMI, H. F. HARLOW, W. T. MC KINNEY
1973    Early stress and later response to separation in rhesus monkeys. *American Journal of Psychiatry* 130(4):400–405.

# The Drug Detoxification Unit as an Ecological System

JONATHAN COWAN and FREDERICK H. MEYERS

Two major forms of outpatient care implemented as a response to the recent epidemic of heroin use are the drug detoxification unit and the methadone maintenance program. The major emphasis of the detoxification unit it to provide short-term help during the period of withdrawal to the heroin user who wishes to terminate or "kick" his habit. This is usually a combination of psychological counseling and drug therapy to relieve his symptoms. According to many programs, this treatment should only span the three-week period of withdrawal, but the addict frequently returns to heroin use before or shortly after the cessation of therapy.

Because treatment is so difficult, many people prefer to treat addiction with a system of controlled access to narcotics, e.g. methadone maintenance (Dole, Nyswander, and Warner 1968). Methadone is a narcotic with a long enough duration of action so that it can be given orally just once a day if the dosage is sufficiently large; it can block the "high" from small doses of intravenous heroin because the patient develops a high degree of tolerance to all narcotics during daily administration of methadone. Another reason for the observed decrease in heroin use with methadone maintenance is that methadone satisfies some of the addict's desire for narcotics. Society benefits from this decrease in heroin use in the form of a lowered crime rate, and in some programs society, rather than the patient, may be thought of as the true "client" for whom the service is provided. Recent federal programs have focused on crime prevention through methadone maintenance. In the methadone maintenance program, psychological counseling is frequently provided, but it is neither as intense nor as important as it typically is in the drug detoxification program.

This article represents an attempt to develop a theoretical framework from which careful study of the drug dextoxification unit can proceed. We hope that further work along these lines will develop a practical guide for those designing future programs and will assist currently operating programs to become more readily self-corrective. We anticipate that the validity of the framework will apply, with some limitations, to methadone maintenance programs, but because of the substantial differences between the two modalities as they are currently employed, they will not be discussed together here in order to avoid confusion.

## OBSERVATIONS

One of the authors has observed formally at two drug detoxification units for a period of nine months. The other author has participated in the founding and operation of four drug treatment programs and has treated drug dependence in his private practice since 1960. As a member of the agency responsible for supervision of methadone programs in California, and in other capacities, he has visited many methadone clinics and drug detoxification units throughout the state.

## THE PROBLEM OF EVALUATION

Investigators in this area have been hampered by their inability to obtain any data on the success of a given program. Evaluation is not always seen as an essential part of a program, and criteria for success are not agreed upon. What is success with this population? Holding a steady job? Being free of drugs? For how long? Evaluation is further complicated because many patients, successful or unsuccessful, are lost to follow-up study after leaving the program. Some change programs, while others attend several at once. At present, then, it is clearly impossible to obtain comparative data on a large number of programs. One must return to the careful observation and systematization of data that characterized the early practice of medicine and current work in anthropology.

In treating this complex problem, one cannot confidently expect that all of the addict's symptoms — physical and psychological — will promptly (or slowly) disappear upon selection and administration of the proper drug, as occurs in many other diseases. Drug treatment may even make dependence worse if the drug given is easily abused. This traditional view of therapy must give way to a view in which the social context of giving a drug is accorded its full importance.

A study of addiction treatment must consider which psychosocial variables are interacting with drug giving and with each other in order to produce the variations in response observed in the detoxification units. Our observations led us to isolate two independent variables — MOTIVATION of the patient and PROGRAM CHANGES in the clinic — that we felt were important determinants of the variations in ATTENDANCE and EFFECTIVENESS (the dependent variables) observed in these units. Both independent variables had a number of different components, which will be specified below. The complexity of their interaction demanded an ecological model for the drug detoxification unit.

## AN ECOLOGICAL MODEL

One can draw a rough analogy between a drug detoxification unit and a forest. Like the different species of trees in the forest whose survival and health are determined by environmental changes and by their mutual interaction, the attendance of the different "motivation populations" at the detoxification unit, and the program's effectiveness with them are determined by the program changes and by the interactions between the motivation populations.

A system can be defined as an interlocking complex of processes characterized by many reciprocal cause-effect pathways. Clearly, both the forest and the drug detoxification unit are systems. If one accepts Bateson's notion (1972:483) that "ecology, in its widest sense, turns out to be the study of the interaction and survival of ideas and programs in circuits," then both of these systems may be properly termed ecological, as they both contain an element of feedback.

As in an ecological climax, to reach a steady state the addict population would have to be divided out among the various detoxification units in response to the differences in "climate" among them. These differences are the sum total of all previous program changes.

Because such an equilibrium has not yet been reached, it is interesting to predict how the attendance of each motivation population will change with the different program changes. It is also important to be able to predict what result these program changes will have upon effectiveness with each motivation population. Because of the difficulties in accurately specifying and quantifying a number of the variables involved (motivation, intensity of program changes, effectiveness), it is not possible to produce the quantitative model that is the goal of formal systems analysis; however, it does seem feasible to endeavor to predict the DIRECTION of a program change upon the attendance and effectiveness of each population, and further to predict the effect of changes in population attendance upon the other motivation populations at the unit.

## THE MOTIVATION POPULATIONS

Any framework that involves motivation as a concept must recognize that motivations are mixed and unclear. Described below are six idealized components of the motivational state of a patient at a drug detoxification unit; they often may exist in conflict with one another in the same patient, in the same way that other patients may have complex psychological problems or several concurrent medical diseases. But just as one may characterize the junkies who inhabit a particular clinic according to certain demographic features (black junkies, middle-class junkies, etc.), so one may describe them in terms of their predominant motivations. Interviews with the patient and his counselor could be used to assess these motivations; research questionnaires could be developed for patient and counselor rating of motivations. Perhaps behavioral criteria could be established to aid in the replicability of these measurements, although independent raters (i.e. neither the patient nor the counselor) would be required. As motivations may change with time (and exposure to the program), repeated rating of the same patient would be necessary.

The motivations described below, while somewhat arbitrary, nonetheless represent what we perceive as a continuum among addicts seeking treatment:

1. *Self-generated desire to kick the habit*. Members of this population have made strong, conscious decisions to end their addictions. They provide considerable energy toward change but need understanding, reinforcement, environmental change, and a good example. Their participation in all aspects of the program is almost completely voluntary, as opposed to the nonvoluntary participation often shown by other populations.

In NONVOLUNTARY PARTICIPATION the patient no longer wishes to take part in one aspect of the program, usually the counseling, with its associated requirements for dealing with his drug dependence. Program changes that increase the pressure on the patient toward reform can exacerbate this. However, other benefits derived from the program — such as abusable drugs, symptomatic relief, or freedom from incarceration — force him to at least meet the program's minimum requirements for participation and produce a state of conflict between his desires. By providing a reason to continue his participation, some program changes increase or POTENTIATE the nonvoluntary participation caused by others. Eventually, as the demands of the program increase and the addict's resentment mounts, he approaches a breaking point beyond which decreased attendance and effectiveness take the place of nonvoluntary participation ("playing the game").

2. *Compulsion by law enforcement.* There are varying degrees of motivation for these patients, corresponding to the seriousness of the possible penalty. Although most of these patients regard their attendance at the clinic as an attempt to mask their symptoms, rather than an abandonment of the junkie life-style, the clinic can be effective in rehabilitating the more highly motivated ones. However, there is a large problem with nonvoluntary participation here.

3. *Compulsion by loved ones.* Nonvoluntary participation is usually not much of a problem with this group, as this is usually not a very strong motivation in our experience. Many of the addicts in this category who do "clean up" (i.e. stop using drugs), do so without the help of the detoxification unit but with the help of the loved one. Those who come to the clinic are usually responding either to the weak and inconsistent pressure of a heroin-using loved one or to the temporary pressure of a nonuser they have recently met; they usually terminate rather quickly.

4. *Reducing the habit to economically feasible proportions.* This category comprises junkies who have suffered a sudden change of fortune — a loss of earning capacity or loss of "connection" (dealer). This person has no intention of giving up heroin use but wants temporary medical help in smoothing the symptoms of abrupt withdrawal. He is interested in obtaining the symptomatic relief afforded by the drugs dispensed by the clinic and can become a nonvoluntary participant for this reason.

5. *Using the clinic as a source of drugs.* These patients try to manipulate the program by feigning symptoms and telling stories in order to obtain drugs, particularly sedatives with a short duration of action (Seconal, Valium) and narcotics (methadone, Darvon), which may be used by the patient or sold on the street. There is, of course, much nonvoluntary participation by this group and very little chance of being effective with it.

6. *Finding companionship and developing connections.* This patient's real desire is to find a place to "hang out" — to meet friends, dealers, or perhaps clientele (if the patient is a dealer). These patients can be discouraged rather easily, as they can hang out in many places; continued nonvoluntary participation is rare.

## ATTENDANCE AND EFFECTIVENESS

Attendance at the clinic should be defined in terms of the percentage of time required for full participation. Obviously, certain manipulations, e.g. requiring the addict to report for his medication daily instead of every two days, can change the number of hours he spends at the clinic per week without changing his desire to attend the program.

The relative attendance of the motivation populations can also change if an individual changes his motivational hierarchy during his period of attendance. Many individuals change from motivation 1 to motivation 5, for example, as they become discouraged about their prospects for cure or become more interested in using the available drugs.

It may be a mistake to think that short-term changes in attendance are of great importance, as many of the goals of the clinic, including personal rehabilitation and reduced crime, can only be accomplished over a long period of treatment. A large patient drop-out rate during the first few weeks of treatment may signal, not a failing in a program, but rather the weeding out of some clients with the latter motivations who are deterred by the strictness of the rules. By limiting the clinic's clientele in this manner, it may become much easier to rehabilitate those addicts in the first two groups, and the program may be more successful as a result. Program changes that make nonvoluntary participation possible may only produce temporary increases in attendance, as Jaffe (1971) demonstrated with two different drug dosages.

In order to establish some common ground for communicating our observations about effectiveness, the following components of rehabilitation are delineated:
1. Relief of withdrawal symptoms.
2. Decreased or no use of heroin, without recourse to other drugs of abuse, e.g. alcohol or barbiturates.
3. Decreased number of arrests.
4. Increased social productivity, e.g. employment and reconciliation with family.

## THE ADDICT AND THE DOUBLE BIND

In the previous discussion, nonvoluntary participation was explained as the result of a conflict between the demands of the program and the benefits derived from participation. However, a program change can produce another cause of nonvoluntary participation: the double bind (Bateson 1972: 194–278).

Here, the junkie perceives two conflicting messages from the program at two different levels of communication. The counselor is ostensibly trying to help him to stop using drugs and communicates this to him verbally and by many of his actions. On the other hand, to prevent becoming too involved with the success or failure of his patients, the counselor may try to appear "cool" or indifferent. The patient may know that many other addicts in the program are still using heroin or are selling the clinic's drugs on the street, and he may suspect that his counselor knows about it and is looking the other way. He sees other patients in the waiting room, looking as if they have just taken heroin, and notices that some of the ex-addict staff members view intoxicated patients with envy, rather than scorn. In many cases, he may even suspect (or know) that his ex-addict counselor is not completely free of occasional heroin use himself. On another level, this communicates that using heroin is really not that reprehensible. The addict is in a situation where he cannot win. This is the double bind postulated by Bateson as a cause of schizophrenia, but with one difference — in this case the patient can leave the clinic instead of playing along with the counselor by participating nonvoluntarily.

## PROGRAM CHANGES

A change in a program is usually brought about intentionally by the staff in an effort to improve the program, although some changes do occur for other reasons, such as budget shifts or expediency. Excluding these reasons, we can describe the ideal program as self-correcting, containing a feedback loop in which present information is used by the staff to correct the future course of events by the appropriate program changes. In order to facilitate this feedback and summarize the data, a number of charts were developed.

Each chart includes one section for changes in attendance and another for changes in effectiveness. Some of the program changes were first suggested by Nightingale, Michaux, and Platt (1972). For convenience, program changes have been subdivided into major categories: goals, operational decisions, intake and discharge policy, counseling and/or therapy, drug giving, and the effects of motivation populations on one another. Because of the complexity of the charts, only one has been included here as an example (see Table 1). Program changes can either increase (I), decrease (D), or not change (—) effectiveness or attendance for each motivation population, or they can cause nonvoluntary participation (N), until the addict reaches the breaking point and leaves the too-demanding

Table 1.   Goals*

| Program changes that increase | Attendance | | | | | | Effectiveness | | | | | |
|---|---|---|---|---|---|---|---|---|---|---|---|---|
| Motivation populations: | 1. Self-generated desire to kick the habit | 2. Compulsion by law enforcement | 3. Compulsion by loved ones | 4. Reducing the habit to feasible proportions | 5. Using the clinic as a source of drugs | 6. Finding companionship and developing connections | 1. Self-generated desire to kick the habit | 2. Compulsion by law enforcement | 3. Compulsion by loved ones | 4. Reducing the habit to feasible proportions | 5. Using the clinic as a source of drugs | 6. Finding companionship and developing connections |
| Explicitness of treatment philosophy, goals, expectations | I | N | D | D | D | D | I | I | I | N | N | N |
| Emphasis on patient rehabilitation versus protection of society | I | I | I | — | D | D | I | I | I | — | N | N |
| Rigidity of established behavioral goals | I | N | N | D | D | D | I | N | N | N | N | N |
| Amount of time allowed for desired progress | — | I | I | I | I | I | D | D | D | — | D | D |
| Emphasis on quantity versus quality of care given | D | D | D | I | I | I | D | D | D | D | D | D |
| Efforts devoted to research versus treatment | D | D | D | I | I | I | D | D | D | D | D | D |
| Efforts devoted to survival and funding versus treatment | D | D | D | I | I | I | D | D | D | D | D | D |

* Program changes can increase (I), decrease (D), or not change (—) attendance or effectiveness for each motivation population, or they can

program. Almost any change that increases effectiveness or attendance can cause nonvoluntary participation if it is pushed too far. As individual sensitivity to these manipulations varies, there is really a continuum between increased and nonvoluntary participation; the chart denotes the predominant effect.

*Goals* (see Table 1):

Increase explicitness of treatment philosophy, goals, expectations.
Increase emphasis on patient rehabilitation versus protection of society.
Increase rigidity of established behavioral goals.
Increase amount of time allowed for desired progress.
Increase emphasis on quantity versus quality of care given.
Increase efforts devoted to research versus treatment.
Increase efforts devoted to survival and funding versus treatment.

The more explicit the policy that rehabilitation of the patient (rather than impressive numbers of patients treated, protection of society, survival, funding, lowering crime, or doing research) is the primary goal, the more successful a program will be, we hypothesize, in selecting and helping those patients who are willing to devote real effort toward self-reform (Table 1, motivations 1 and 2). Programs that devote much of their effort to nonrehabilitative goals may well put patients into a double bind. Increasing the strictness of the program regulations may cause many of the other participants to find this an unattractive alternative and perhaps may help to select for highly motivated populations.

*Operational Decisions:*

Increase size of program.
Increase impersonality and formality of interactions with patient.
Increase frequency or amount of required participation.
Increase severity of penalty for violation of program rules (medication, etc.).
Increase knowledge and experience of staff. Decrease staff turnover.
Increase confidence of personnel and patients in methods used.
Increase patient's job skills.
Increase drug education programs.
Increase legal help available to patient.
Increase size of waiting room, proximity to street. Decrease supervision by staff.
Increase accessibility of another program.
Increase honesty in announcing reasons for program changes.

In a similar way, the first four operational manipulations communicate to the patient in more concrete terms the degree of emphasis on his rehabilitation.

Increasing the program's efforts in drug education is fraught with danger under these circumstances. Unless the patient has a healthy respect for drugs, he may be tempted into further use. However, if the educator is not frank about the pleasurable aspects of drug taking, he (and the clinic) may lose the confidence of the patient.

Greater availability of legal help to the patient, especially the intervention of the clinic on behalf of those with pending legal problems, often clears the way for an uninterrupted attempt at rehabilitation (Alperin, Langrod, and Lowinson 1972) and may convince the patient that the clinic is interested in his welfare. However, this may involve nonvoluntary participation. Patients who have cases pending are usually unpromising prospects for treatment because of the resentment against society that this engenders; an extension of help to these people must be weighed accordingly.

The presence of an unsupervised waiting room close to the street invites motivation population 6. Their unchecked presence can create a double bind for more motivated patients.

Frankness with respect to the reasons for a program change is usually helpful; double binds are easily created by program changes that are announced as being for the patient's benefit but can be perceived by the patient as being for the staff's convenience (Bateson 1972:225).

*Intake and Discharge Policy:*

Increase selectivity for success of intake policy.
Increase urine surveillance prior to admission.
Increase frequency of discharge because of rule violation.
Increase rigidity of readmission policy.

Increasing the selectivity of the intake process is difficult to implement. In reviewing the results of a methadone program, Rosenberg, Davidson, and Patch (1972) found that older addicts with longer, more expensive habits tended to drop out less frequently.

Urine surveillance prior to admission can eliminate those nonaddict patients who are hoping to obtain drugs from the clinic and thus can eliminate some nonvoluntary participation. Some of the dangers of urine surveillance are discussed below.

The lack of a fairly rigid discharge policy creates for motivation populations 1 and 2 a double bind with respect to the program rules and encourages other populations to linger on despite rule violations that evidence their lack of sincerity. Because the latter populations are those most likely to be dropped from the program for rule infractions, a more stringent readmission policy reduces these populations.

*Counseling and/or Therapy:*

Increase individual attention.
Increase amount of counseling, group therapy, therapeutic communities.
Increase moral pressure of counseling, especially during initial sessions.
Increase efforts to change life-style.
Increase conversation about positive aspects of drug use.
Increase proportion of professional counselors versus untrained ex-addicts.
Increase use of urine surveillance as feedback device, increase intensity of feedback.
Increase use of attendance record as feedback device.

Increasing the total amount of counseling required or its moral pressure discourages participation by populations less motivated toward rehabilitation, but it also increases their nonvoluntary participation. Efforts toward changing the life-style of the addict are probably more effective than increasing moral pressure, as it is easy to communicate the relevance of life-style to drug use without becoming identified with moral disdain for drug use, which the patient resents. Discussions of the morality of drug laws usually only harm the counselor-patient relationship unless the counselor agrees with the addict, in which case the patient is placed in a double bind. Discussions of the positive aspects of drug use and reminiscence about past drug-related experiences are also best avoided.

The effectiveness of ex-addicts as counselors is still widely debated. The major question here is the thoroughness of the counselor's attitude change. For some, ending their drug use may be accompanied by a complete change of attitude (the "holy addict" syndrome) and they may become restrictive and demanding counselors at first. They may either remain so or become very lax as they become discouraged, and they may drift back to drugs themselves. Other ex-addicts do not follow the "holy addict" path but continue to use some drugs fairly frequently and even heroin occasionally. Judgment of the ex-addict counselor's effectiveness with the different motivation populations should be made on an individual basis and reviewed frequently.

Urine surveillance (along with strict rules about drug use) is probably one of the simplest ways to eliminate certain motivation populations.

However, this procedure can cause nonvoluntary participation. Severe chastisement or expulsion for an occasional slip by a patient may be unwise, as failing in the course of trying to control the compulsion can be a valuable learning experience. The patient should not, however, be allowed to involve another patient in his failure either directly or by means of verbal or nonverbal communication. He must suppress the positive aspects of the experience and acknowledge that it was a failure. The constancy of an addict's attendance is probably a better indicator of his sincerity than are the spots in his urine. Under sustained pressure to attend, nonvoluntary participation becomes very difficult.

*Drug Giving:*

Increase physical comfort, freedom from craving for narcotics.
Increase supervision of drug taking.
Increase in discrimination of drug prescription, number of drugs given.
Increase abuse potential of available drugs.
Increase difficulty in identifying active drug.

Drug therapy is sometimes useful in order to make the addict undergoing withdrawal comfortable. A sick patient is a very difficult subject for therapy, especially if he believes that the clinic could give him more medication. Physical comfort is not a linear function of the dosage or number of drugs given, and there comes a point when the side effects and interactions of these agents limit their usefulness. It should be remembered that the patient has a drug problem: we create a potential double bind for the junkie who genuinely wants to kick the habit every time we prescribe drugs for a drug problem.

Giving out too many drugs — using them as "bait" to attract addicts to the program — can increase the number of patients drawn from population 5 and potentiate nonvoluntary participation by this and other populations. A dramatic illustration of this occurred when one program under observation decided to suspend the dispensing of Valium: its patient population was cut in half over a period of weeks.

One obvious measure to improve the program's control over this situation is to disguise the identity of the abusable drugs by using generic rather than "brand name" preparations. These drugs can be switched frequently and intermixed with placebos and active placebos such as antihistamines and vitamins. In addition to using the placebo effect to maximum advantage, this makes the drugs more difficult to sell. By keeping the addict uninformed about which drugs are available, this can also reduce the addict's manipulation of the therapist in order to get drugs.

In many of these programs, paraprofessional counselors, including ex-addicts, are in charge of drug prescription. They often prescribe too many drugs, are indiscriminate in their choice of agent, and may be far too easy for the patient to manipulate. To combat this, training programs and frequent review of prescription practices of the paraprofessional can be instituted. Divorcing the roles of the counselor and the drug prescriber will also decrease the manipulation of the counselor-patient relationship.

One traditional way of prohibiting the abuse of some of these agents is to increase the supervision under which the drug is taken. In one clinic, many patients could hardly wait until they were outside the clinic's doors before swallowing all the medication they had been given. This was especially dangerous on the day before a weekend, when this clinic would dispense three days' medication. We observed the expected relationship between serious automobile accidents and the use of nominally therapeutic drugs by clinics under study. There is some danger that increased supervision as well as disguising the drugs given will cause nonvoluntary participation by the latter populations rather than eliminating them from the program.

*Effects of Motivation Populations on Each Other:*

Increase attendance of motivation populations 1 through 6.
Increase nonvoluntary participation.

We can assume that often a perceptive junkie can guess fairly accurately the motivations of another from his gestures, conversation, and behavior in the clinic and on the street. Members of a particular motivation population give moral support to one another; patients often change their reason for attending the clinic in order to conform to the crowd. This produces a corresponding change in the ratio of motivation populations there. In other words, the presence of those motivation populations who want to use the clinic for their own ends (populations 4 through 6) produces a double bind that acts on those who are more interested in dealing with their own problems (populations 1 through 3), and vice versa, to a lesser extent.

Nonvoluntary participants are especially facile at suggesting that they are just "playing the game," as this is perceived as particularly important to their status; there is a large nonverbal vocabulary for communicating this. People who have already dropped out of many other aspects of society find this attitude toward the program very easy to adopt. They are therefore quick to gain converts and to create a double bind for populations 1 through 3.

Finally, it should be remembered that the resources of the clinic and the energy of the counselor are necessarily limited. One motivation is often treated at the expense of another.

When examined from a quantitative point of views this last set of program changes gives the model a property worth noting — limited positive feedback with some generalization. Any program change that initially increases any of the latter three motivation populations or the nonvoluntary participants may produce a subsequent increase in all of these groups and a decrease in the other populations. A similar situation holds with any change that increases any of the first three populations.


## DISCUSSION

It is easy to assume that drug detoxification units should exist mainly for the treatment of those junkies who genuinely want to kick the habit and perhaps the other highly motivated ones, and that they therefore should be designed to exclude many of the other populations. Only these addicts have a large chance of successful rehabilitation, and it follows that they are much more rewarding as patients.

There are valid reasons for extending such care to other populations. Populations 2 and 3 (to a lesser extent) may deserve help because there is a significant chance that they can be rehabilitated as skilled therapy gradually increases their desire to kick the habit. Rehabilitating only population 1 would barely make a dent in the social problem because there are so few in this category. Rehabilitating these three populations would reduce crime and relieve the judicial system of some of its load.

This last argument also applies to the "rehabilitation" of the other motivation populations. However, because successful rehabilitation is extremely rare with these patients, stronger arguments are needed. One line of reasoning states that providing care now to these populations introduces them to the availability of therapy. As a result, perhaps at some future time, when their motivation toward genuine change in their life-style has increased, they may be more willing to accept therapy. Furthermore, the addict who wants help in reducing his habit is probably due the same relief that any other person who is in pain because of his own negligence (such as the accident victim) deserves. We can accord him this even if we do not look upon addiction as an illness.

The strongest argument in favor of including these populations (especially population 5) in the health care delivery system is a philosophical one, stated very forcefully by Wurmser (1971:98) with particular reference to methadone maintenance.

Many opponents of methadone treatment... say: It is better to impose compulsory abstinence with a high risk of return to jail than to support this self-indulgence of drug-dependency. What does this philosophical choice mean in sober reality? It means that we prefer to hound addicts on the street as criminals over offering them generous opportunities to remain addicted, though under supervision. Our premise then is: we value compulsory abstinence higher than voluntary addiction; yet it means also: we value freedom from drugs higher than civil liberty. The practical consequence is that we consider the criminalization of addicts, their roaming the streets, their fantastic depradations of society and their crowding together in jails as the lesser of two evils, and the medical condoning as the greater one.

Acceptance of these arguments may create a conflict for the drug detoxification unit — the necessity to provide care for all populations against the knowledge that to do so damages its effectiveness with the most "deserving" of them. Perhaps some thought should be given to eliminating this interaction by separating the motivation populations into physically isolated detoxification units under the same administrative structure.

Drug detoxification units can no doubt profit from frequent evaluation and carefully considered changes in strategy. Further work toward developing a complete ecological model of these units may provide valuable guidance in optimizing such changes. Observation and interviewing at a number of these clinics would seem to be a logical first step toward refining such a scheme.

Understanding the addict's motivation may have importance in the study of addiction treatment. The interaction of motivational factors with the specific design of the detoxification unit should be considered in developing methods for the evaluation of present treatment facilities and the design of future programs.

## REFERENCES

ALPERIN, L., J. LANGROD, J. LOWINSON
  1972  "The role of legal services in a methadone maintenance treatment program," in *Drug addiction: clinical and sociolegal aspects*, volume two. Edited by J. Singh, J. Miller, and H. Lal, 163–168. Mt. Kisco: Futura.

BATESON, G.
  1972  *Steps to an ecology of mind.* New York: Chandler.

DOLE, V., M. NYSWANDER, A. WARNER
  1968  Successful treatment of 750 criminal addicts. *Journal of the American Medical Association* 206:2708–2711.

JAFFE, J.

1971   "Methadone maintenance: variation in outcome criteria as a function of dose," in *Proceedings of the Third National Conference on Methadone Treatment*. Edited by M. Perkins, 37–44. Washington: United States Government Printing Office.

NIGHTINGALE, S., W. MICHAUX, P. PLATT

1972   Clinical implications of urine surveillance in a methadone maintenance program. *International Journal of the Addictions* 7:403–414.

ROSENBERG, C., G. DAVIDSON, V. PATCH

1972   Patterns of dropouts from a methadone program for narcotic addicts. *International Journal of the Addictions* 7:415–425.

WURMSER, L.

1971   "Some psychological comments on prejudice against methadone maintenance," in *Proceedings of the Third National Conference on Methadone Treatment*. Edited by M. Perkins, 98–99. Washington: United States Government Printing Office.

# Notes from the Interface:
# A Commentary on the Anthropology
# and Mental Health Symposium

K. J. PATAKI–SCHWEIZER

Since the classic period of the 1930's and 1940's anthropology has witnessed the rapid emergence and slow decline of several schools of thought in this field. From the perspective of a psychologically oriented anthropologist interested in medicine and mental health, I will comment on certain general research trends, observed through the session on "Anthropology and Mental Health" (at the IXth International Congress of Anthropological and Ethnological Sciences). Why this engagement? Primarily becouse we seemed to share a sense of convergence of research, a merging of interests and data that suggests a *bridging of the universalistic-particularistic — more recently the "etic-emic" — distinction* so long assumed to be virtually inherent in the social and behavioral sciences. This rather profound change is suggested by several general patterns and trends, all demonstrable from the papers and discussions of this session, although they are equally demonstrable from the general professional literature. These trends or themes include the following:

1. Increasing sophistication, rigor, and retroductive power of mathematically-derived methodologies. The evidence that certain statistically-achieved correlations have extremely deep implications for clinical practice and theoretical models cannot now be avoided.

2. Overlap of accruing "psycho-pathological" data and case studies from more and more cultures and subcultures, clinic- or field-derived from various disciplines. This is, in effect, a convergence of cross-cultural data

I am grateful to the participants and discussants of the symposium for their stimulating and constructive comments during and after the sessions, and especially to James M. Schaefer, Francis L. K. Hsu, Hans Huessy, Bela Maday, Joseph Westermeyer, and Joseph Hartog.

and of methods for assessing them from behavior earlier classified or considered unique, or perhaps just too bizarre for firm integration within a given disciplinary structure.

3. The effects of what might be called "reflective anthropology." Those characteristics of the informant-interviewer feedback loop that directly affect the nature of information are no longer to be ignored or classified as ephemeral, epiphenomenal or peripheral.

4. The accumulating data or at the very least a corpus of material from that body of experience generally termed "altered states of perception" or "altered states of consciousness," such as trance, drug-induced conditions, and various methods of meditation. The extreme popularity of some examples does not lessen the importance of this area of information nor those areas of experience from which they are obtained.

5. An increasing convergence of information on various states and classifications of "mental illness" and "deviant behavior" from anthropology, psychiatry, clinical psychology, and related fields into an apparent "folk" taxon of nonnormative behaviors with an implicit "folk-remedial" delivery-system model for health care. Of course, profound contrast exists between the health care delivery system of traditional Asmat in southwest New Guinea, for example, and a San Francisco drug clinic. I am speaking here of accessibility — a direct, mutual meaningfulness for recipient and deliverer — and of certain shared cross-cultural characteristics for which the term "folk" may be used.

6. An increasing use of highly individualistic sources for many general statements which have their influence upon the professional, as well as the lay, consumer; that is, a willingness to consider and use data from idiosyncratic if not unique cases, in apposition with mathematically and formally derived correlations and associations referred to in (1) above.

7. Various payoffs from the "applied" area or "neo-utilitarian theory." Feedback from the vast range of "applied" programs of the past decade has provided new data, data controls, paradigms, and research insights. This feedback has also allowed for assessment of such programs by various disciplines (despite the profound truncation of our national research programs in the past few years). As a result, that which was initially and intentionally seen as primarily "useful" may now also be considered as firmly adaptive and not "lightweight," too "exotic" or "ethnographic," "anecdotal" or — the ultimate calumny — "nonscientific."

8. An apparent emergence of "nontypological," "nonmodular" experiments in explanation and thinking. The implications of this focus are far-reaching. It exhibits a growing willingness to consider explanations based on rationales other than the familiar Greco-Roman one. The epistemo-

logical implications are striking, especially since (a) the data often call for such explanatory sallies and (b) policy decisions are gradually being made from such settings (e.g. local minority-group decisions or Western research models and criteria among non-Western practioners).

9. The use of "systems theory," and concern for "system," "process," "transaction," "ecology," a renewed interest in *"epidemiology"* — *that is, post-modal grids for research*. Surely this has a feedback effect on the data collected and the contexts used for explanation.

10. A vast information field, apparently with its own dynamics, emerging through extended research, technological innovations, cybernetic thought, and mass media, with profound effects upon our psyches as well as on our formal and institutionalized communication processes. The effects of these are everywhere as abundant as they are curiously redundant when classified according to earlier paradigms such as "culture-and-society," "culture-and-personality," "culture, social-structure, and personality," "social-genetic," "normal-abnormal."

These trends indicate a convergence of research effort and the emergence of linkages and networks of linkages within the behavioral sciences for areas of information hitherto classified as disparate or unrelated. In part this *de facto* "classification" has been the (epistemological) spinoff of overly-structured disciplinary boundaries that have kept us from an important no-man's-land by maintaining the "inert symbiosis" Schwimmer decries. This convergence also indicates changes in the use, and apparently in the perceived nature, of several anthropological and psychiatric/psychological concepts, notably those of culture, social structure, personality, and aberrant and deviant behavior. These changes are emerging in part through reflection on the growing body of behavioral data, statistical associations, and often unique ethological insights mentioned above.

Stress has resulted also, sometimes an acute disciplinary stress, which need not lead to acute intellectual anomie. If wisdom and solutions come from the folk domain, from the most abstruse theoretical realms, and from the daily existential domain, then some new state of insight and utility should emerge. Radical shifts in the modes of presenting data and of discourse, and even in the use of language, appear to be associated. I should not wish to imply the "death of relativism" or of disciplines; these are much too melodramatic to provide focus or even context. Yet the apparent bridging of the "emic" and the "etic "domains, apparently in part from the study of the nature and function of symbols and symbolizing, and the shifting away from a preferred particularistic or universalistic postition quite apart from the naïveté often ascribed, imply some sort of revolution. Moreover, neither universalistic nor particularistic focuses are ignored as a source of data; the issues involved are meaning, comprehension, and direction. Perhaps all this implies the best sort of revolution, one that is self-corrective and firmly constructive in the long run; such a revolutionary bridging, orientation, or jump is implicit in the major innovative thought of all cultures. Such an intense intellectual dynamism is firmly constructive because it can provide broader, more powerful methodologies, research, available data, criteria for assessment, even systems of thought, and use for immediate needs. It is integrative and relevant (to use that hapless word) whether for an acute sorcery-related schizophrenic in New Guinea, economic development in a third world "minority" group, or individual confrontation and acceptance of death by a Western professional. It implies "a balance between what previously seemed incompatible, and integration of bodies of data which, until very recent theoretical findings, we were forced to consider in isolation."[1]

  If I look at our session and the preceding paragraphs from the imme-
diate viewpoint of mental health, anthropology, and research as I see them, I recognize the conceptual simultaneity of an injury (that is, an insult to body and psyche) and the ability to rally from injury; the possible dominance in response of body over psyche or vice versa, depending upon cultural heritage, methodology in treatment, and human idiosyncrasy; an acknowledgement of the immediacy of transcendental and pervasive questions that are everywhere and every time part of human life; the need for engagement and resolutions in the daily exigencies and challenges of life, including efficient and sensitive social organizations; and the crying need for better paths to knowledge, love, and happiness. There are firm invitations offered here for continued commitment with a renewed and dynamic social-behavioral science that can merge the militantly scientific with the militantly humanistic, the child with the elder, the doer with the thinker; and the question of just how one articulates the "newness" of this mesh can simply remain open. I do not think I am alone in feeling grateful to this symposium and to this Congress for providing impetus and nexus for one small joint effort towards connection, continuity, and direction.

---

[1]   From Erik Schwimmer's 1973 article in the *Journal of Symbolic Anthropology* 1, page vii, discussing "inert symbiosis."

# Biographical Notes

ENRIQUE ARANETA, JR., graduated in medicine from the University of the Philippines in 1948. He taught neuroanatomy and embryology (1948–1956) at the University of the Philippines (College of Medicine) and at the Far Eastern University Institute of Medicine. He did a residency in neurology (1957–1959) at Albany Medical Center Hospital. He was an Assistant Professor of Neurology (1961–1962) at the Far Eastern University Institute of Medicine. He did a residency in psychiatry (1959–1960, 1962–1964) at Albany Medical Center Hospital. He was medical superintendent, Fort Canje Hospital, and psychiatric consultant, Government Hospitals, British Guiana (1964–1966). He was unit chief, Psychiatric Service, V.A.H., Albany (1966–1969); and also served as Chief of Psychiatry and Neurology Service at Hampton V.A. Center, Virginia. He held the position of Adjunct Professor of Behavioral Science at Allport College, Oakland University, Michigan (1970–1973). He is now an Associate Professor of Psychiatry at the University of Florida, Gainesville, and works as staff psychiatrist at the V.A.H. in Gainesville. Dr. Araneta's major interest is in clinical and transcultural psychiatry.

OTTO BILLIG received his medical doctorate from the University of Vienna in 1937. He trained in psychiatry at the University Hospital in Vienna and at Highland Hospital in North Carolina. In addition to membership of several psychiatric societies, he also belongs to the Archaeological Institute of America and has served with the Nashville Arts Council and the Peabody College Art Museum. He is a Professor of Psychiatry at Meharry Medical College and a Clinical Professor of Psychiatry at Vanderbilt University School of Medicine. In this volume Billig combines his fifteen year interest in schizophrenic art with the talents of B. G. Burton-Bradley.

BURTON G. BURTON-BRADLEY, an Australian citizen, received his M.D. from the University of New South Wales and his F.R.C.Psych. from the Royal College of Psychiatrists. His diploma in Anthropology is from the University of Sydney, following fieldwork in New Guinea. He taught psychiatry at the University of Malaya and has been Associate Professor of Psychiatry at the University of Papua and New Guinea. He is Adviser in Ethnopsychiatry to the South Pacific Commission. He was Research Fellow, Culture and Mental Health Program at the University of Hawaii in 1969, and Abraham Flexner Lecturer at Vanderbilt University in 1973. His main interest is Papua New Guinea transcultural psychiatry on which he has 70 publications.

JONATHAN D. COWAN graduated from Brown University where he obtained degrees in both arts and science. For the last three years he has been a doctoral candidate in the Department of Pharmacology at the University of California in San Francisco. Presently he is working on effects of drugs on learning and memory. Together with his departmental chairman, Frederick H. Meyers, he suggests a model for modifying the behavior of individuals and groups in a drug treatment unit.

MARLENE DOBKIN DE RIOS received her master's degree in Anthropology from New York University in 1963 and her doctorate from the University of California-Riverside in 1972. Presently she is an Associate Professor of Anthropology at California State University-Riverside. Her fieldwork in Peru has been published in book form: *Visionary Vine: Psychedelic Healing in the Peruvian Amazon*. In addition to her interest in the hallucinogens and folk healing, she has also studied the role of witchcraft beliefs in psychosomatic illness.

ELLEN DOERMANN started the first two years of her undergraduate work at the University of Miami, and completed her studies at Vanderbilt University, earning a B. A. in Fine Arts and Psychology. Additional instruction in stained glass windows and batiking followed in Basel, Switzerland (1972). She has since served with an advertising agency as a member of the staff of creative writers.

GUY DUBREUIL graduated in Psychology from the University of Montreal and obtained his graduate anthropology training at Columbia. His research activities reflect his wide interests: he has worked in Martinique, Canada, and New Mexico on topics ranging from family dynamics to psychopathology. He is now Professor and Chairman of Anthropology at the University of Montreal.

H. WARREN DUNHAM. No biographical data available.

JOSEPH HARTOG is a psychiatrist with the George Williams Hooper Foundation at the University of California in San Francisco. He has done fieldwork in Malaysia and written on a variety of mental health topics relative to that country. His paper here indicates a movement from proven methodologies to one which may have more value in this age of rapid culture change.

FRANCIS L. K. HSU is currently a Professor of Anthropology (and Chairman of the Department) at Northwestern University, Evanston, Illinois. Born in China, educated in China and England, he came to the United States in 1944. On the faculties of Columbia University and Cornell University before joining Northwestern University in 1947, he is a specialist in Psychological Anthropology and Comparative Studies of Large Civilizations, with emphasis on China, Japan, India, and the United States. His main research emphasis is not on areas as such, but on the unifying psychological factors (testable or inferable) underlying the behavior patterns in each culture which make most of them predictable and which distinguish one culture from another. He characterizes his work as "Grammar of Culture." He has travelled extensively in Europe (including Russia and four other Eastern European countries), Asia and America, and has lectured widely in different parts of the United States and abroad to both academic audiences and the general public. Dr. Hsu is the author of over 100 articles in learned journals and some eleven books.

HANS R. HUESSY is a psychiatrist at the University of Vermont. Concern with rehabilitation of the psychiatric patient has led him to collaboration in a variety of nonhospital treatment modalities. In this volume his historical reconstruction of mental health resources in the United States assists us in understanding the present state of affairs.

MAMORU IGA went to college in Japan, where he was born. Soon after World War II he attended Brigham Young University in Utah where he received his master's in English. In 1955 he received his doctorate in sociology at the University of Utah, after which he did postdoctoral work at Harvard University. His studies have led him to collaborate with physicians, including a psychiatrist and a pathologist, both of Japanese-American heritage. At the present time he is a Professor of Sociology at California State University-Northridge. Half his many publications over the last several years have been on suicide, especially among Japanese and Japanese-Americans. In this volume he uses the case study method to gain yet another perspective on this subject.

DOUGLAS A. JACKSON received his B.A. in Psychology in 1968 from the University of California at Riverside, and his M.A. in Family Social Science from the University of Minnesota in 1973. He is currently working on his Ph.D. at the University of Minnesota. He has been involved in cross-cultural research on death customs and for two years has taught family life courses at Minnesota. His major interests are in the areas of family life education, marriage and family counseling and research.

WOLFGANG G. JILEK is a psychiatrist now practicing in British Columbia. His various interests in ethnopsychiatry range from social issues to psychopathology; he has done fieldwork in Africa and North America. His paper here focuses on linkage theory, drawing from an amazing diversity of investigators to explain data which he has collected among indigenous Indian people in western Canada.

LOUISE MATHILDE JILEK-AALL received her medical degree at the University of Zurich in 1966. She then studied tropical medicine at the University of Basel. Later she trained in psychiatry at McGill University in Montreal and obtained a master's in Anthropology from there in 1972. Her research has included ethnopharmacology in Tanzania and ethnopsychiatry among Indian people in Canada. Presently she practices psychiatry in British Columbia. During a field trip Jilek-Aall became intrigued with an epilepsy-like condition among the Wapogoro; her curiosity is reflected in the clinical description and psychosocial correlates of the condition contained in this volume.

MARTIN M. KATZ attended Brooklyn College and obtained his doctorate in Psychology and Physiology from the University of Texas in 1955. For over a decade he has worked in various fields of social psychiatry. During the last several years he has focused especially on the manifestations of psychopathology among various ethnic groups. Presently he is the Chief of the Clinical Research Branch for Extramural Programs at the National

Institute of Mental Health. His paper here, written in cooperation with Kenneth O. Sanborne, is a synthesis of extensive and well-known work which has been done in Hawaii.

JOHN LANGROD received his B.A. *magna cum laude* from the University of Puerto Rico in 1960 and his M.A. from New York University in 1962. He has taught social psychology at the Polytechnic Institute of Brooklyn and is currently at work on his dissertation at the New York University's Center for Human Relations. In 1955–1956, he was law clerk and investigator to Mark Lane in cases involving the East Harlem community. Subsequently, he did research concentrating on migration stress among Puerto Rican families and on urban drug abuse for the New York Medical College, the National Conference of Christians and Jews, and Columbia University, where he was director of a study of methadone maintenance at Harlem Hospital. Currently, he is Director of the Albert Einstein College of Medicine Methadone Maintenance Treatment Program. His publications include articles on multiple drug abuse, addiction in the Puerto Rican community, the group therapy approach, community opposition to drug treatment centers, and ancillary services to methadone maintenance.

DONALD LIGHT, JR., teaches sociology at Princeton University where he specializes in education and mental health. His research has focused on the psychiatric profession as a powerful force which shapes ideas and institutions in mental health care. He is writing a book on psychiatric training which examines how young physicians get socialized into the psychiatric paradigm of illness and health. He is also beginning a cross-national study of mental health services under a grant from the Ford Foundation.

WILLIAM T. MC KINNEY, JR., is a psychiatrist interested in experimental psychopathology in nonhuman primates. His present position is in the Department of Psychiatry at the University of Wisconsin in Madison. His paper here brings us up to date on the resurgence of a field that, while fallow for several years, has benefited from recent methodological and technological advances.

BEATRICE MEDICINE, a native of Standing Rock Reservation in South Dakota, received her undergraduate education at South Dakota State University, her M.A. in Sociology and Anthropology from Michigan State University, and is currently finishing her doctorate at the University of Washington. Meanwhile, she has worked as a teacher among the Navajo, Dakota (Sioux), and Pueblo groups. She has worked as a psychiatric social worker and has taught at several universities in Canada and in the United States. The latter appointments include Michigan State University, the Universities of Montana and South Dakota, and San Francisco State University and Dartmouth College. She is currently teaching at Stanford University. Her publications are in the areas of education, linguistics, ethnology, and social anthropology. She has presented papers at the International Congress of Americanists, among other professional organizations.

FREDERICK H. MEYERS received a B.A. from the University of California, San Francisco. Following internship and an additional three years at the University of Tennessee Medical Units, Memphis, he returned to the Department of Pharmacology, UCSF, where he is now Professor. In addition to laboratory studies on autonomic and CNS pharmacology, he has an active interest in the study and treatment of problems generated by drug abuse.

JAMIE NAIDOO. No biographical data available.

K. J. PATAKI-SCHWEIZER received his B.S. from the University of Chicago and then both his master's and doctorate in Anthropology from the University of Washington. His fieldwork consists of a study of human ecosystems in the New Guinea Highlands and resettlement programs in Malaysia. After working as an anthropologist with the George Williams Hooper Foundation at the University of California in San Francisco, he is presently a Senior Lecturer in the Department of Social Medicine at the University of Papua, New Guinea. His statement herein reflects careful attention and participation at the symposium, discussions during the Congress, review of his audio-tapes from the symposium, and reflections on all of these with Dr. Hartog and other colleagues.

PAUL BODHOLDT PEDERSEN attended college at the University of Minnesota and obtained his doctorate in Asian Studies, with a minor in Counseling, at Claremont Graduate School in California. He is also a clergyman in the Lutheran Church and has served in Malaysia and Indonesia as a missionary. His prolific writings reflect his experience and interest in the Malay Archipelago. Currently he is with the Foreign Student Advisor's Office at the University of Minnesota. His clinical work, teaching, and research now address the problem presented in his paper: counseling in the cross-cultural context.

NANCY ROLLINS received her M. D. from Tufts College Medical School in 1949 and completed psychiatric training in Boston. Most of her professional life has been with the Department of Psychiatry of Children's Hospital Medical Center in Boston, where she has engaged in clinical practice, training, and supervision. She is also Clinical Instructor in Psychiatry at Harvard Medical School. She is certified by the American Board of Psychiatry and Neurology in adult and child psychiatry. Special interests are in psychosomatic disorders, adolescent problems, family therapy, psychiatric diagnosis, and Soviet studies. She has been three times to the Soviet Union, twice as an individual investigator on the Medical Cultural Exchange program. Her publications include clinical studies of anorexia nervosa and observations in the Soviet Union.

PAUL C. ROSENBLATT received his B.A. from the University of Chicago in 1958, and his Ph.D. in Psychology from Northwestern University in 1962. After teaching psychology, sociology, and anthropology at the University of Missouri, Columbia, and psychology and anthropology at the University of California, Riverside, he moved to the University of Minnesota, where he is now Associate Professor of Family Social Science and Psychology. His principal scholarly interests are close social relations and theory translation. His recent publications, many of them coauthored with students or former students, deal with such topics as the development of close social relations, the effects of children and childlessness on families, sex differences and birth order differences in cross-cultural perspective, and coping with anger and aggression in mourning.

PEDRO RUIZ attended college in Cuba, his homeland, and graduated from medical school at the University of Paris in 1964. He received his psychiatric training at the University of Miami. Following the community take-over of Lincoln Hospital in the Bronx, a citizen's search committee chose him to be director of the Lincoln Community Mental Health Center. Under his aegis, mental health services in south Bronx have been decentralized; consumer participation and community control are prominent features of the programs which he has established. He has an academic appointment as Associate Professor with Albert Einstein College of Medicine. Charged with providing services to a largely Puerto Rican neighborhood, he wed the community experience and cosmology of local spiritual healers to the technology and resources of health professionals. Ruiz and his research associate, John Langrod, report their experience with this innovative relationship.

KENNETH O. SANBORN is the Executive Director of the Institute of Behavioral Sciences in Honolulu, Hawaii, and works also in cooperation with the Clinical Research Branch, National Institute of Mental Health, Rockville, Maryland.

JAMES M. SCHAEFER attended the University of Montana and received his Anthropology doctorate from the State University of New York at Buffalo in 1973. The cross-cultural method and alcohol usage have comprised his major interests to date. He is now in the anthropology department at the University of Montana. His paper here reviews the current status of multi-cultural studies, a method which has undergone considerable modification and sophistication over the last several years.

PHILIP SINGER studied economics and philosophy at Syracuse University, the University of Oslo in Norway, and Delhi University in India. In 1961 he received his doctorate in Cultural Anthropology from Syracuse University. He has studied suicide, psychiatric treatment methods, and folk healing, in addition to a variety of social and culture change issues. At this time he is Professor of Anthropology in the Allport College of Human Behavior at Oakland University, Rochester, Michigan. During fieldwork in Guyana, he mediated a collaborative clinical effort between a psychiatrist and a Kali cult leader. All three members of this coalition wrote a paper on their activities, a summary of which appears herein.

JOEL MATHLESS TEITELBAUM, after graduating from college in the United States, received his master's in Economics from Manchester in 1964. Following his fieldwork in Tunisia, he received his doctorate in Social Anthropology from Manchester in 1969. He next did health-related field research in Appalachia. A Fulbright Fellowship then permitted him to continue his work in Tunisia. He now is an Assistant Professor of Anthropology and Ethnonutrition at the Pennsylvania State University. In addition to his extensive fieldwork in Tunisia, his close association with a Tunisian physician provided an entree and a perspective for his work in this volume.

JOSEPH E. TRIMBLE attended Waynesburg College in Pennsylvania, received his M.A. at the University of New Hampshire, and attained his doctorate in Social Psychology at the University of Oklahoma in 1969. His interests have involved him in work on minorities in the United States (especially American Indians) and measure of aptitude by psychological testing. He has taught psychology at the University of Oklahoma where he also holds an Adjunct Professorship in Health Sciences. He is currently a research scientist at the Social Change Study Center in Seattle, Washington. With Bea Medicine, he reviews the practical consequences of our contemporary mental health theories and offers an ecological model for conceptualizing behavior.

R. PATRICIA WALSH received her B. A. degree from the University of Maryland in 1968, and her Ph.D. in Social Psychology from the University of Minnesota in 1974. She is currently an Assistant Professor at Loyola University, Los Angeles. She has coauthored research regarding anger and aggression in mourning.

JOSEPH WESTERMEYER, M.D., is an Assistant Professor in Psychiatry at the University of Minnesota in Minneapolis. His varied study interests include opium use in Southeast Asia, culture and mental illness (with cross-cultural focus on Laos and the United States), alcohol use among the Chippewa Indians, and drug use and mental disorder in Minneapolis. Publications include "Lao Buddhism, mental health and contemporary implications," *Journal of Health and Religion* (1973); "The drug scene: acute drug syndromes," *Postgraduate Medicine* (1972); "Political homicide and conflict resolution in Laos," *American Anthropologist* (1972).

ERIC D. WITTKOWER, M.D. received his medical training at the University of Berlin, Germany, graduating in 1924. He was made a teacher (*privatdozent*) in psychosomatic medicine in 1932. He emigrated to Great Britain in 1933 where he carried out research at the Maudsley Hospital and Tavistock Clinic, London, and acquired British degrees. He also continued his psychoanalytic training at the London Institute of Psychoanalysis. During the war he served as army psychiatrist mostly engaged in officer selection and in sociopsychiatric research.

He joined the Department of Psychiatry at McGill University, Montreal, Canada, in 1951 as Assistant Professor and became a Full Professor in 1953. He now holds the rank of Professor Emeritus.

His main research interests have been: psychosomatic medicine, psychoanalysis, and transcultural psychiatry. He has published several books and over 200 articles. He has been a member of the World Health Organization Expert Advisory Panel on Mental Health, and president of various scientific socities. He is associate editor of numerous journals and editor-in-chief of the *Transcultural Psychiatric Research Review*. In 1956 he founded the Section of Transcultural Psychiatric Studies at McGill University. His field research was carried out in Haiti and Liberia.

JOE YAMAMOTO graduated from medical school at the University of Minnesota in 1949, after having earlier been forcibly removed from Los Angeles early in World War II and interned in a concentration camp for Japanese-Americans. He trained as a psychiatrist in Minnesota and was later a psychoanalytic candidate in California. For the last twenty years he has practiced and taught in academic settings; his research interests have focused primarily on social and transcultural psychiatry. He is a Professor of Psychiatry at the University of Southern California in Los Angeles. In the last few years he has studied a broad array of topics regarding the Japanese, from *morita* therapy in Japan to identity crisis among Japanese-American adolescents. His paper here brings light to suicide and acculturation among Japanese-Americans.

# Index of Names

# Index of Subjects